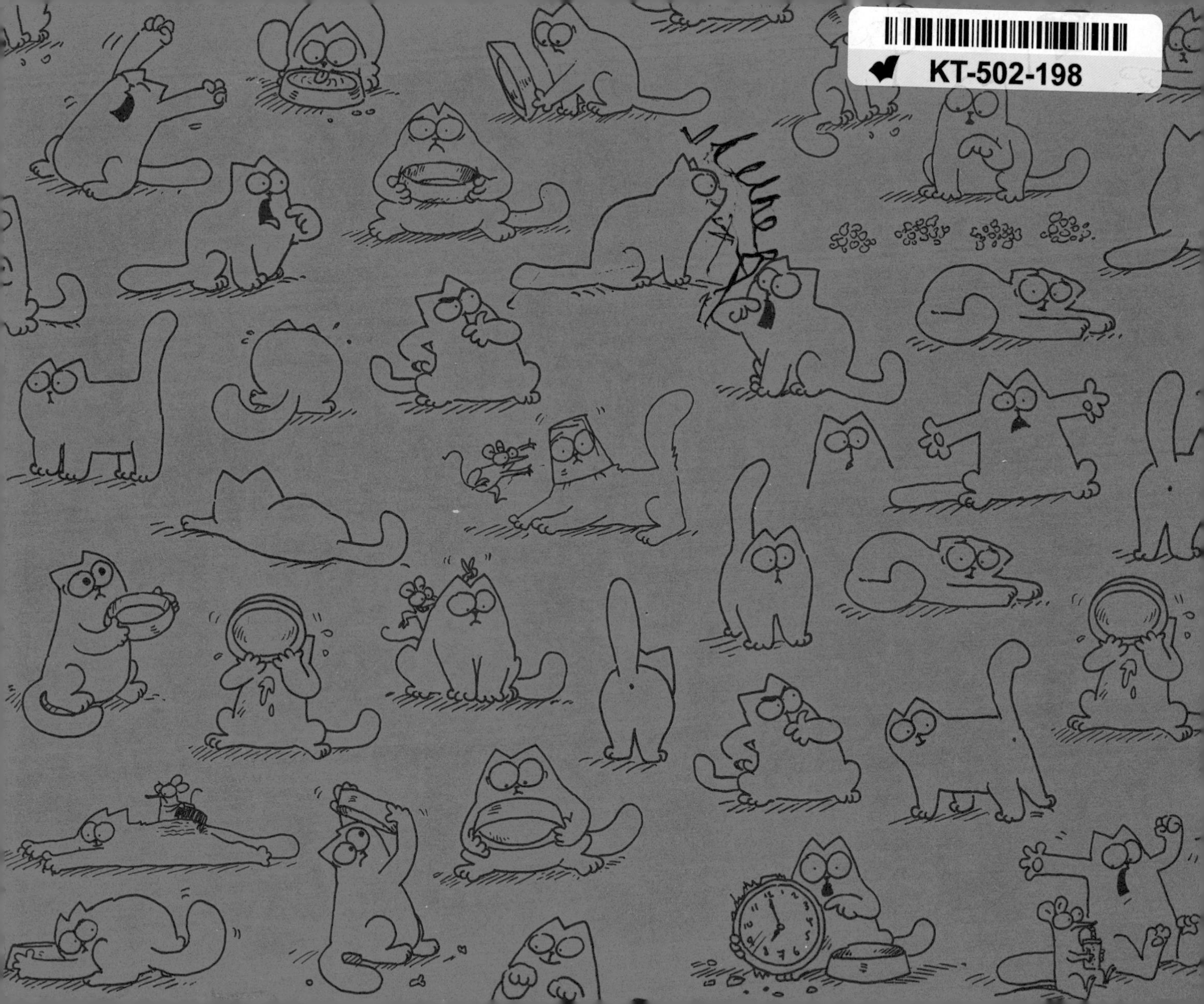

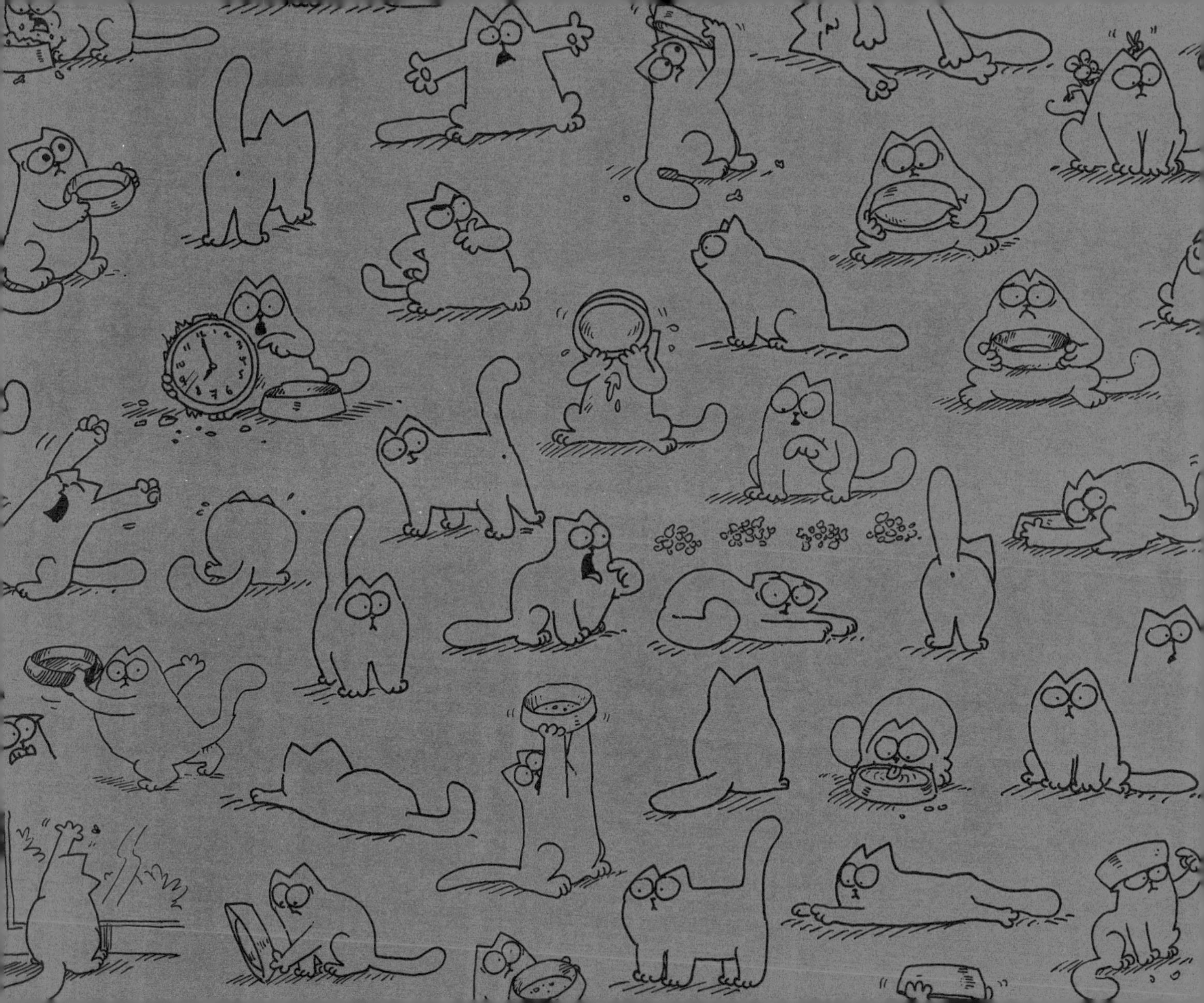

Simon's Cat

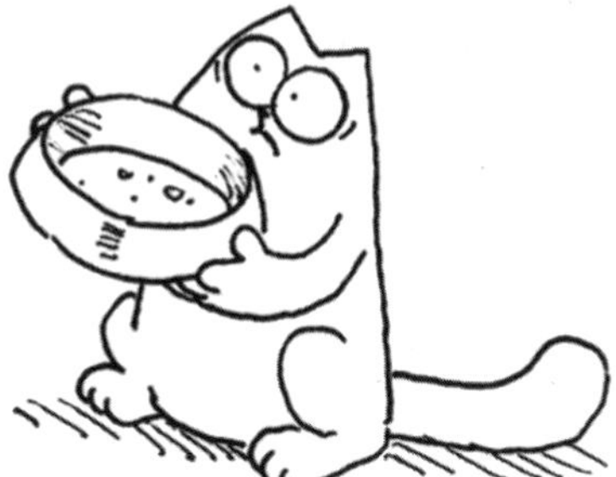

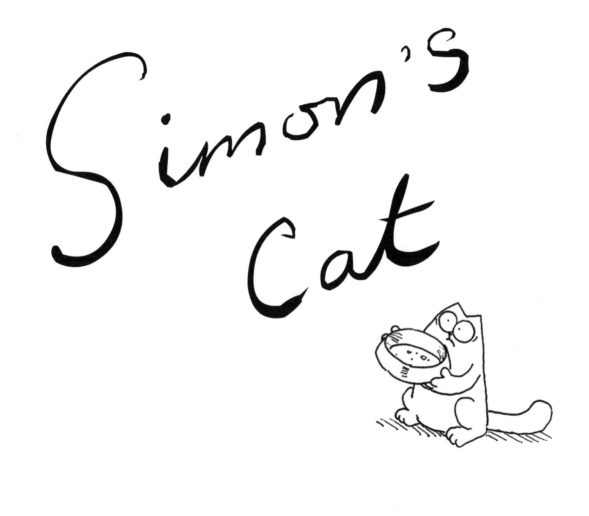

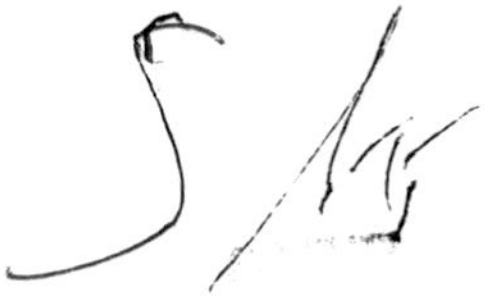

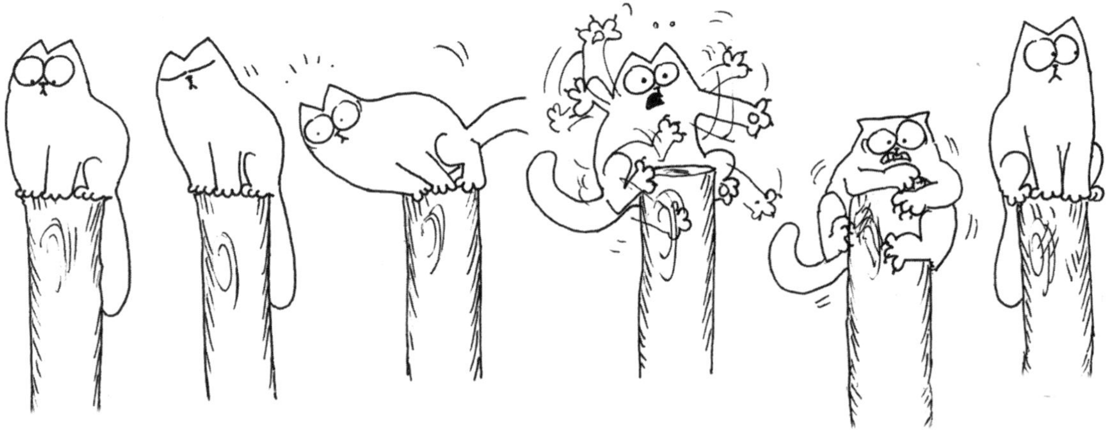

Simon's Cat

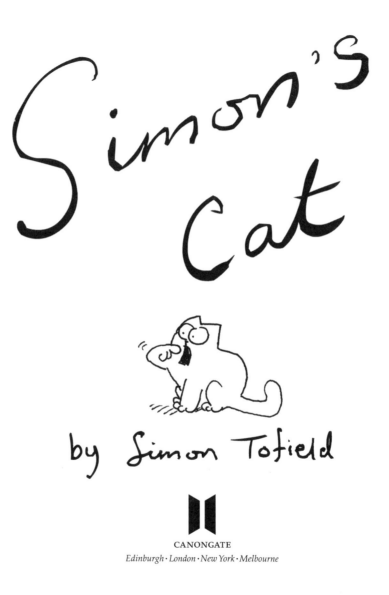

by Simon Tofield

CANONGATE

Edinburgh · London · New York · Melbourne

Published by Canongate Books in 2009

6

First published in Great Britain in 2009 by Canongate Books Ltd,
14 High Street, Edinburgh EH1 1TE

www.meetatthegate.com

British Library Cataloguing-in-Publication Data
A catalogue record for this book is available
on request from the British Library

ISBN 978 1 84767 481 4

Typeset by Stuart Polson

Printed and bound in Great Britain by Scotprint

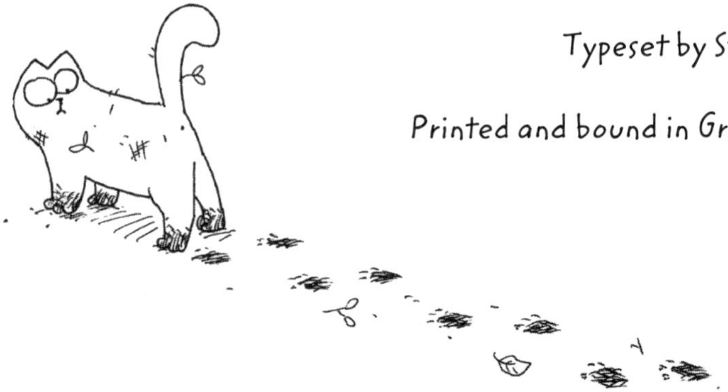

To Mum, thank you for everything.
This book is for you.

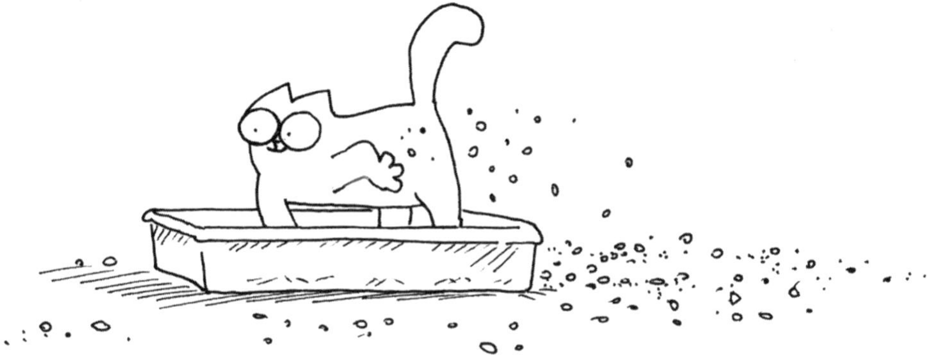

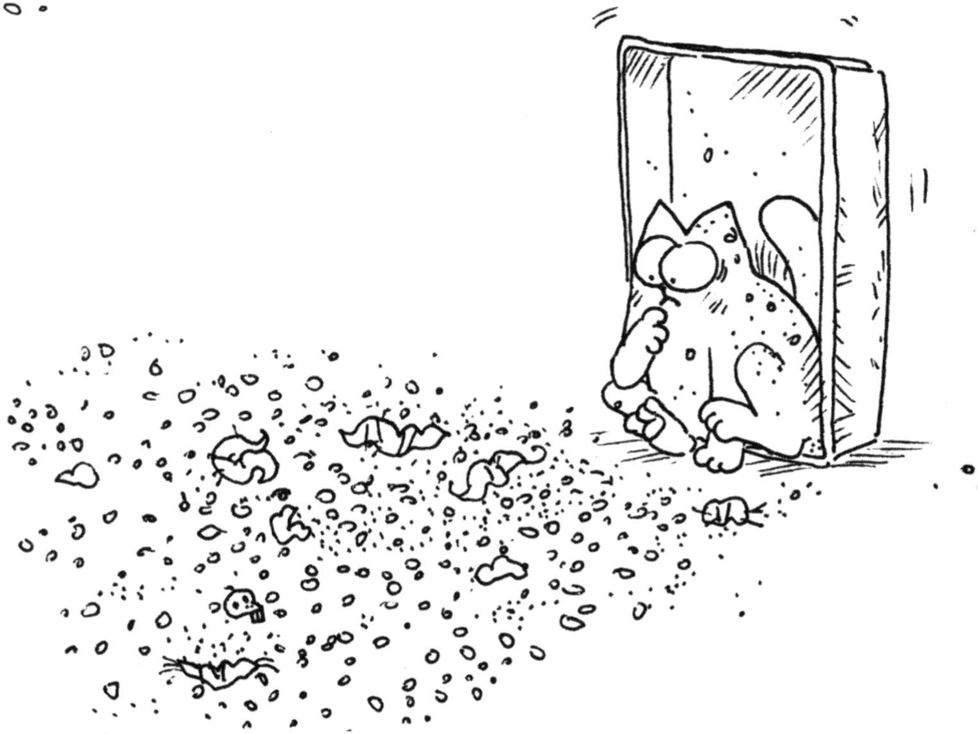

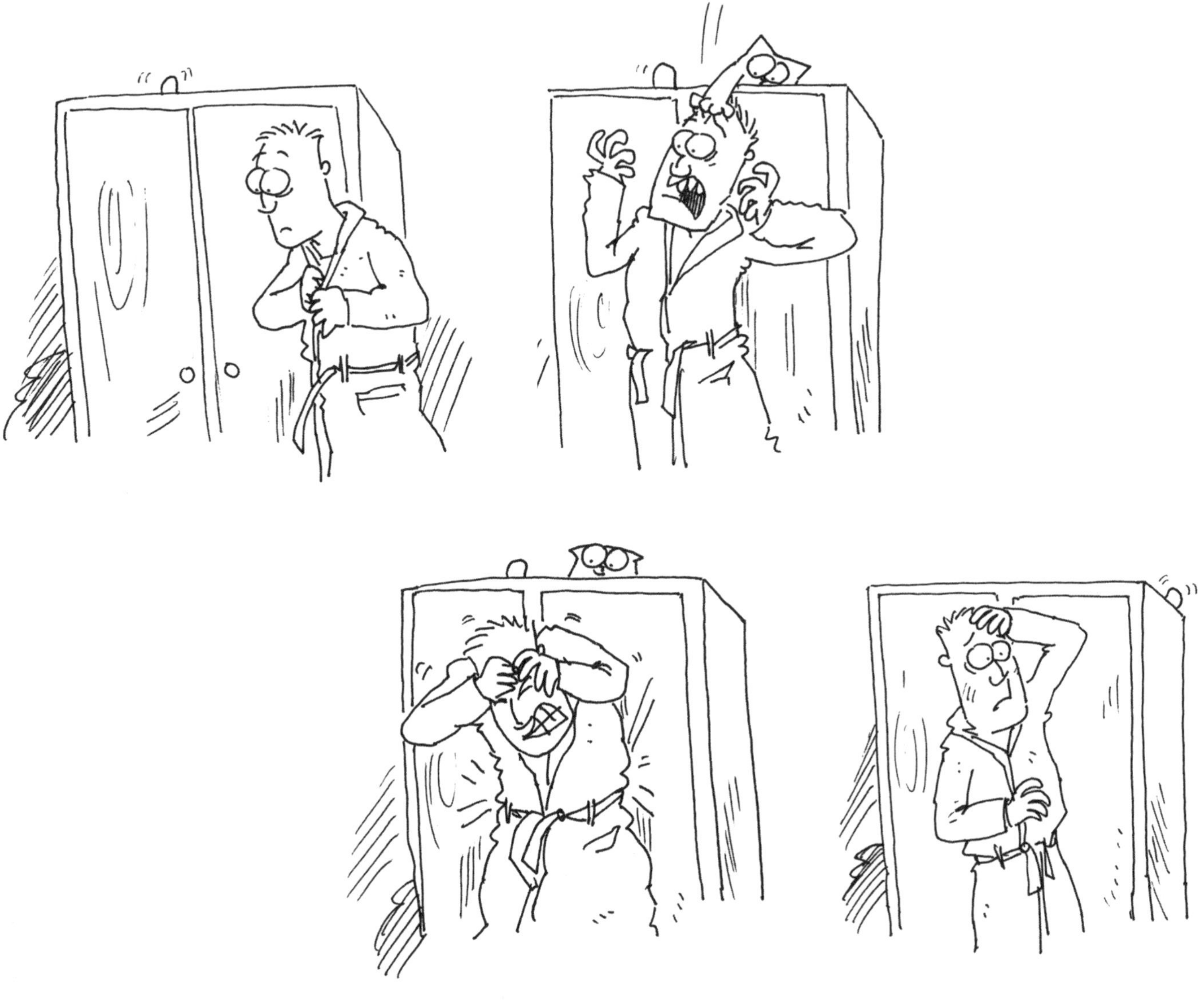

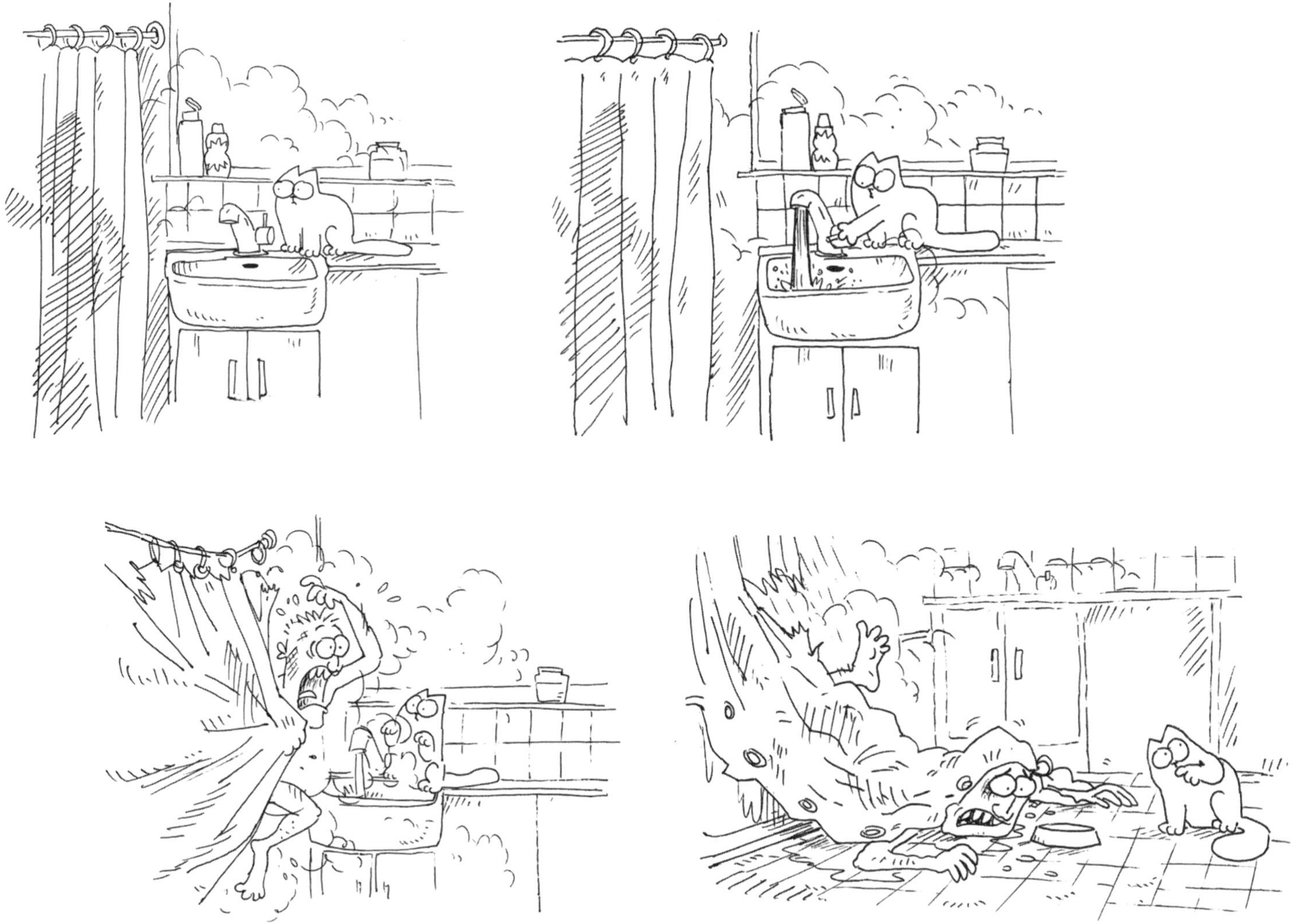

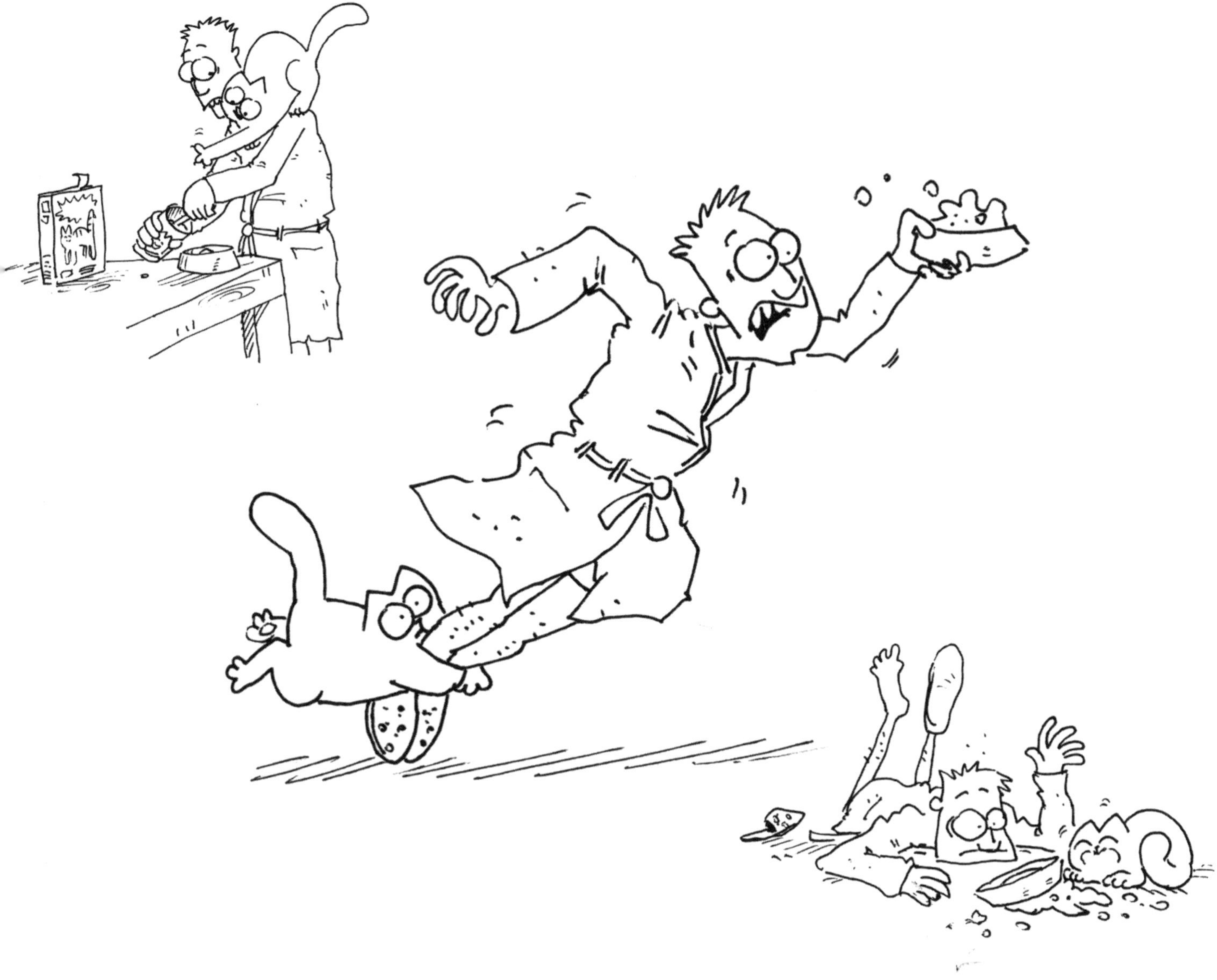

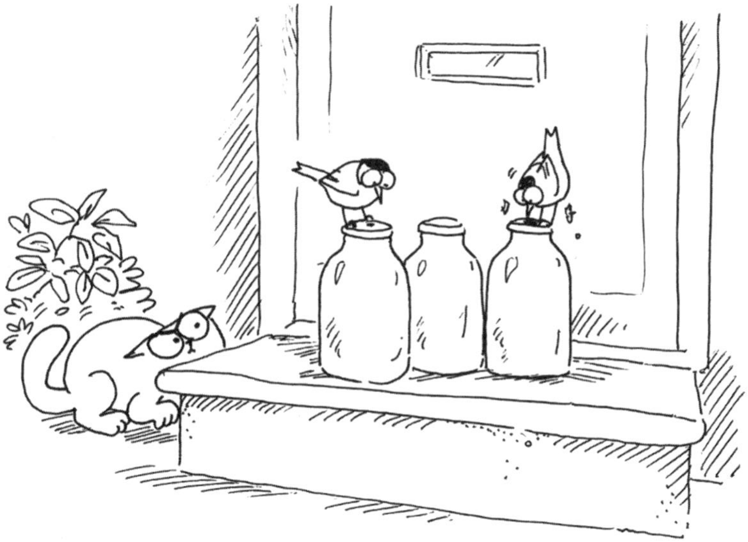

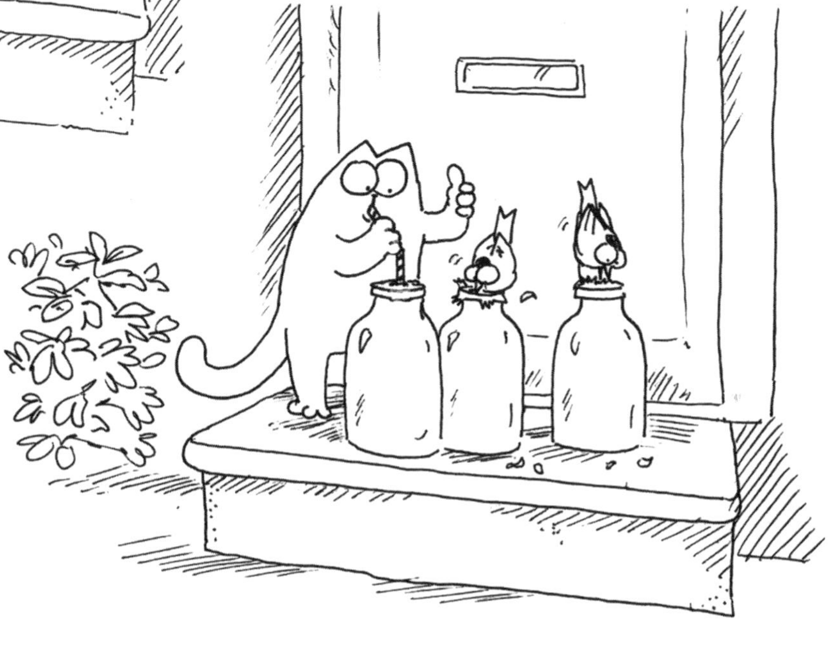

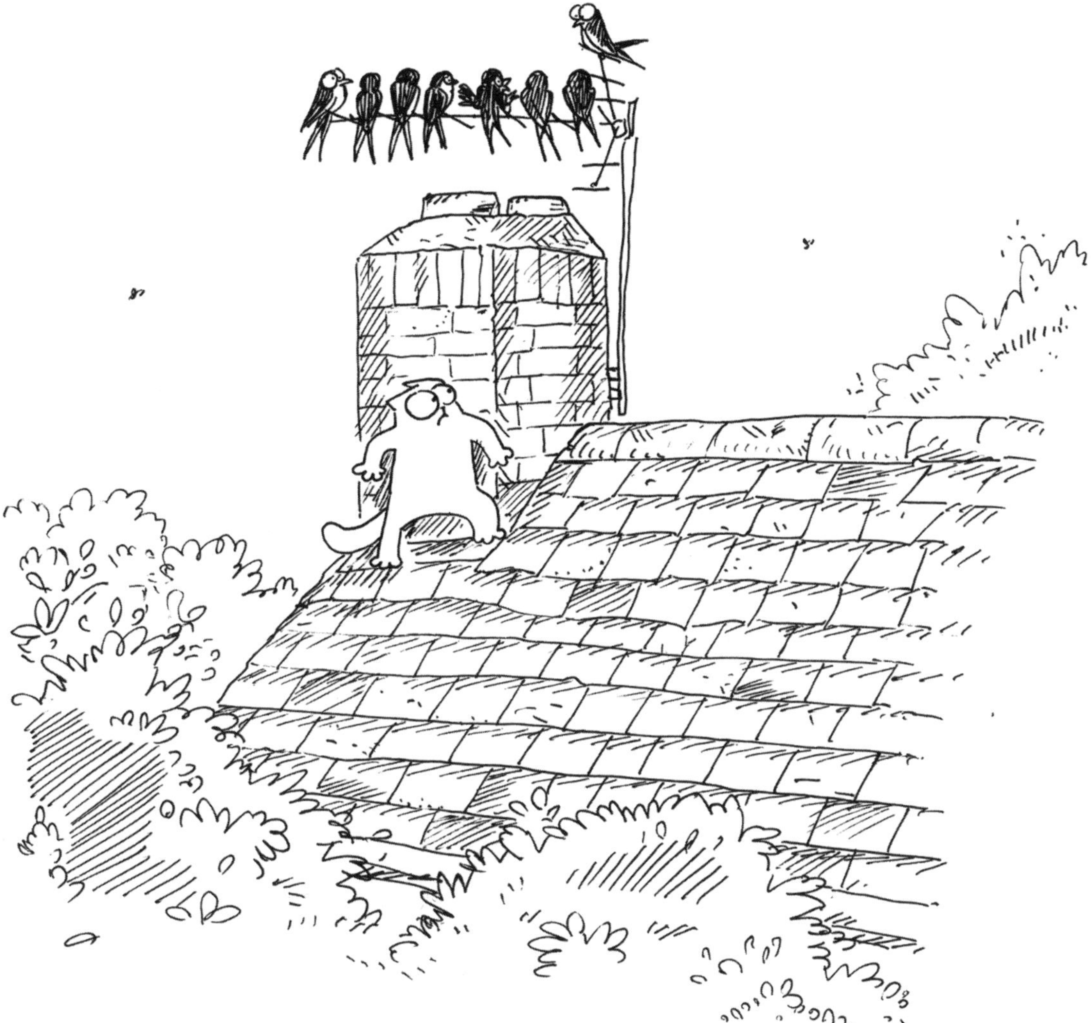

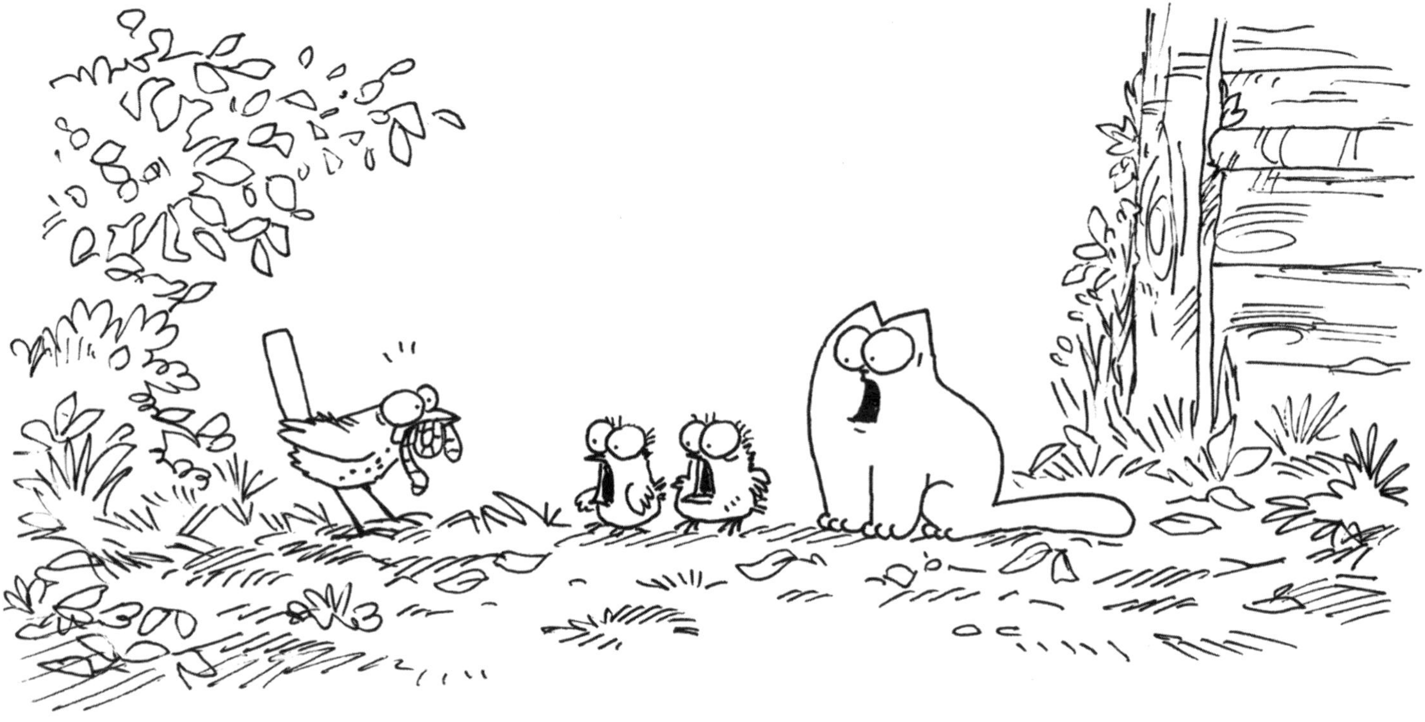

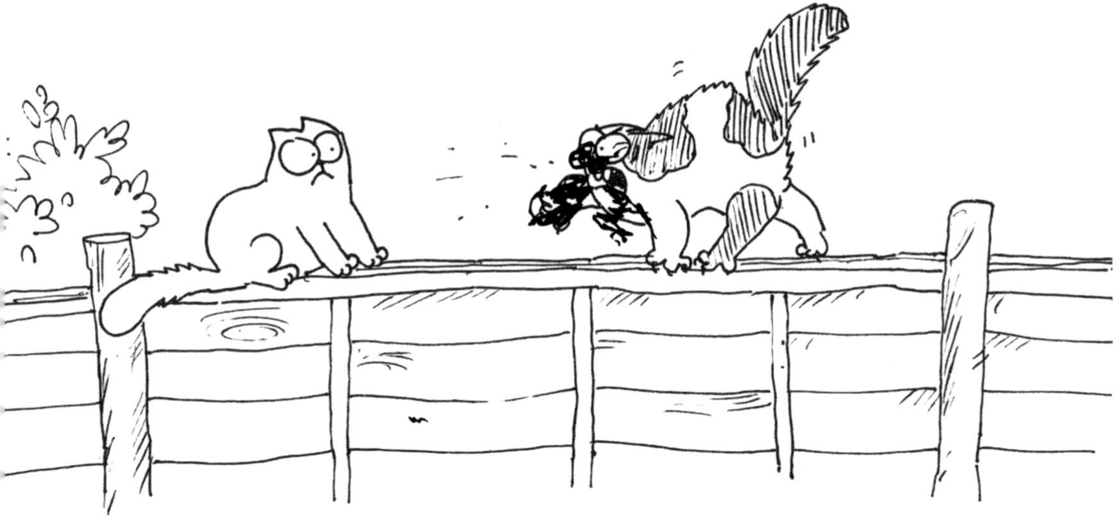

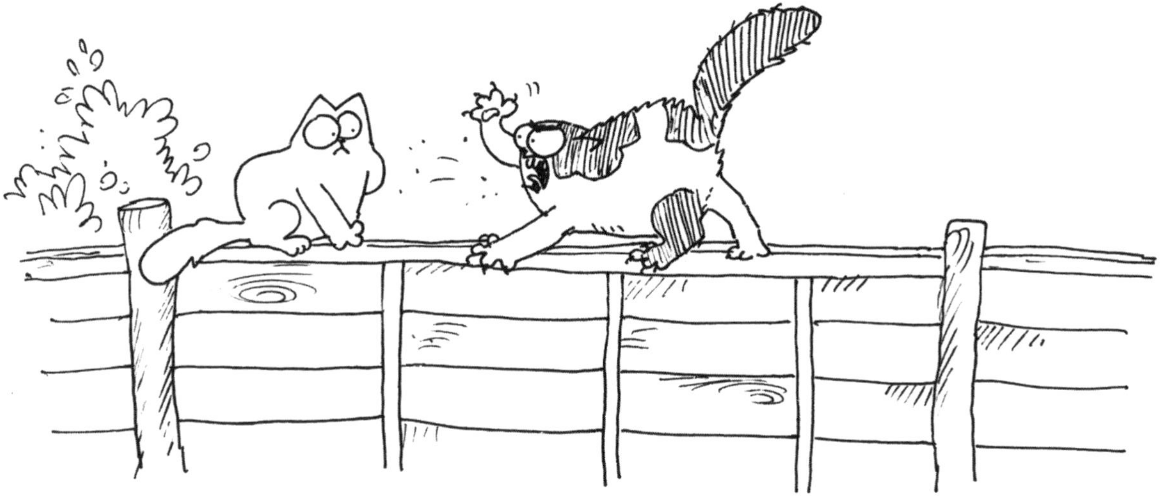

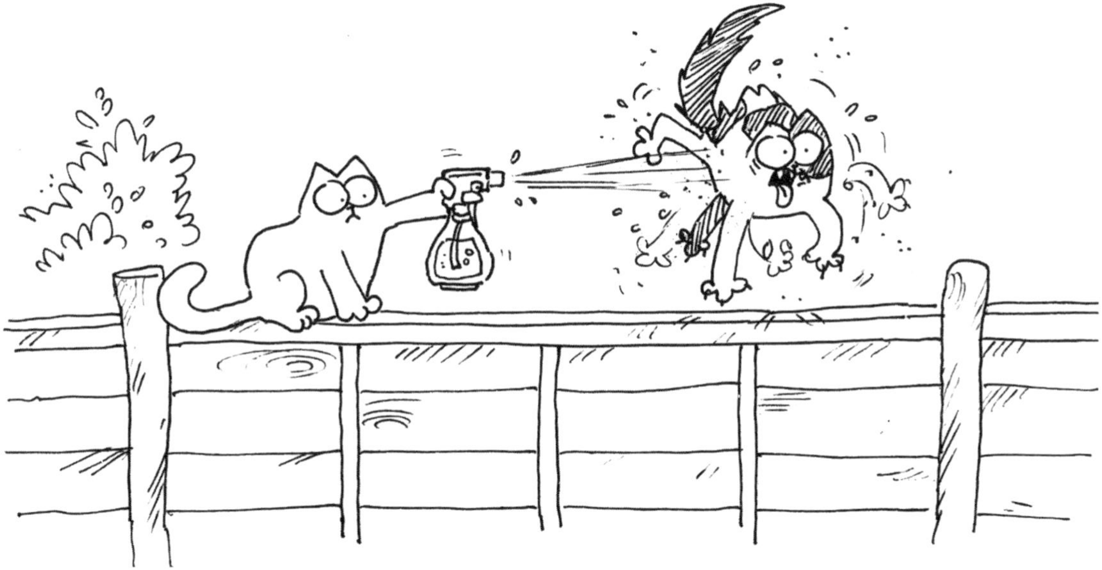

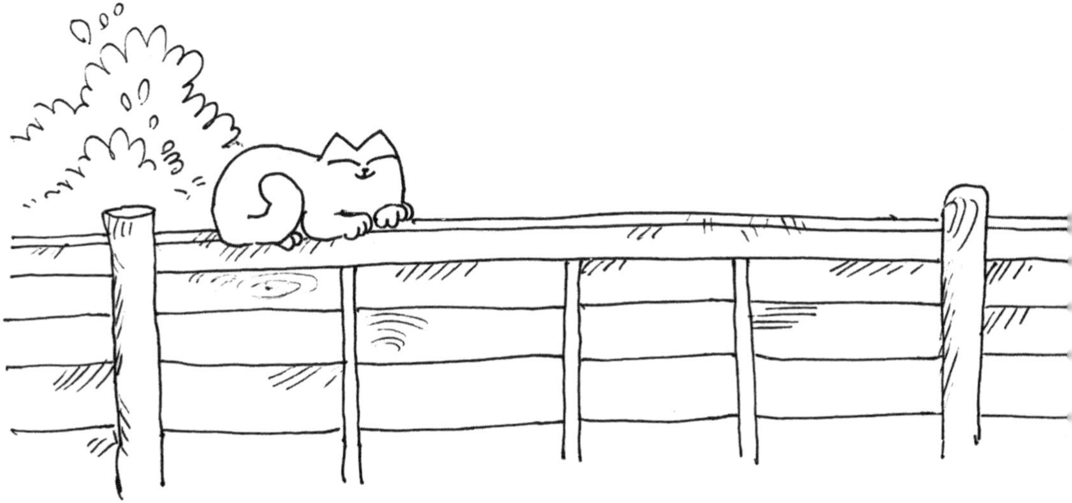

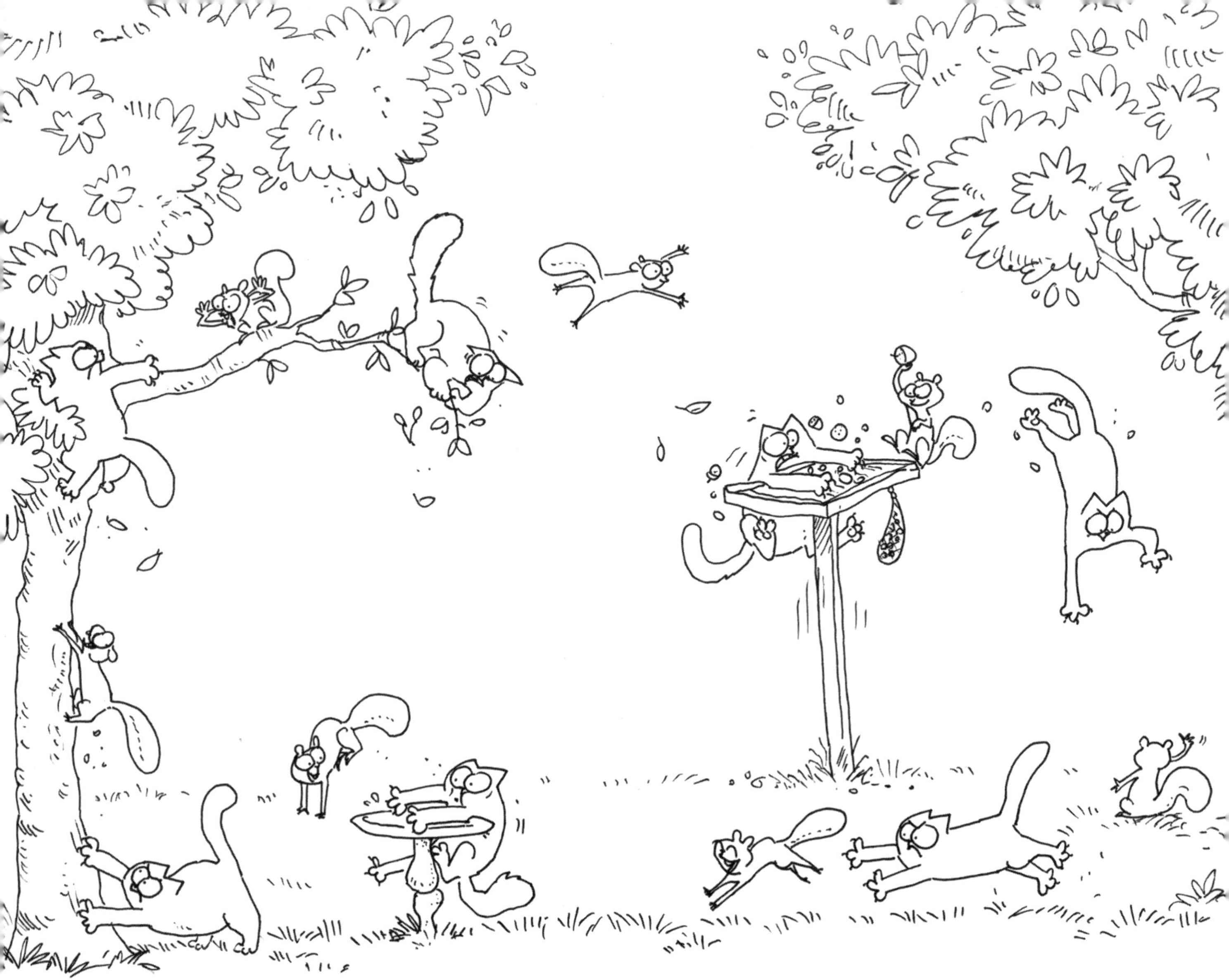

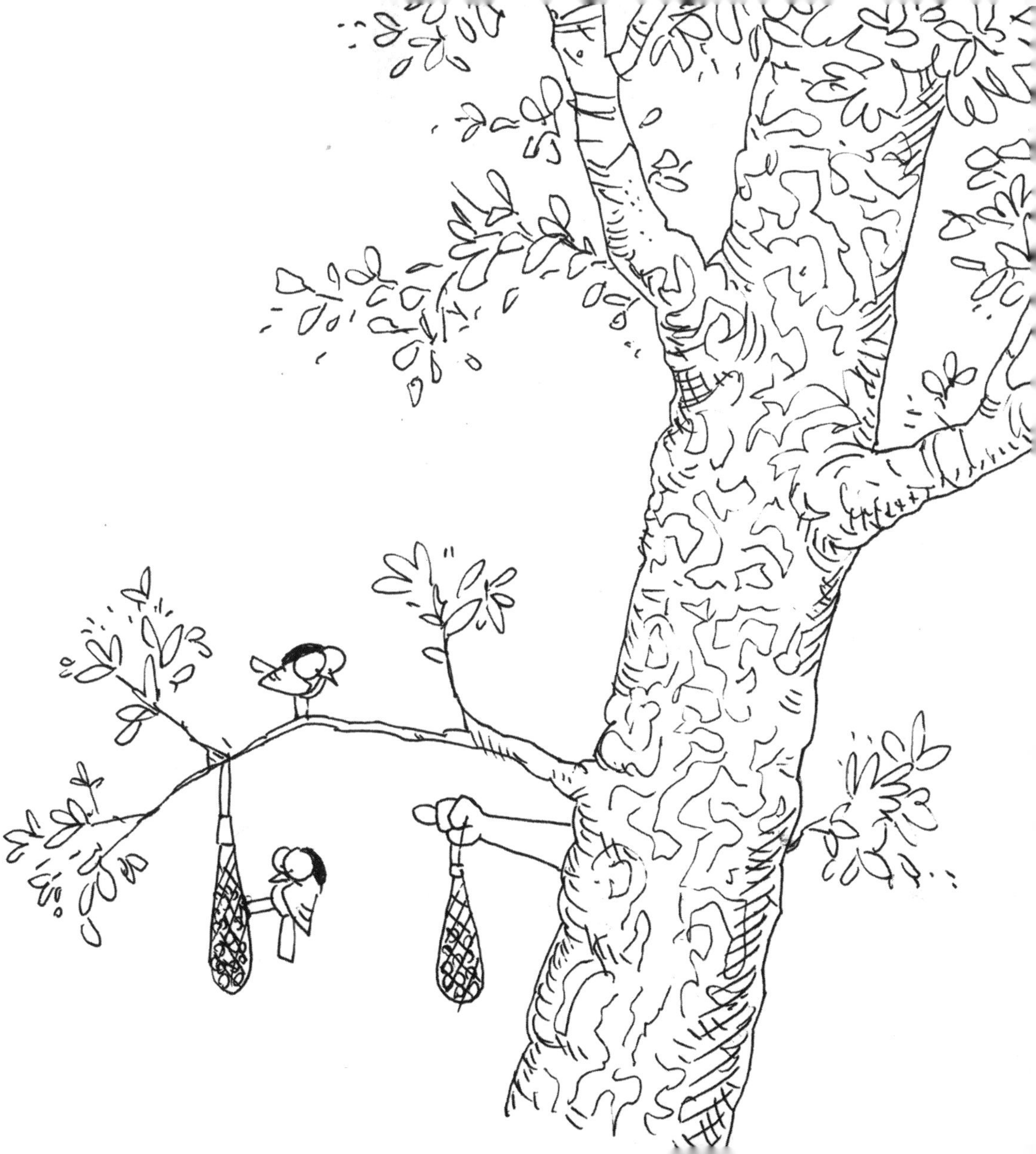

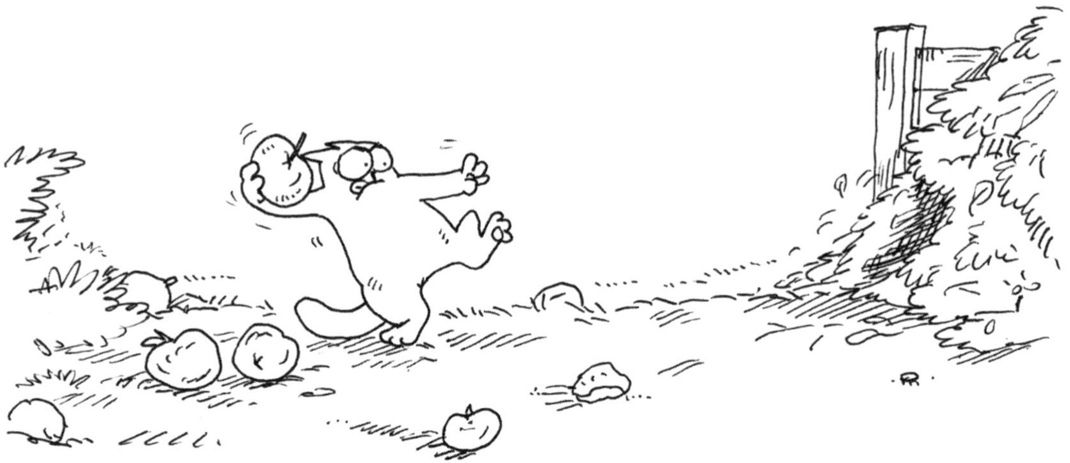

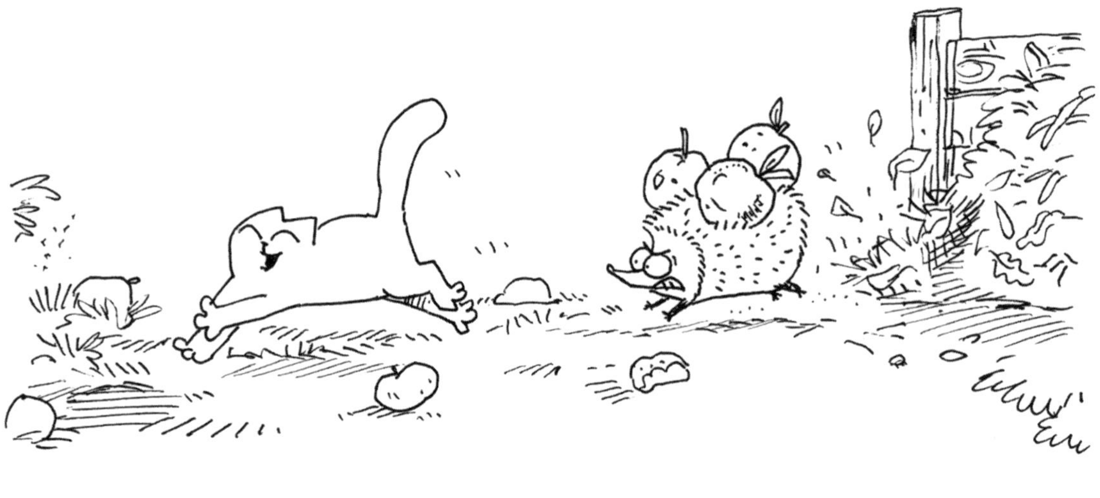

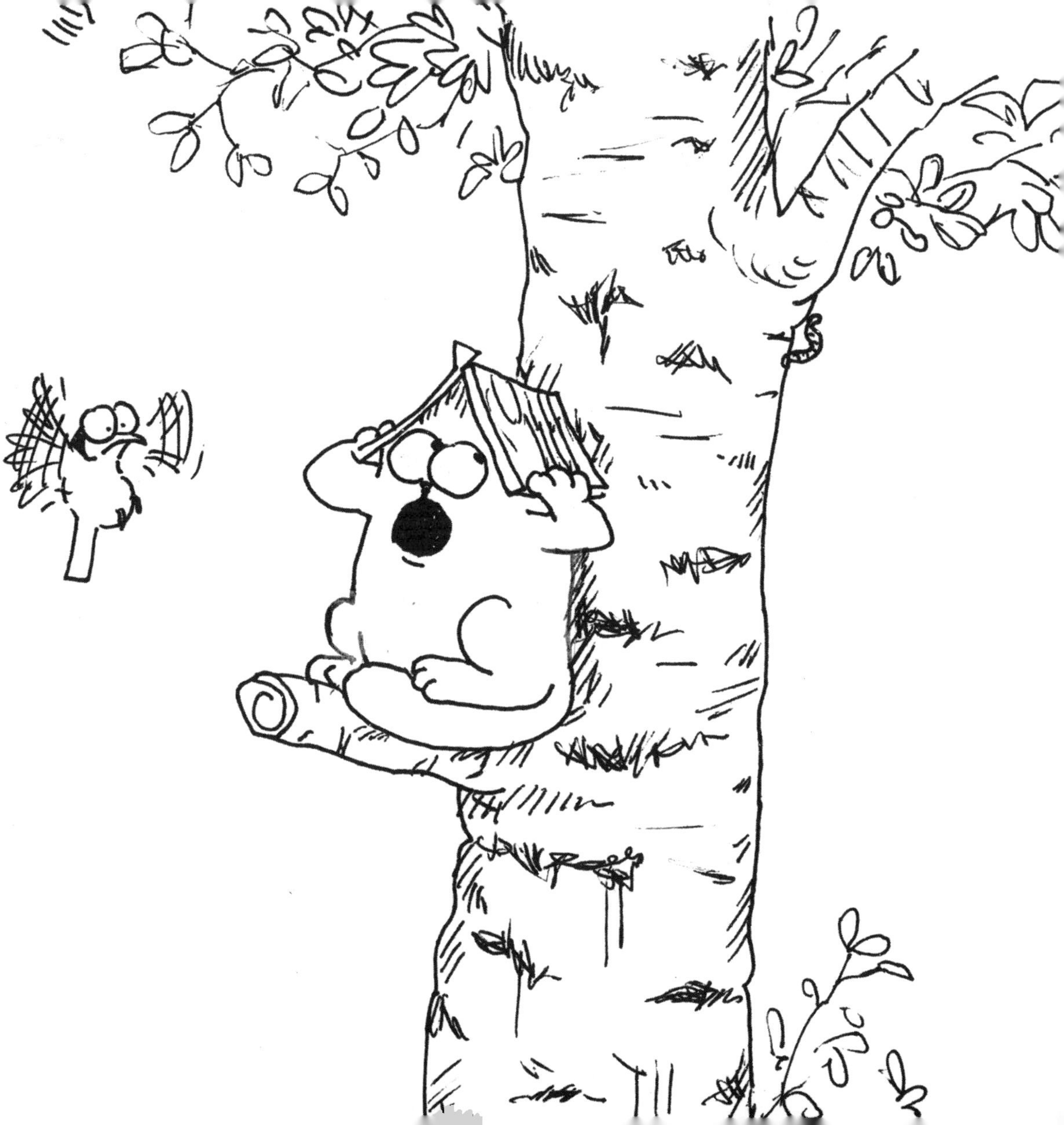

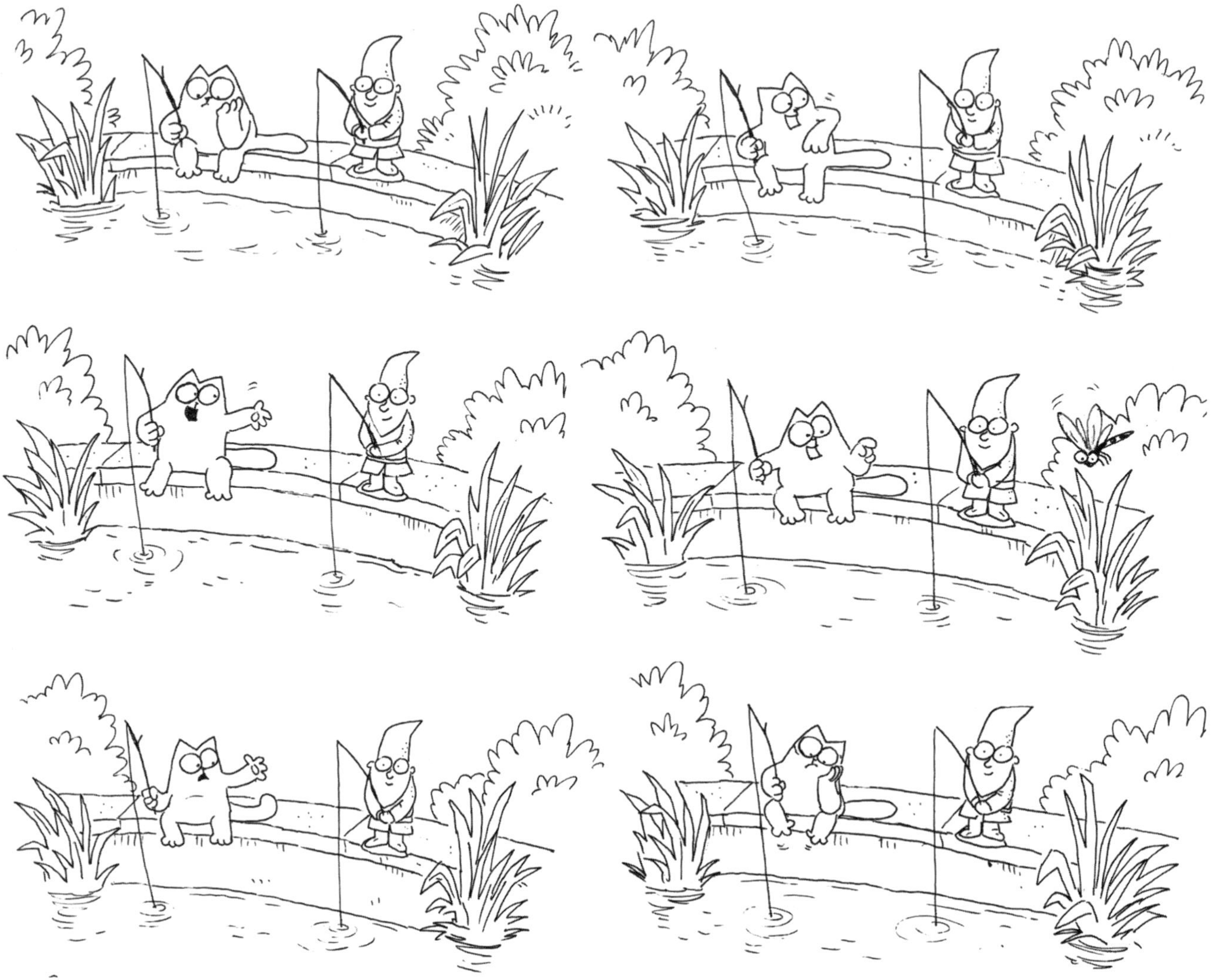

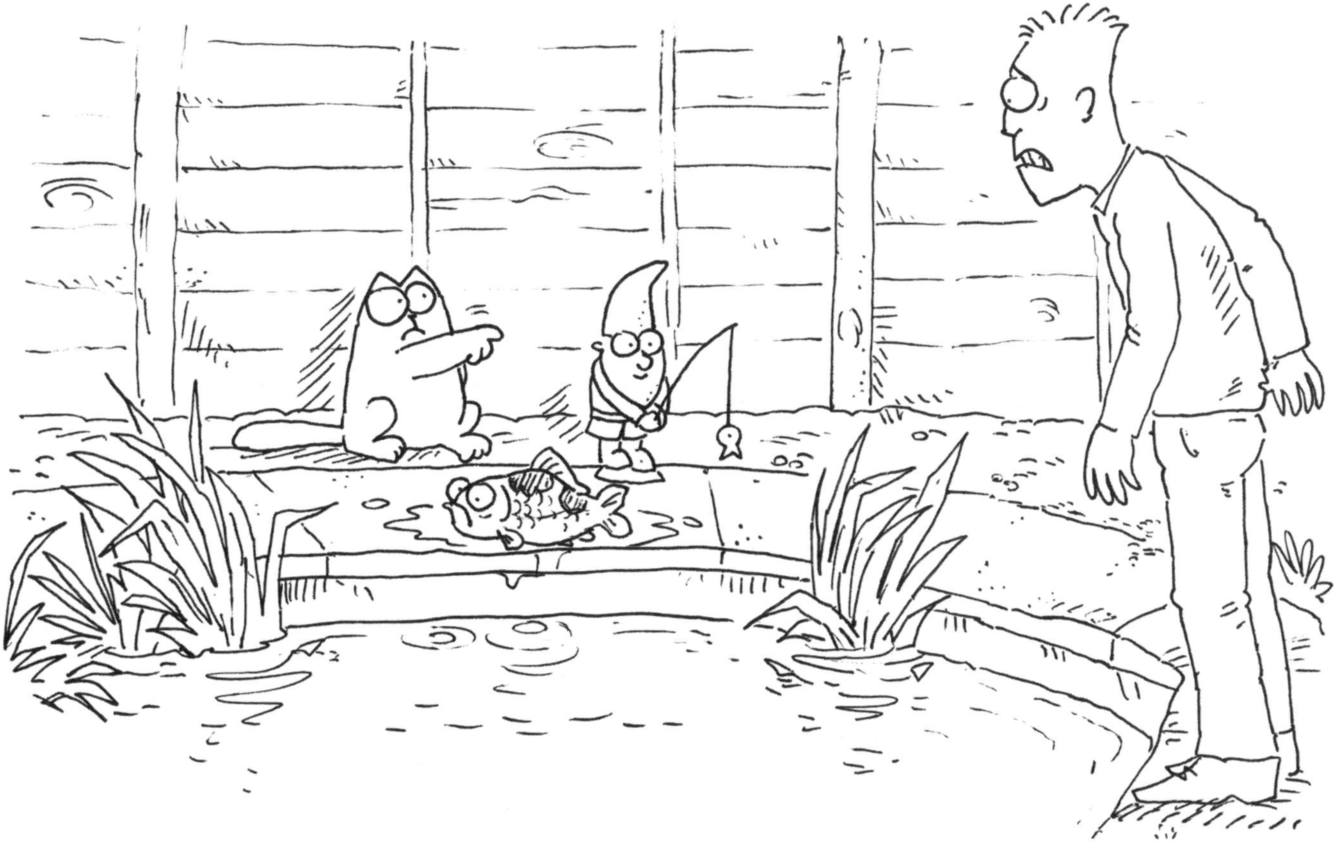

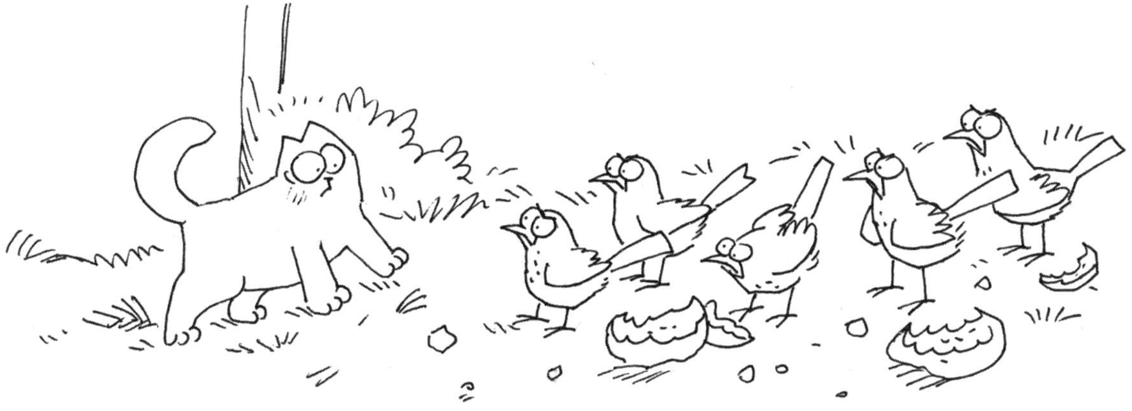

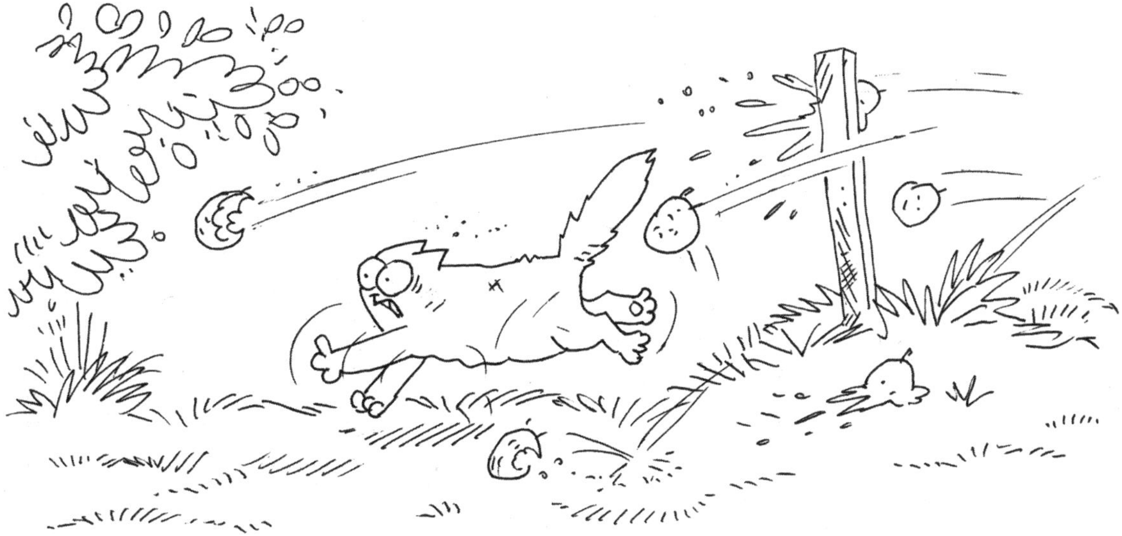

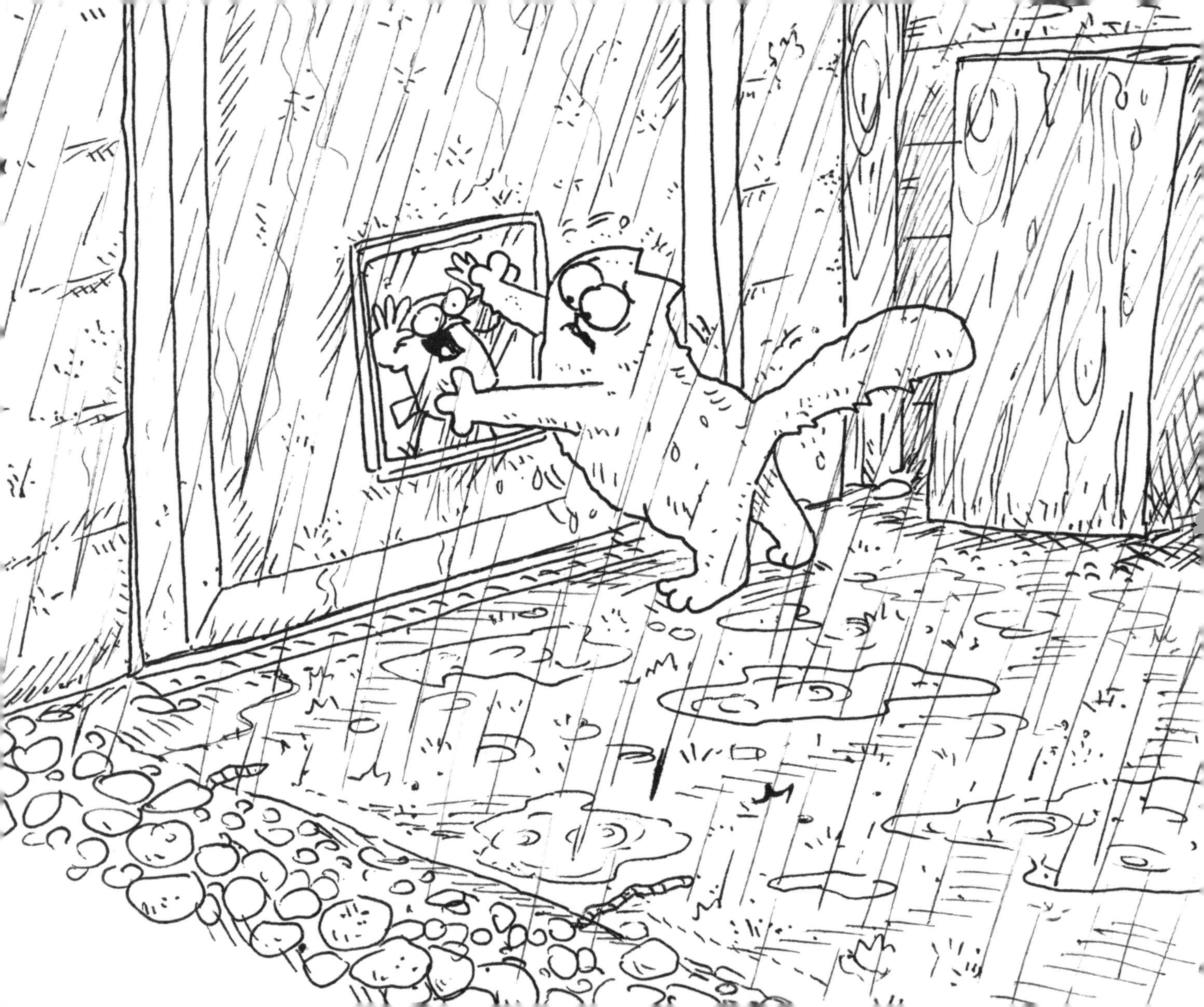

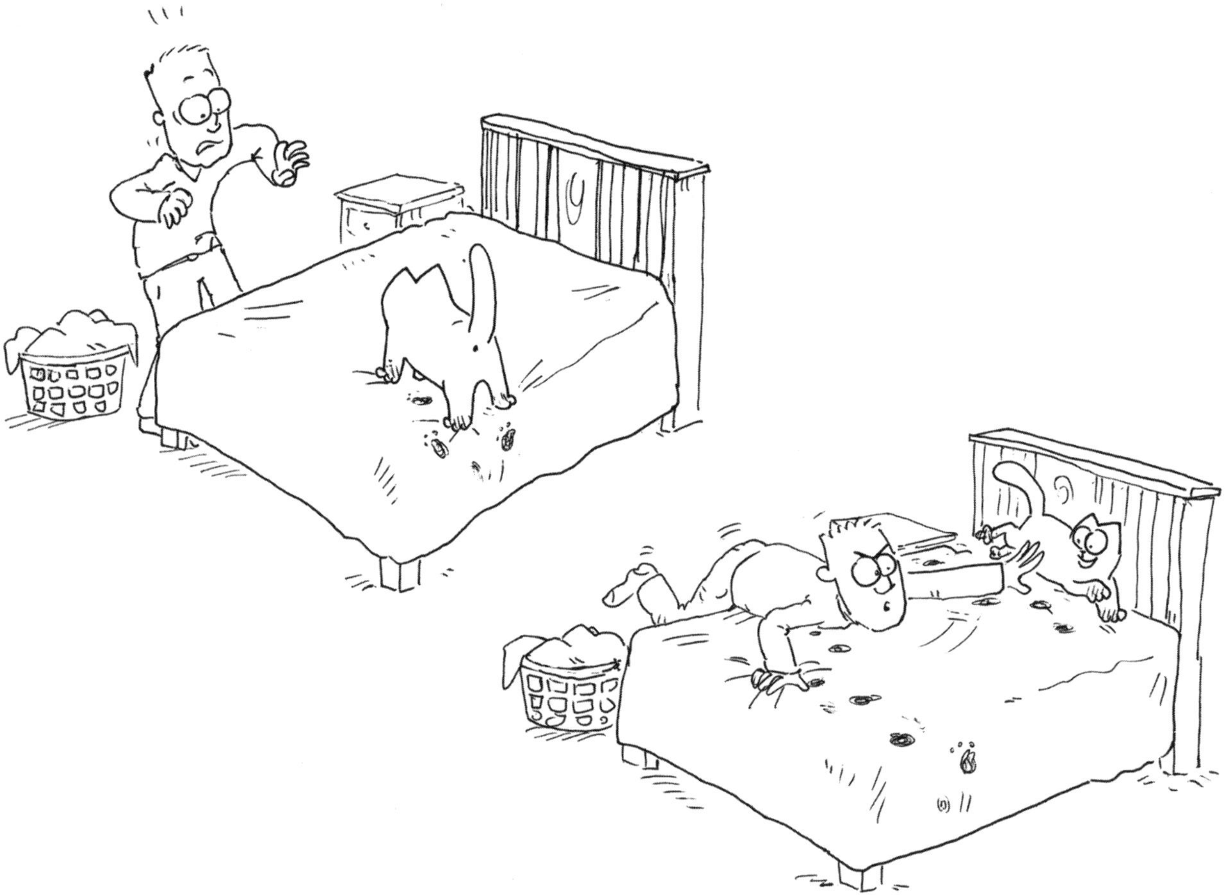

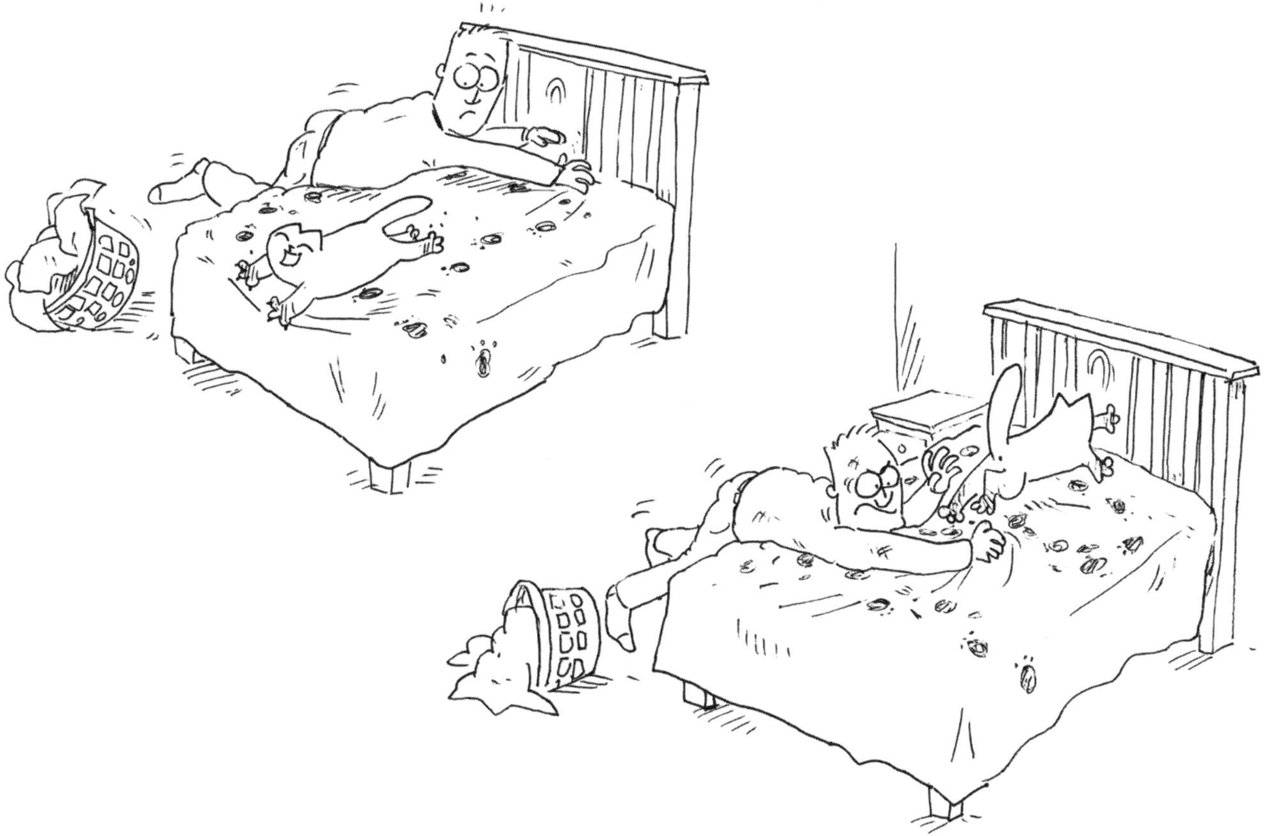

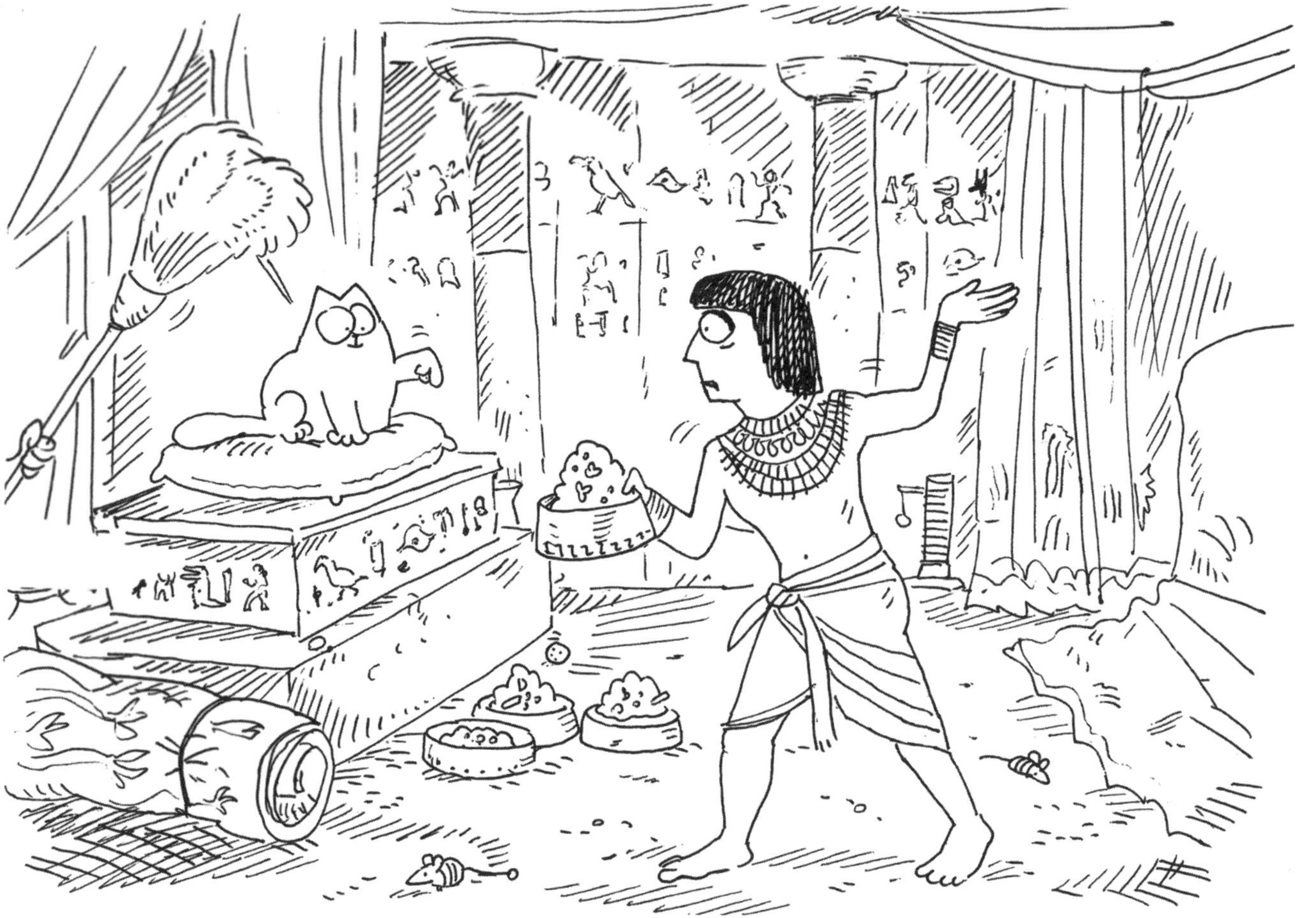

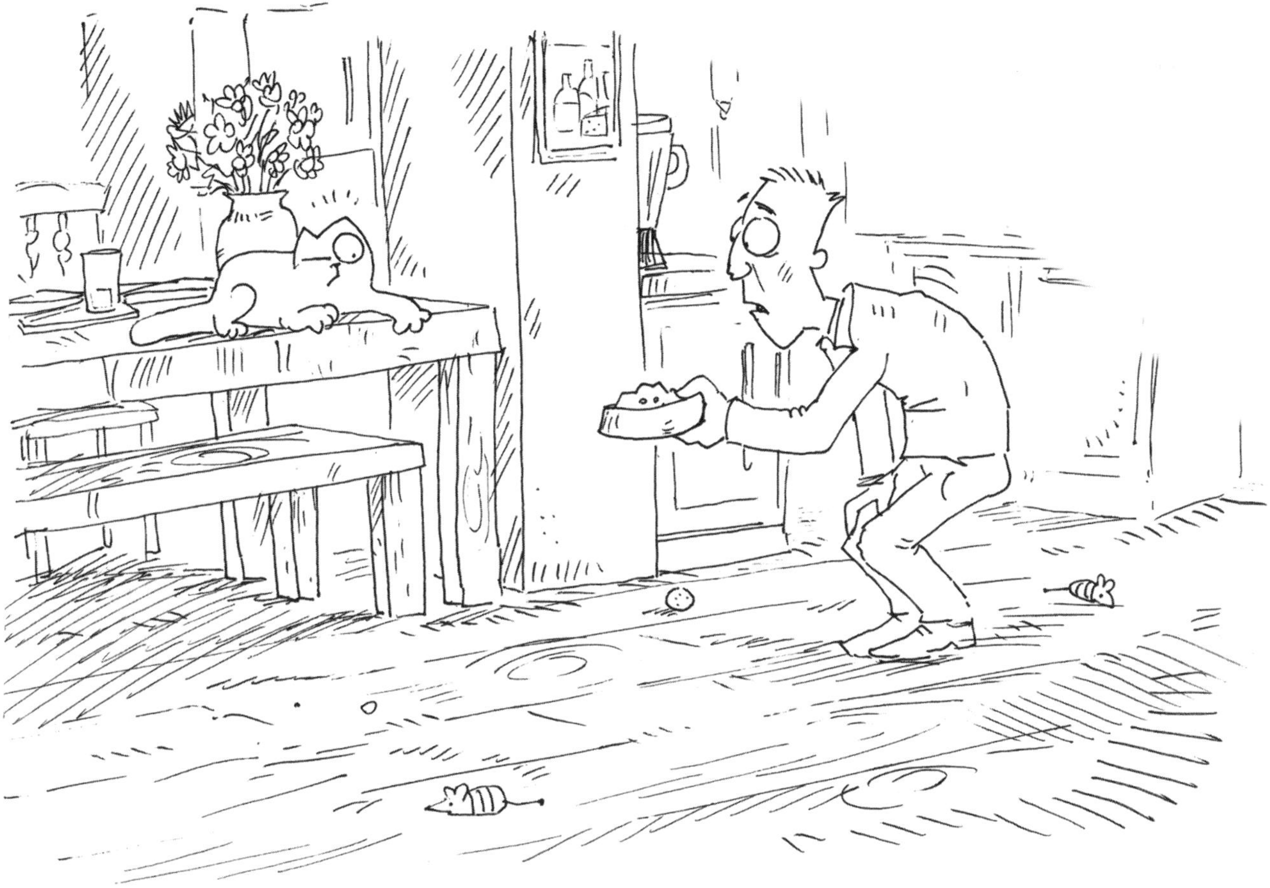

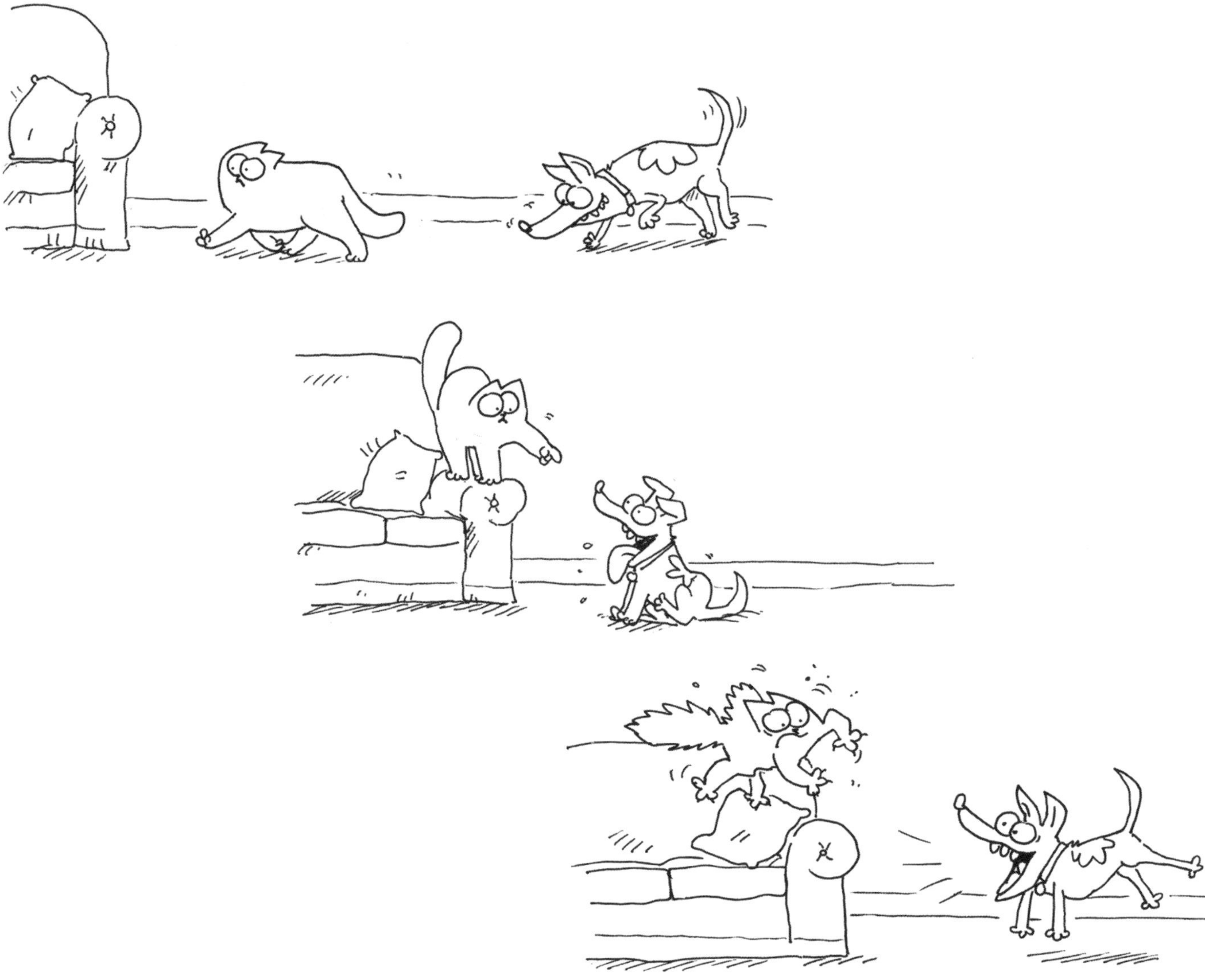

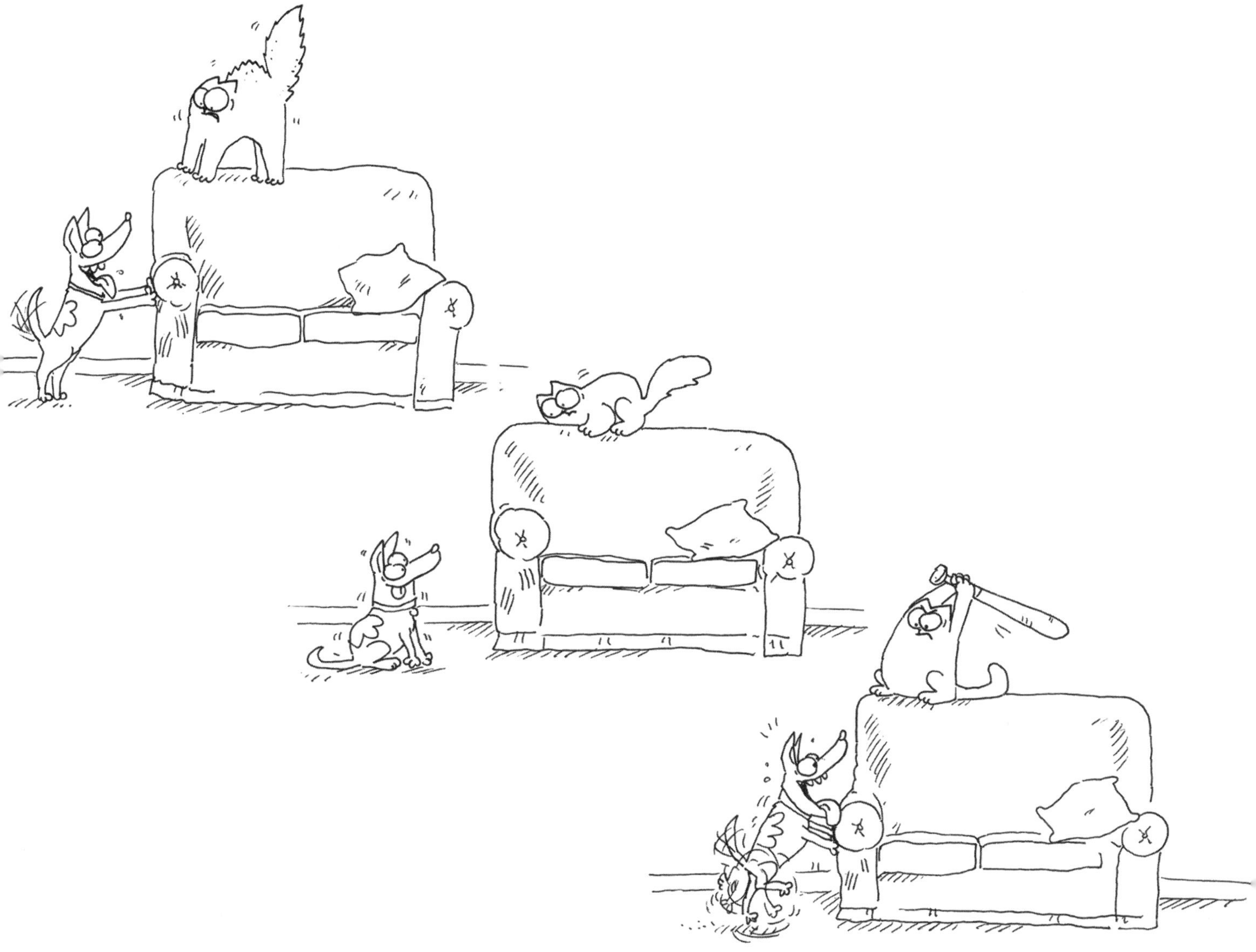

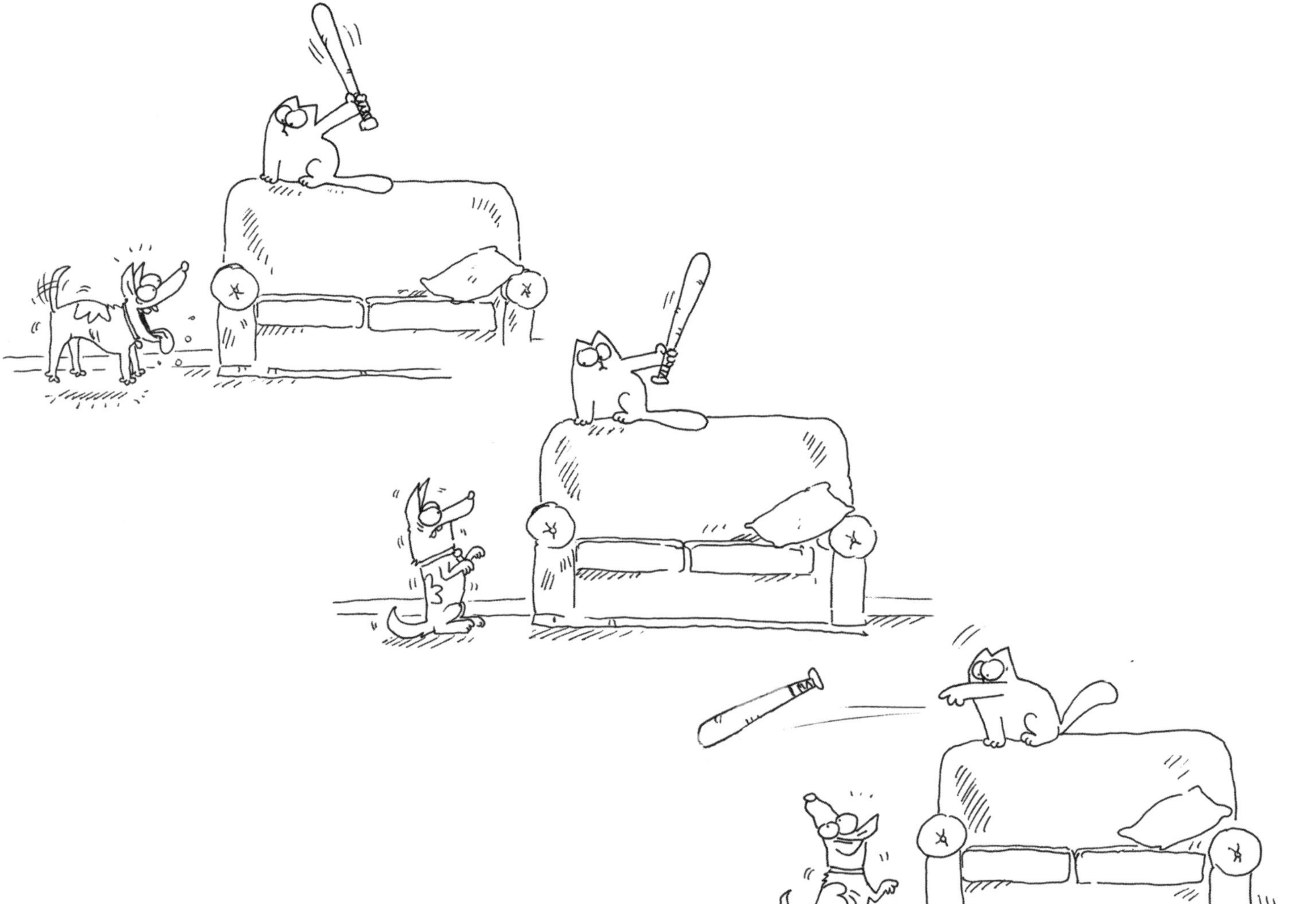

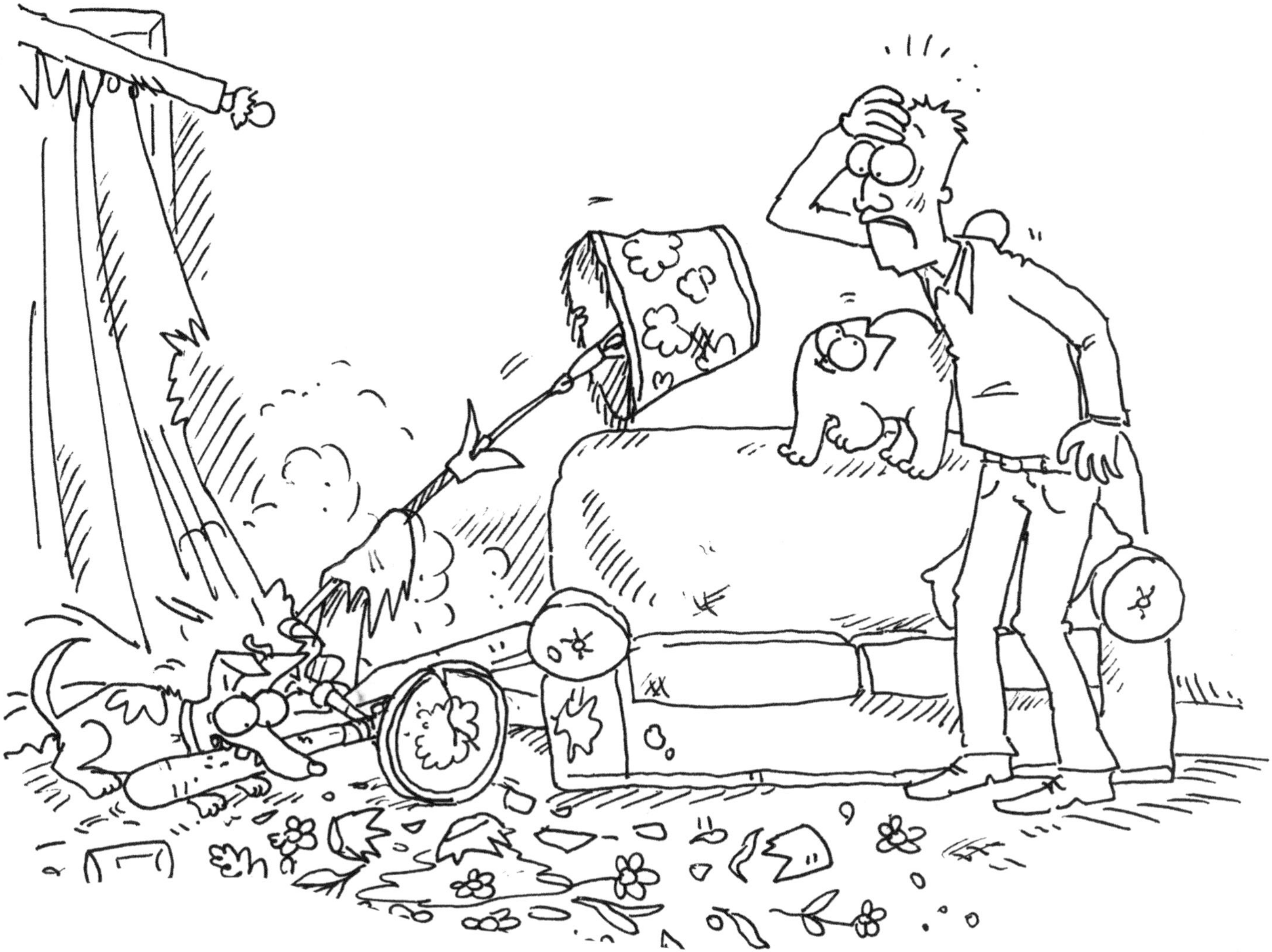

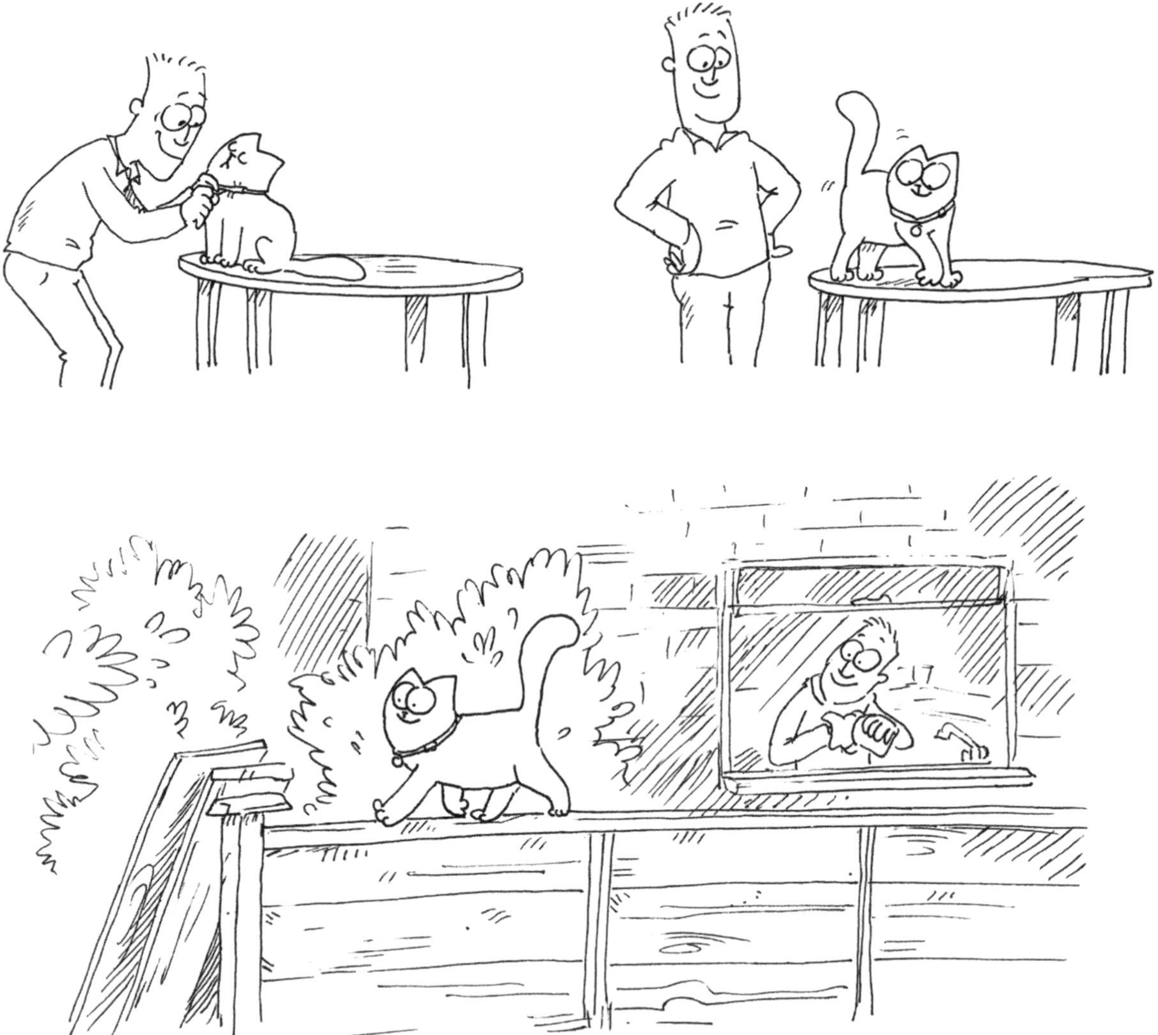

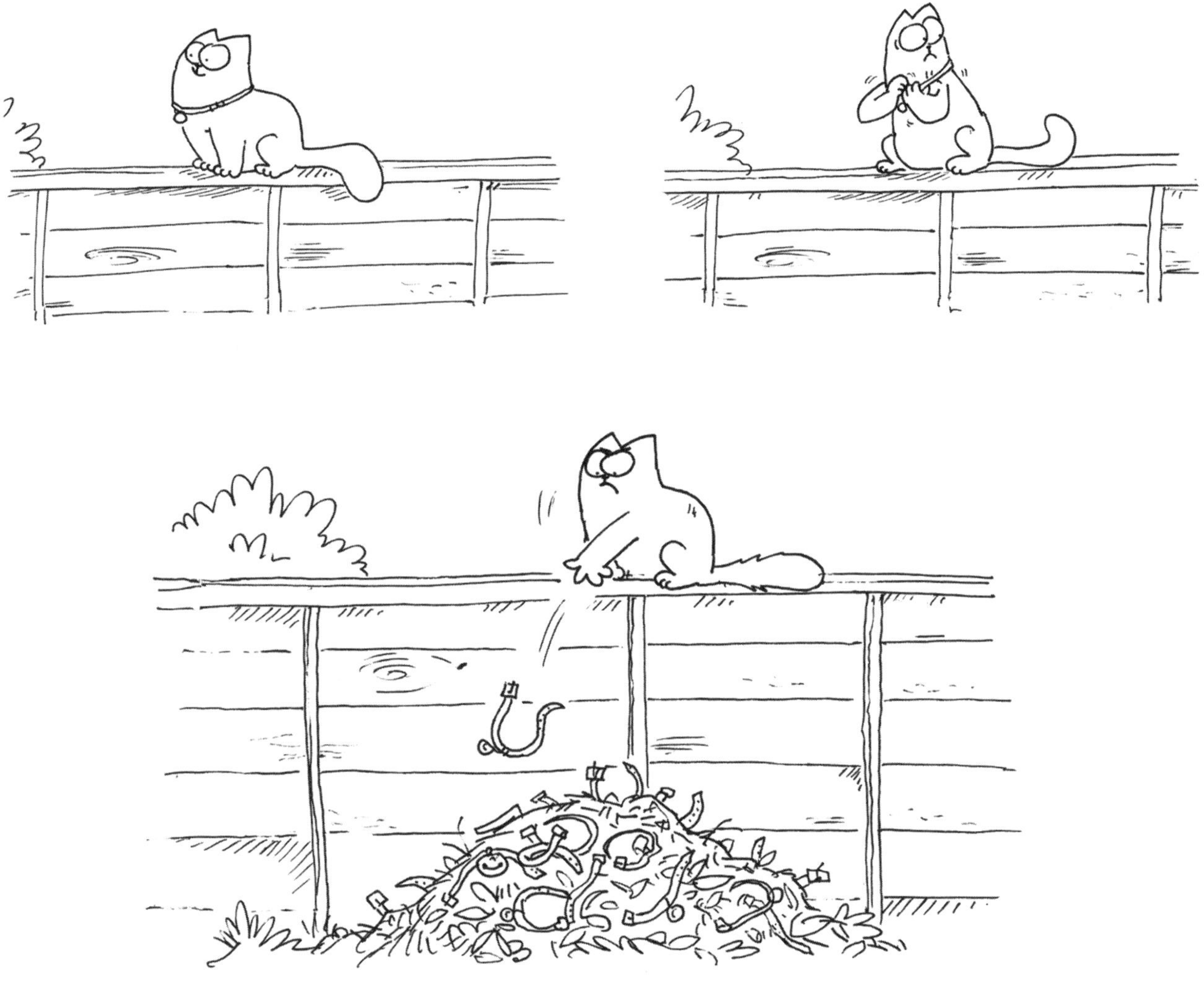

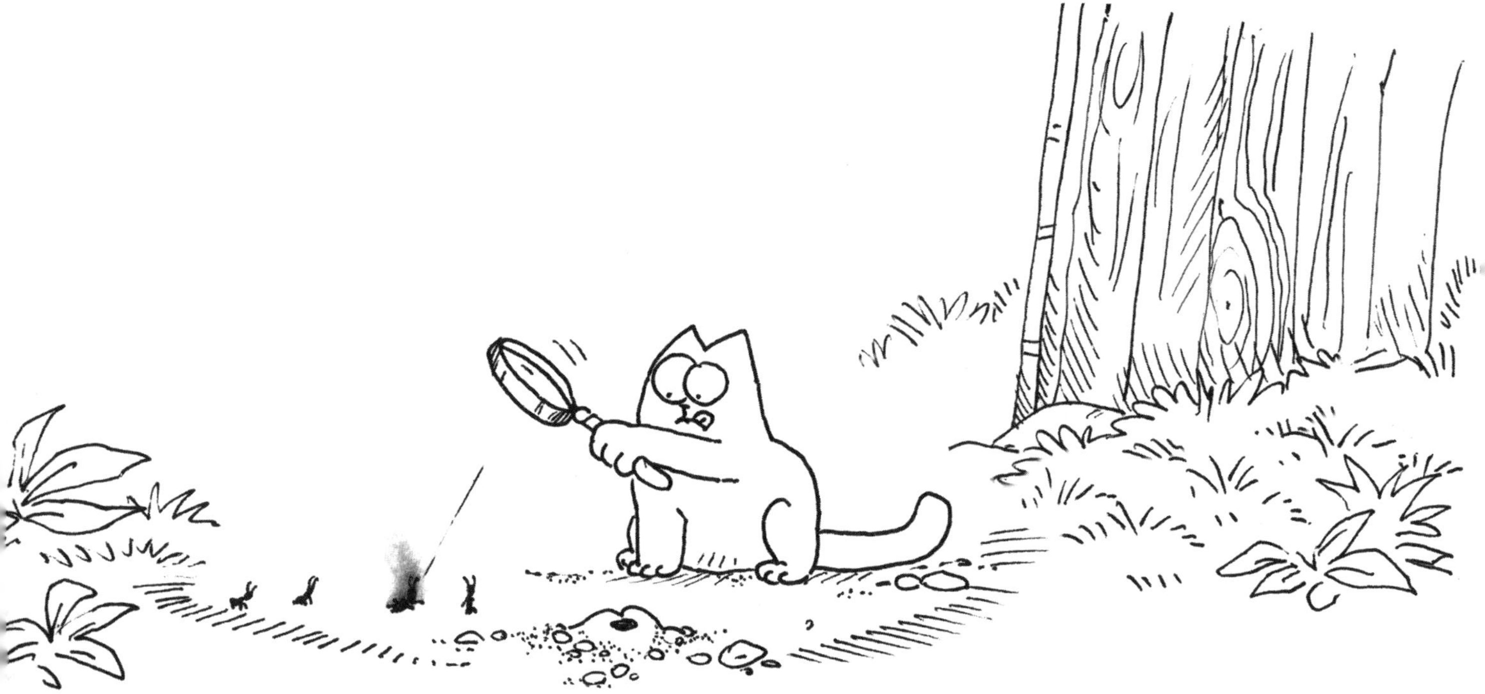

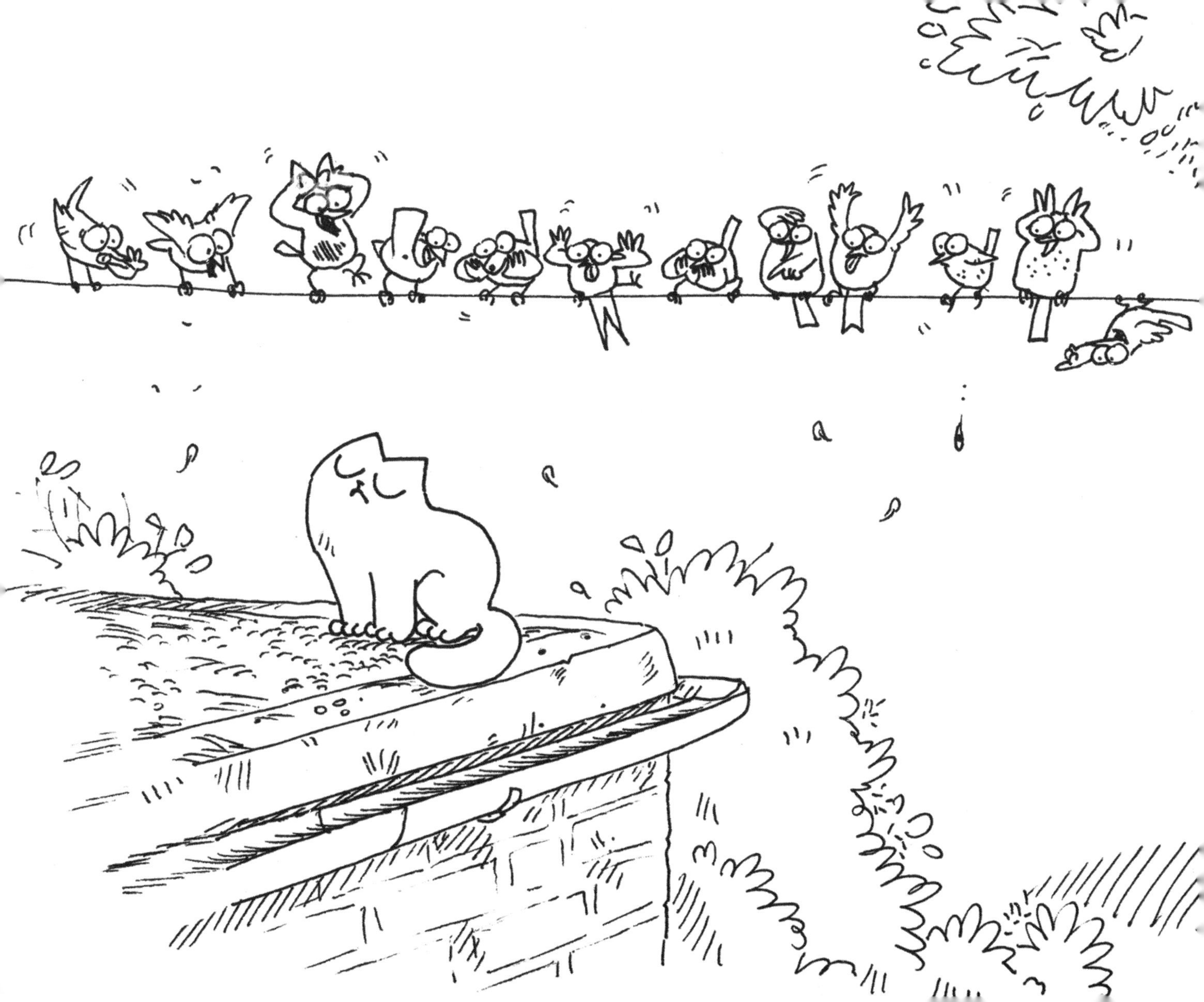

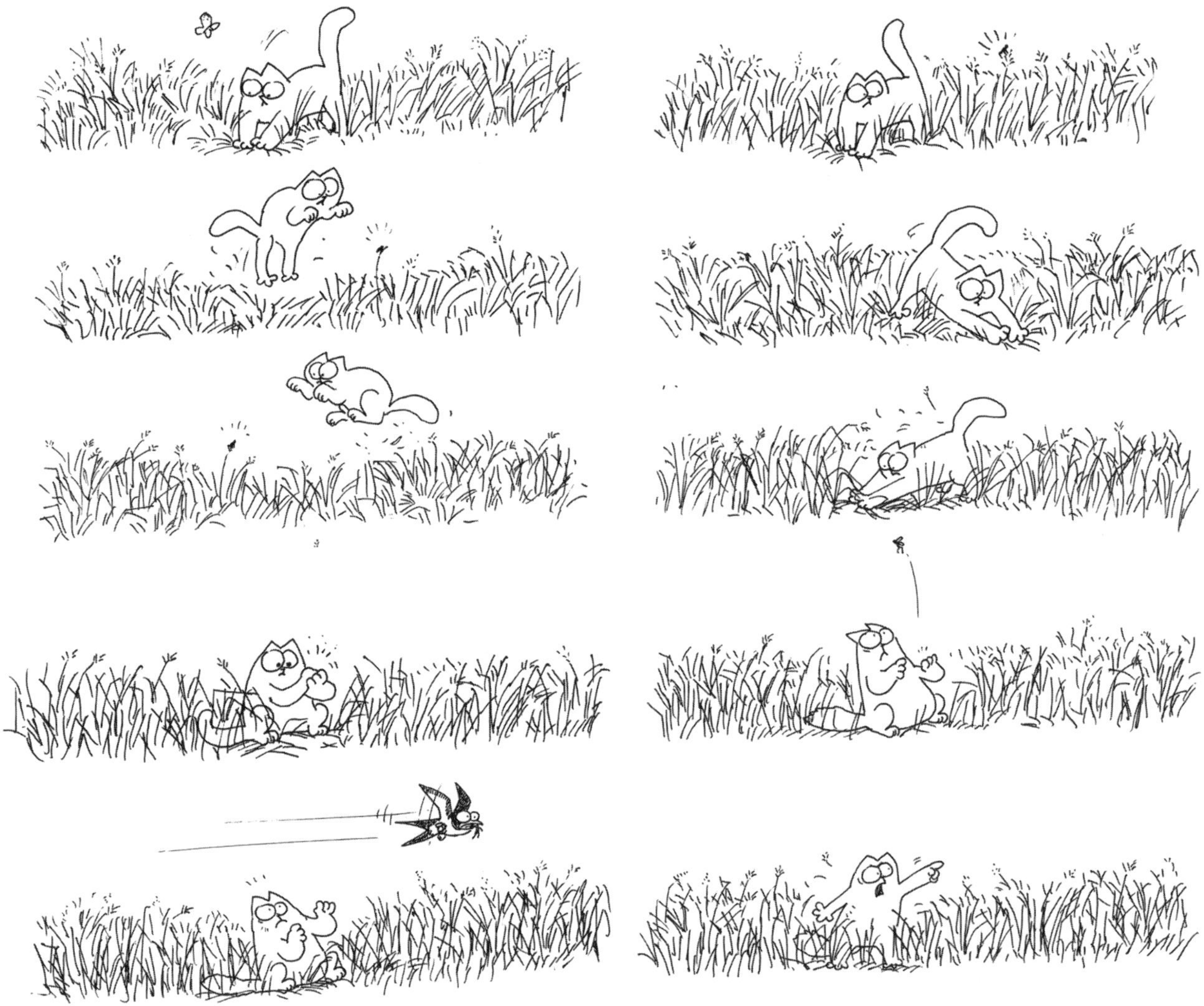

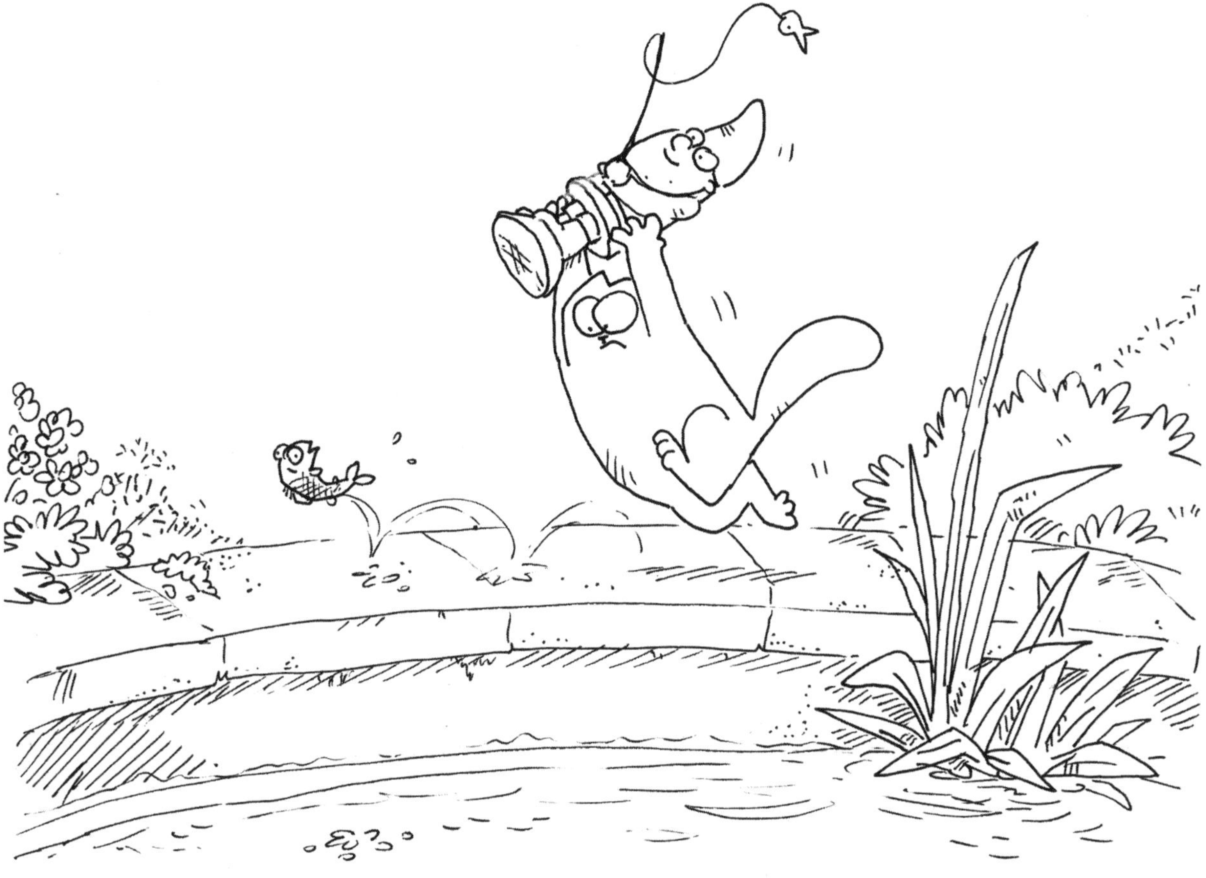

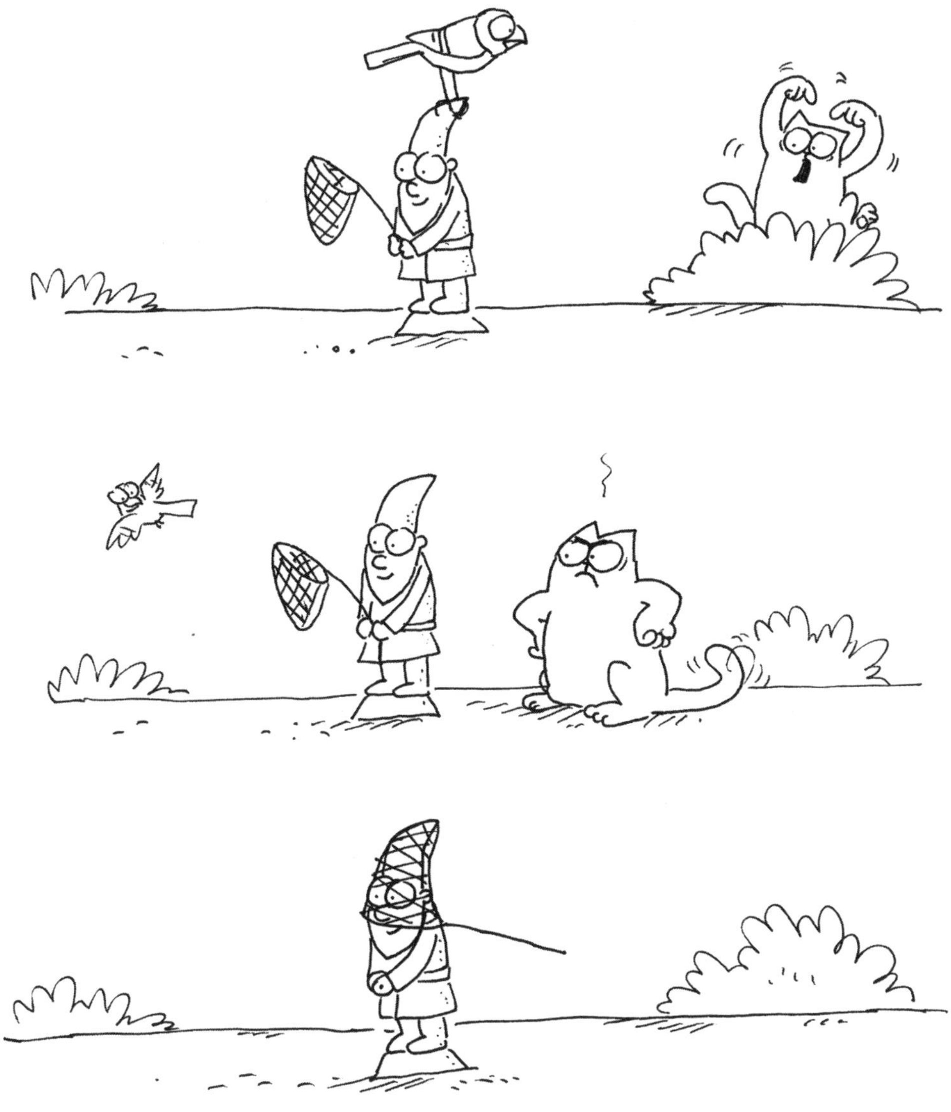

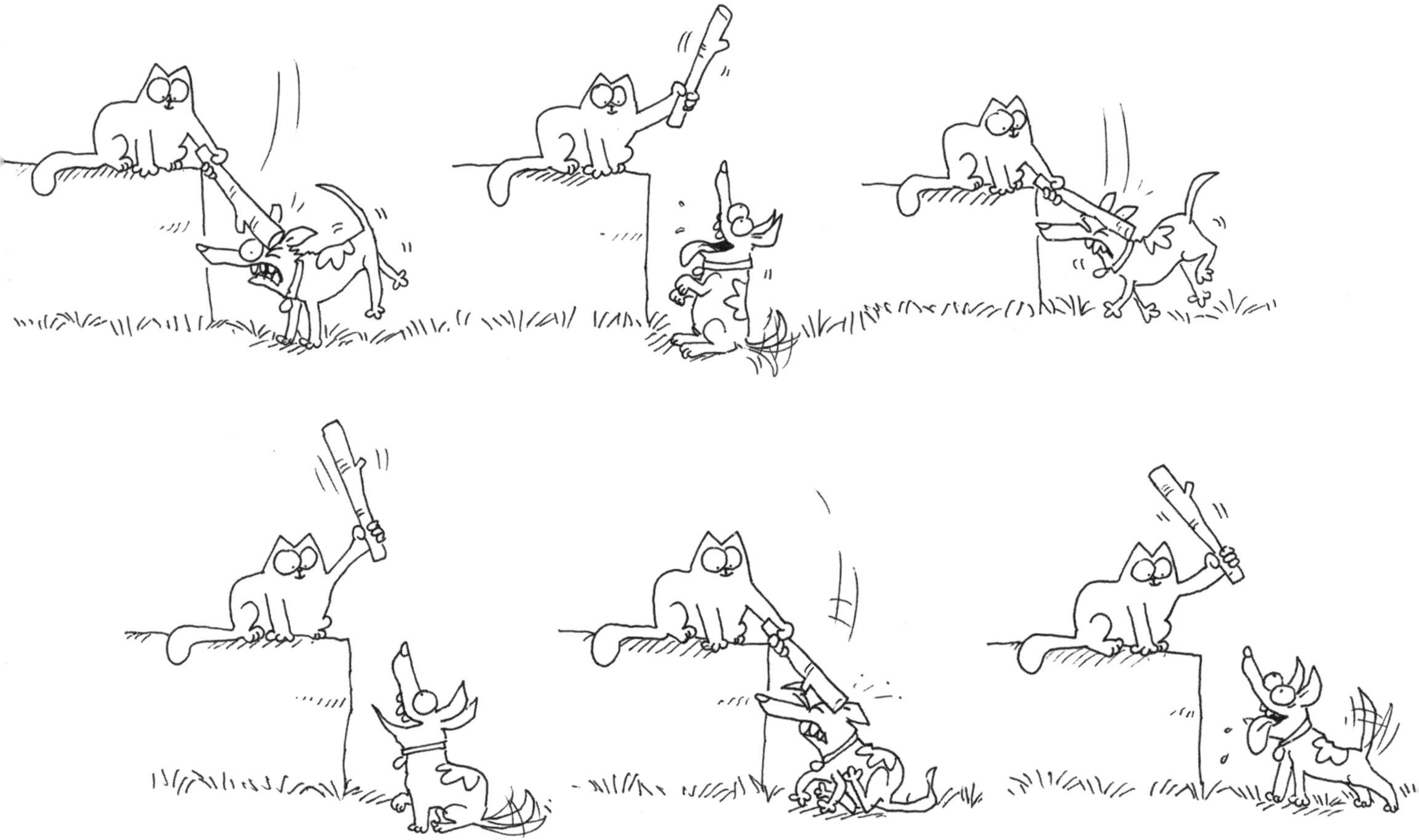

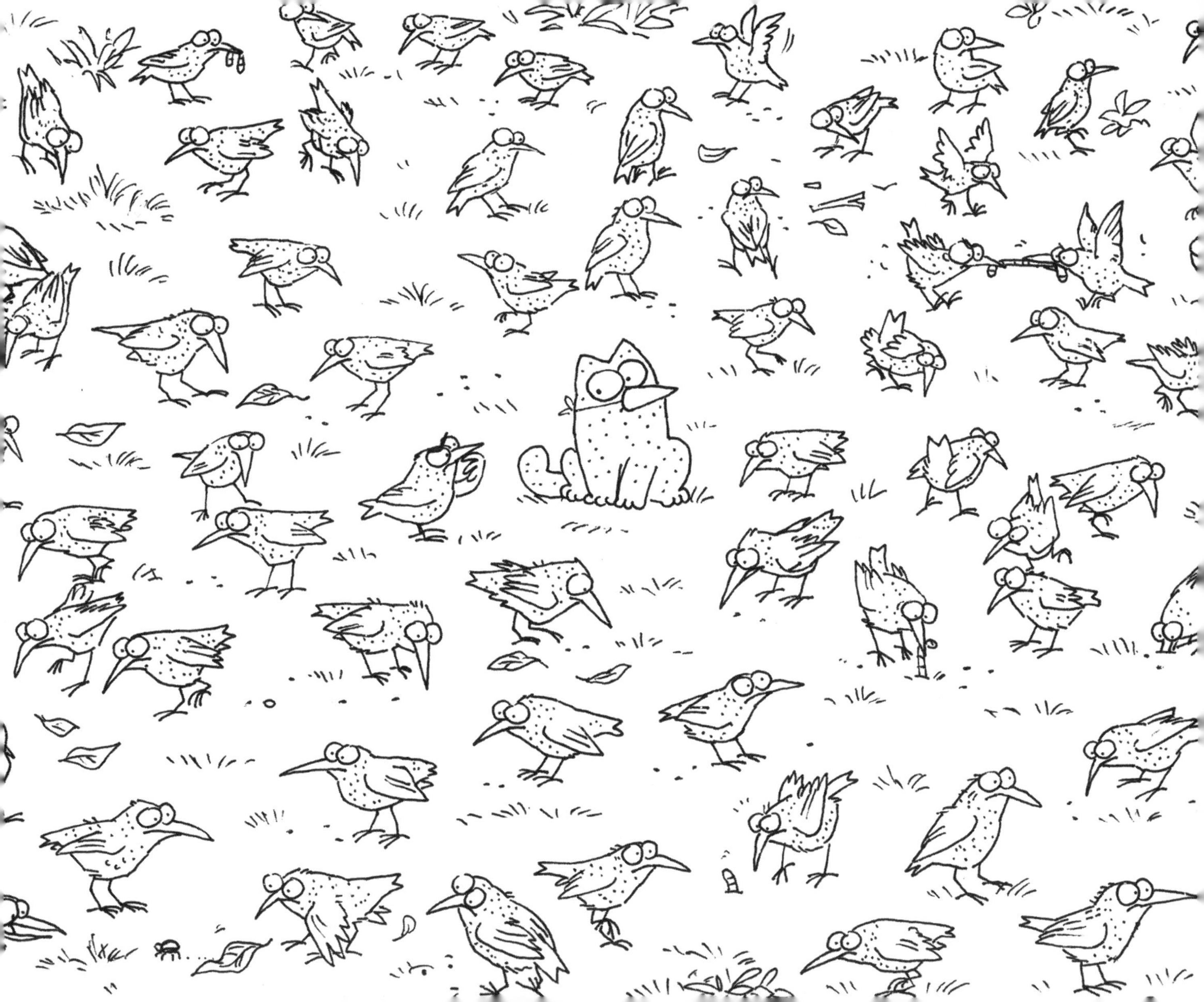

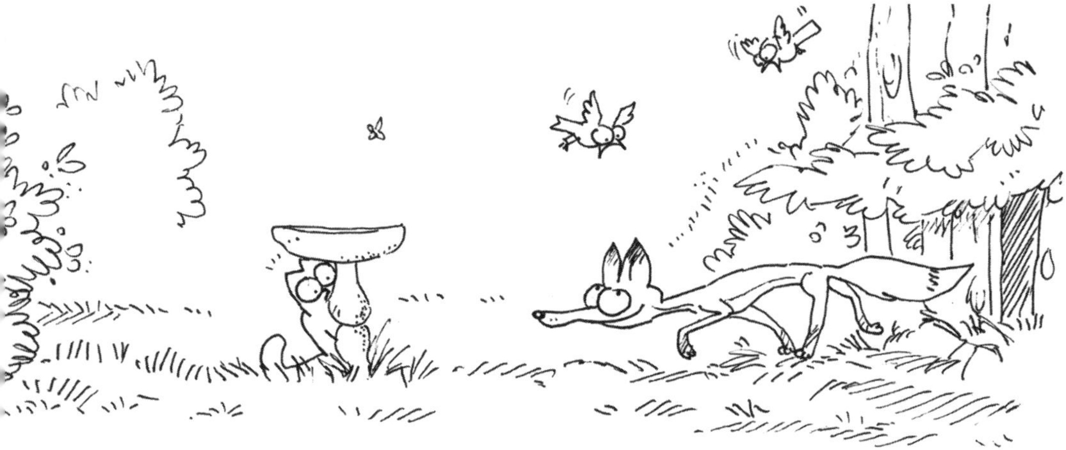

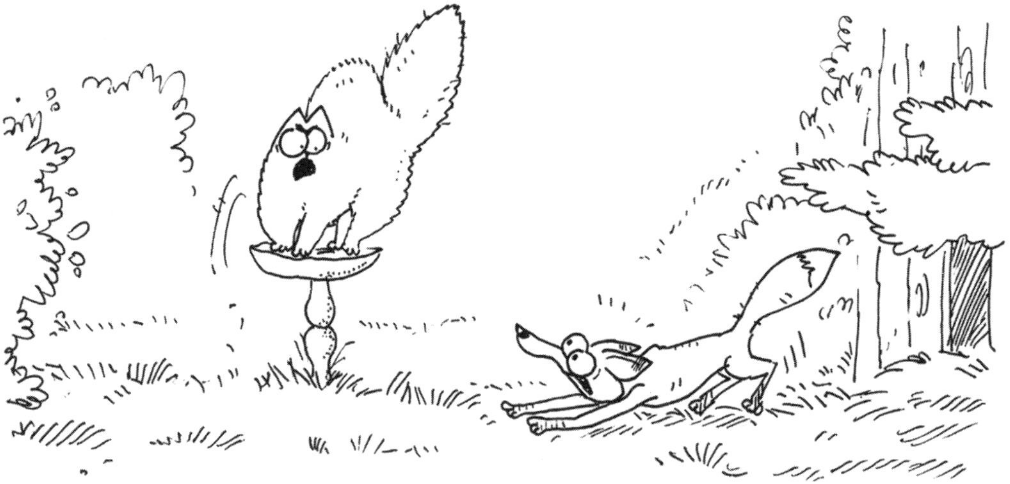

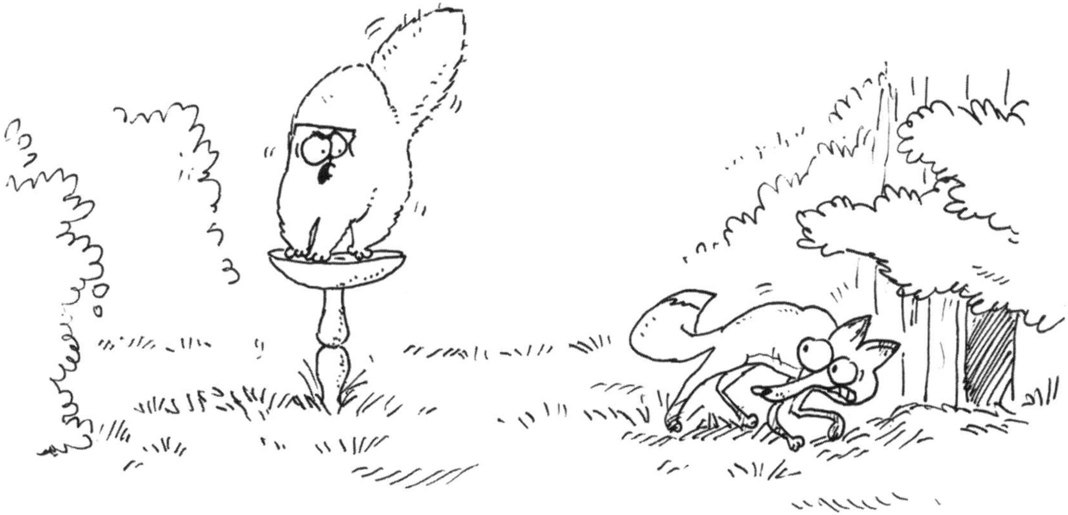

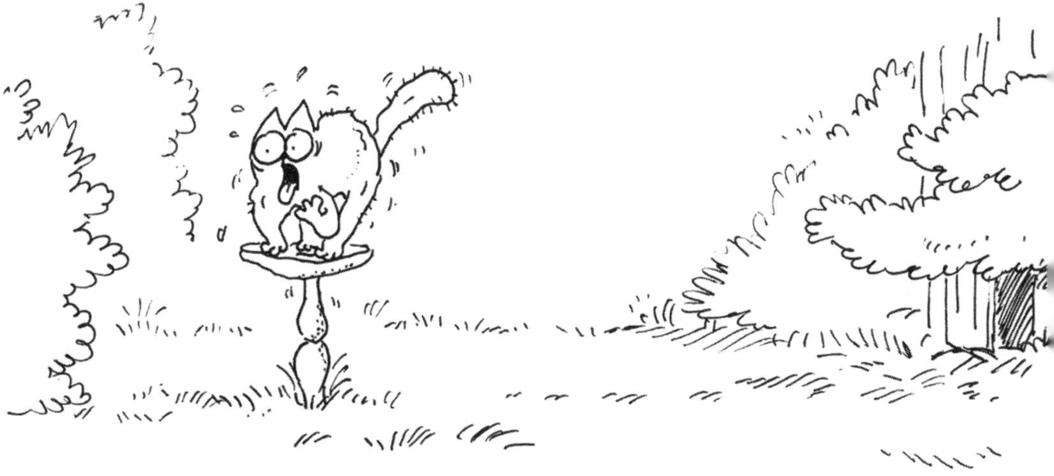

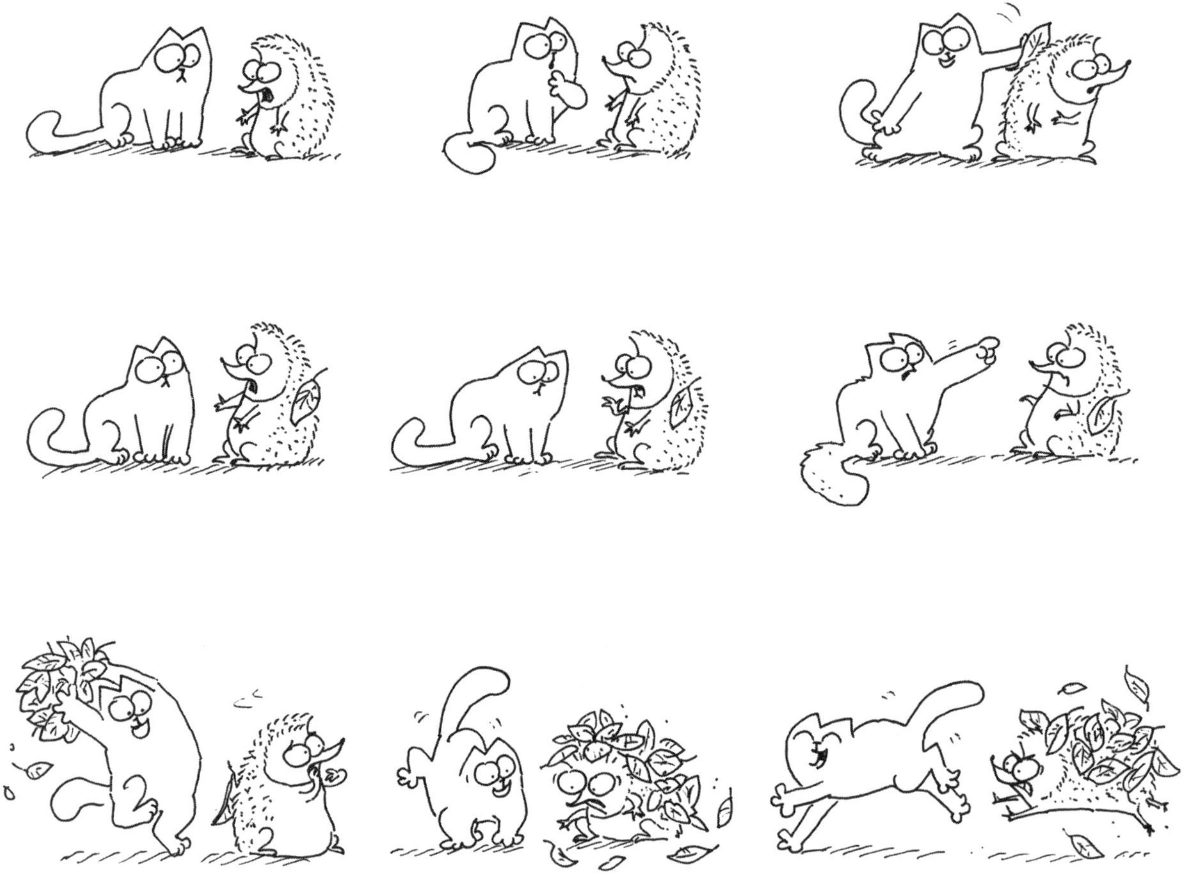

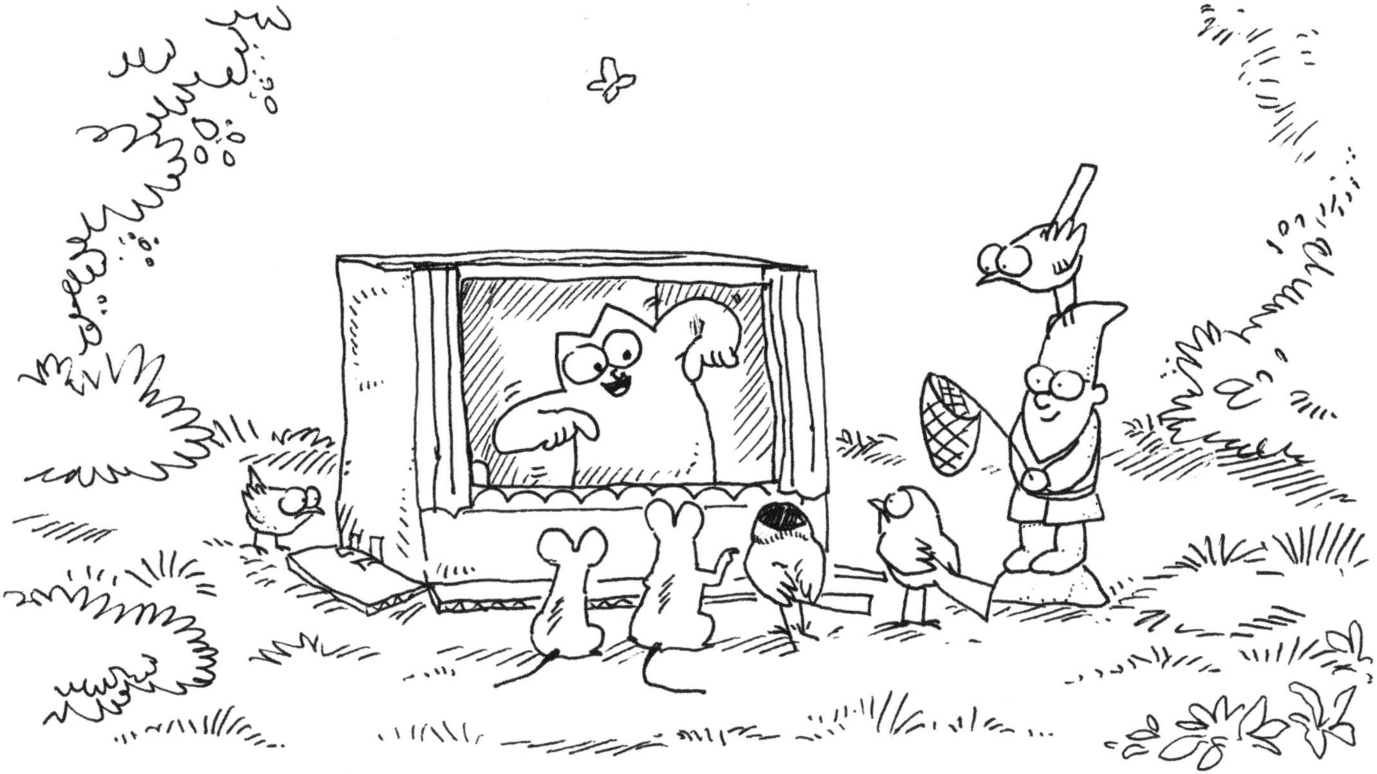

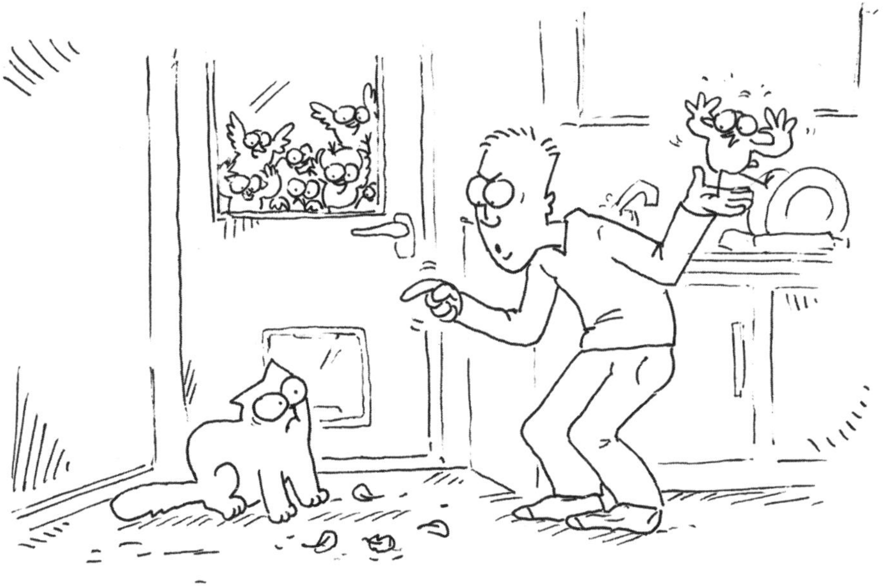

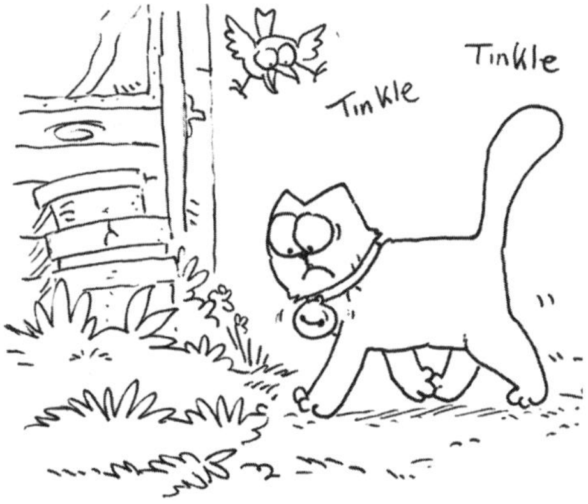
Tinkle
Tinkle

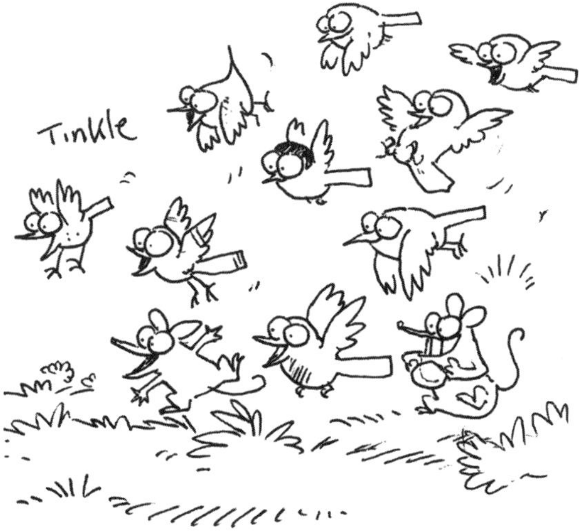
Tinkle

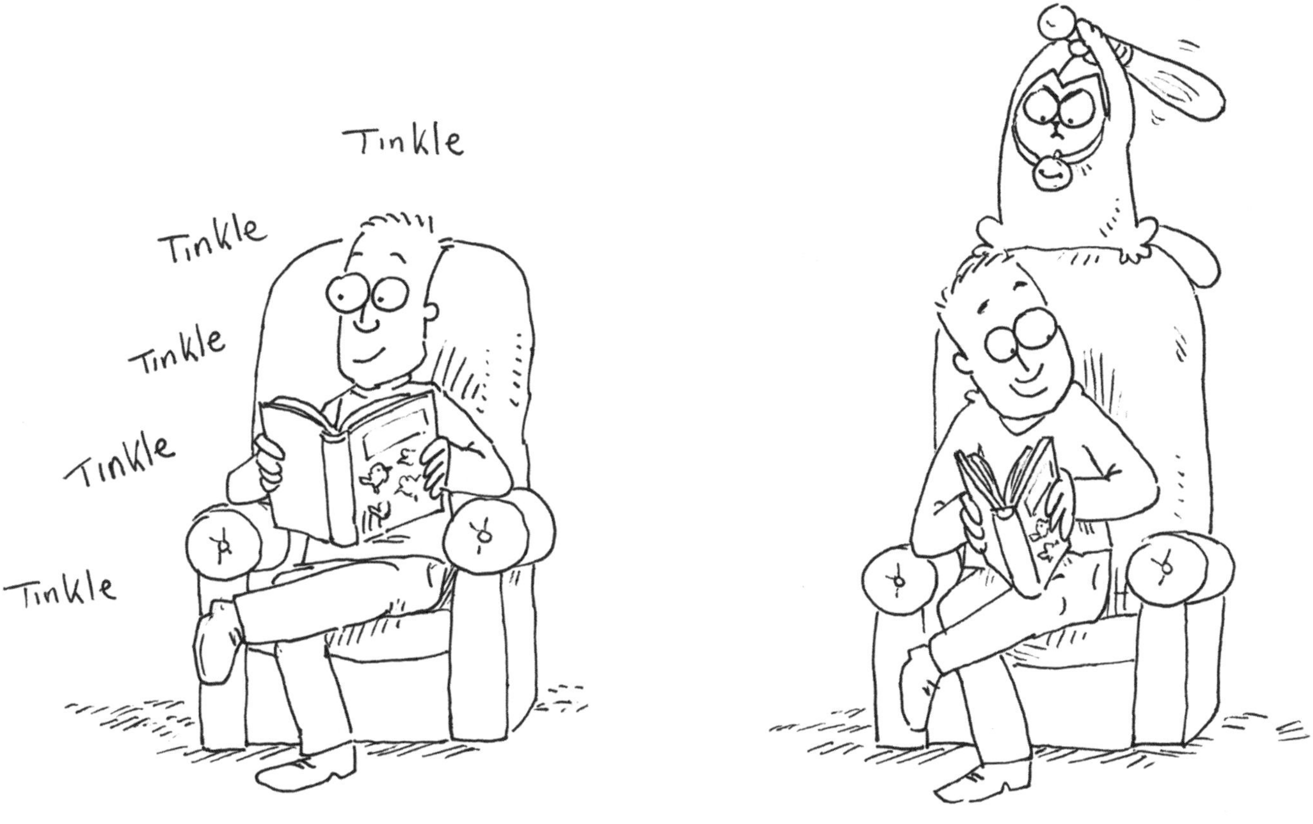

Tinkle
Tinkle
Tinkle
Tinkle
Tinkle

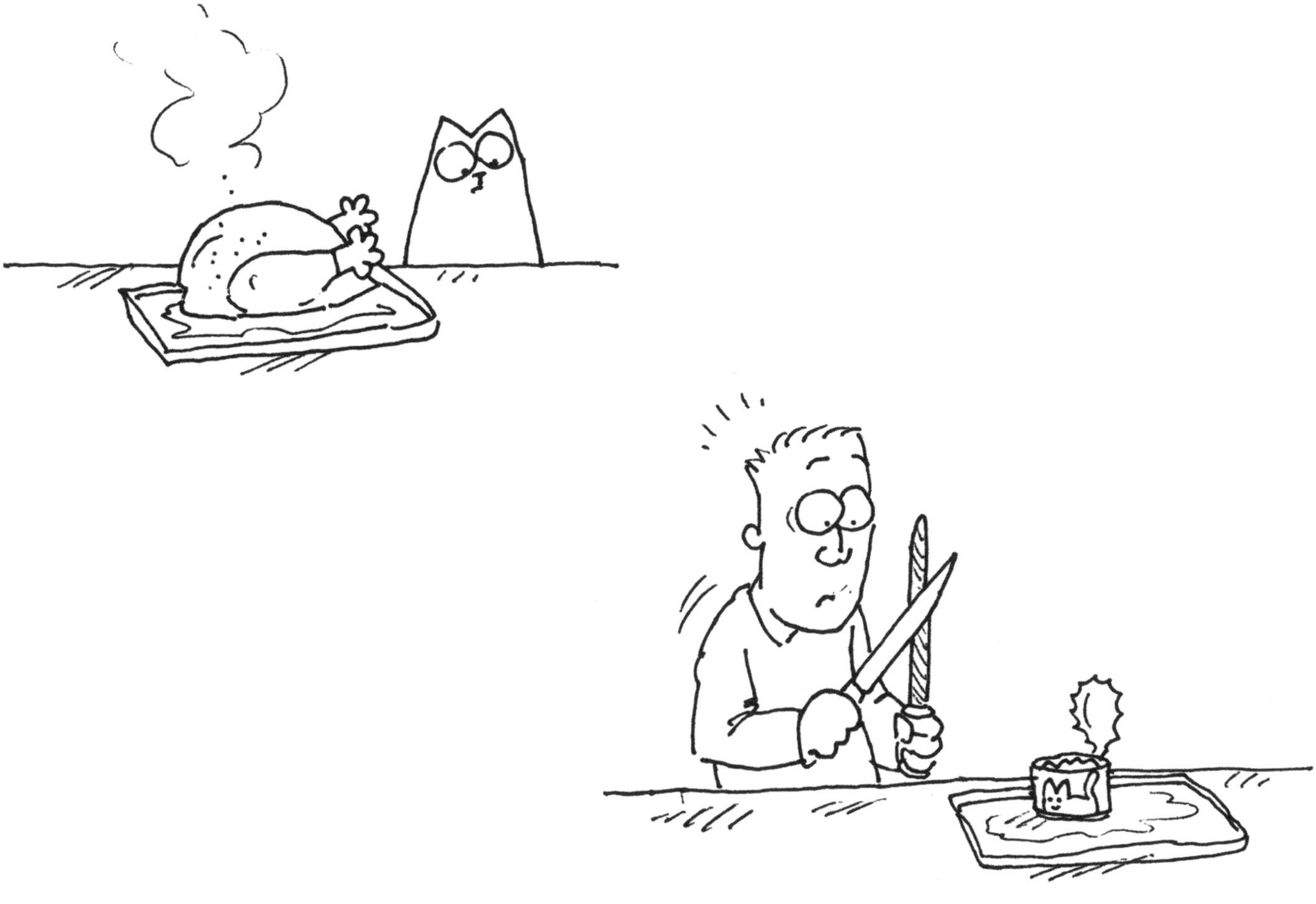

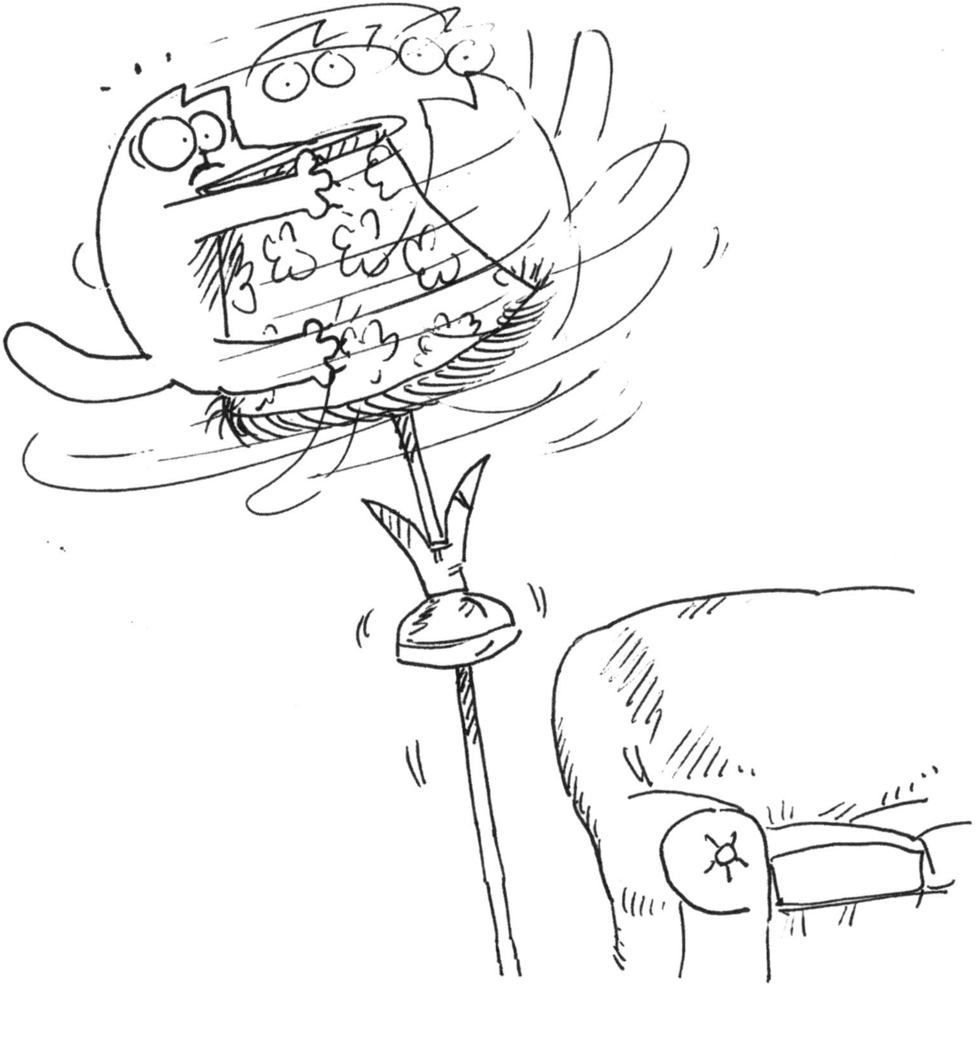

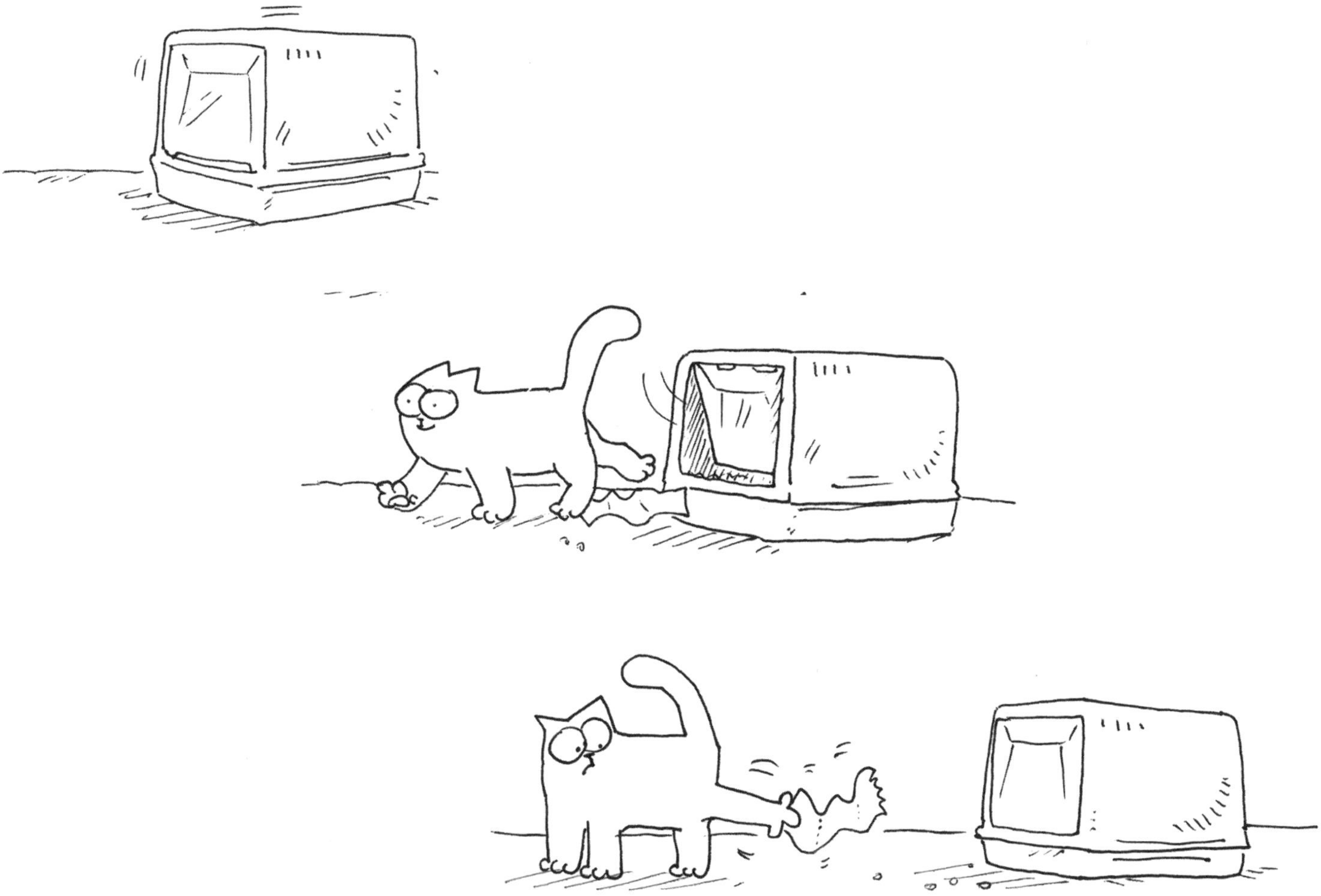

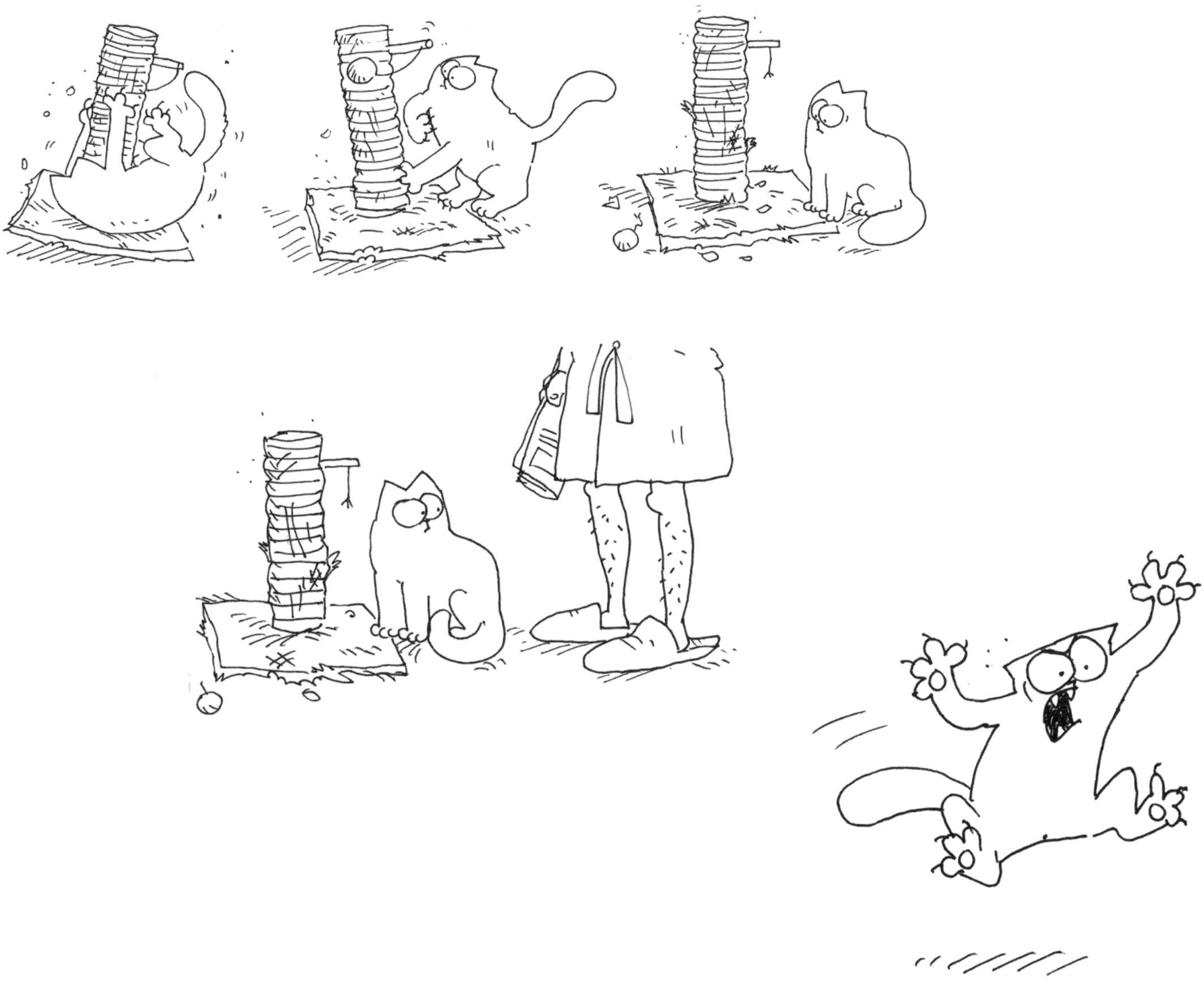

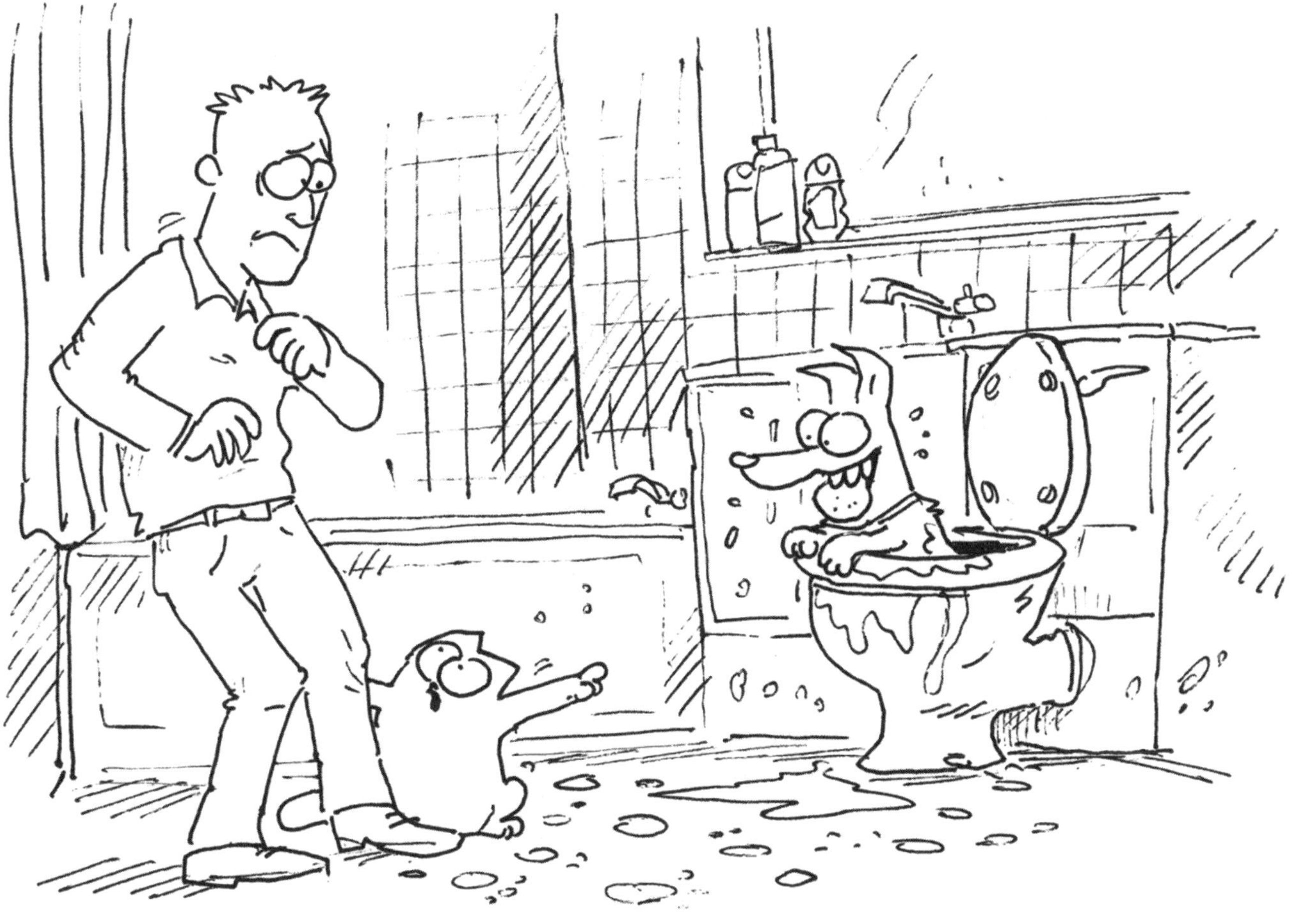

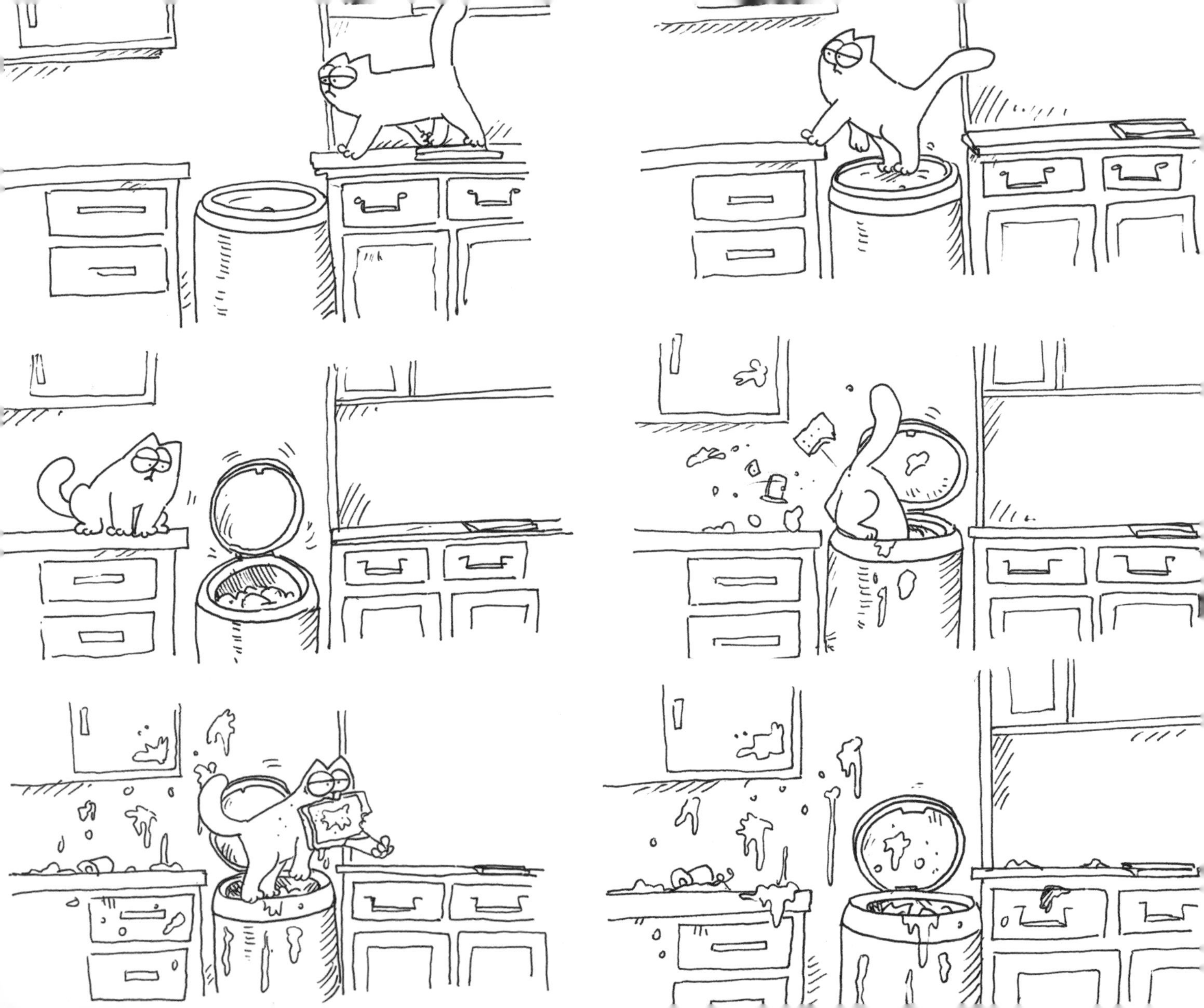

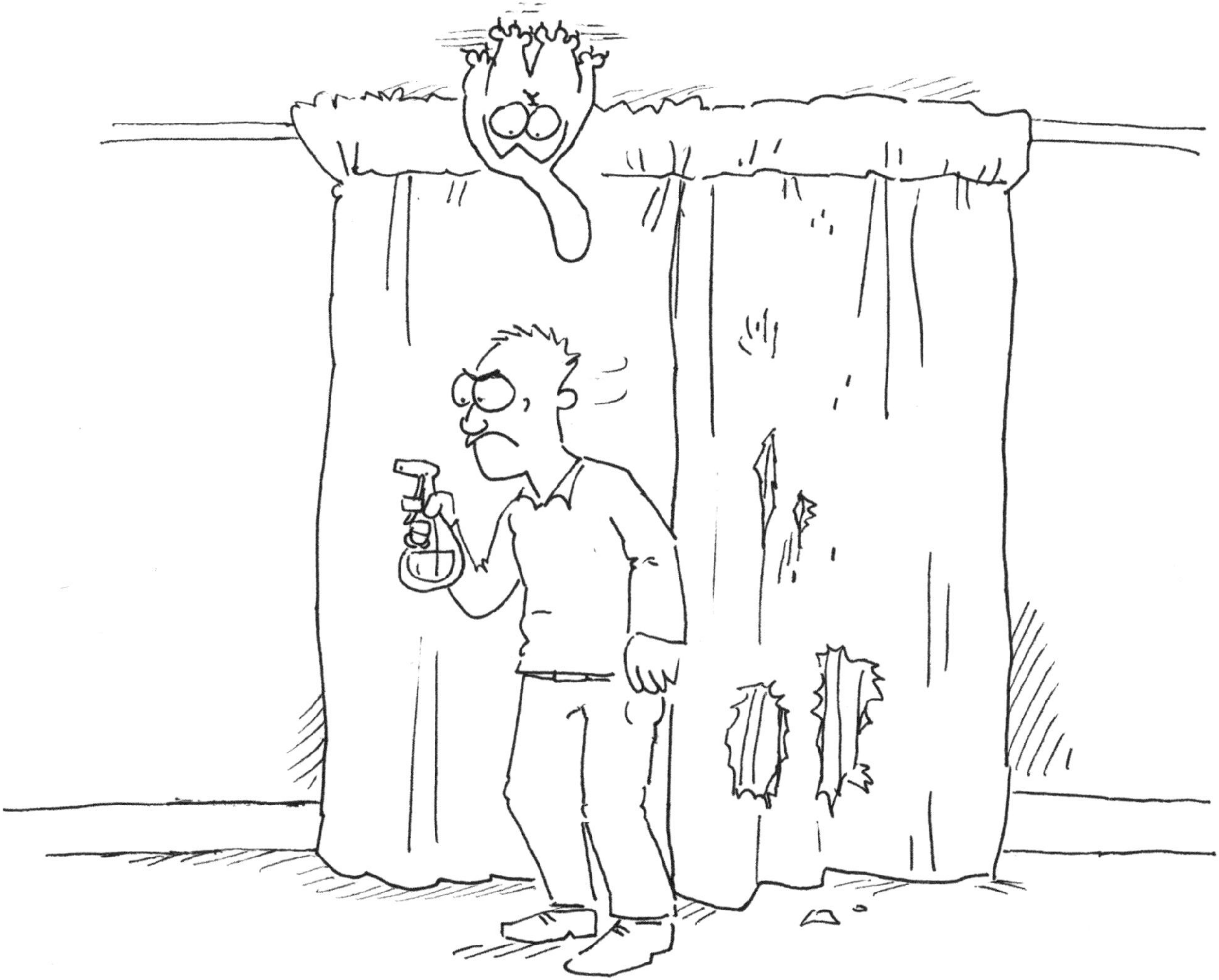

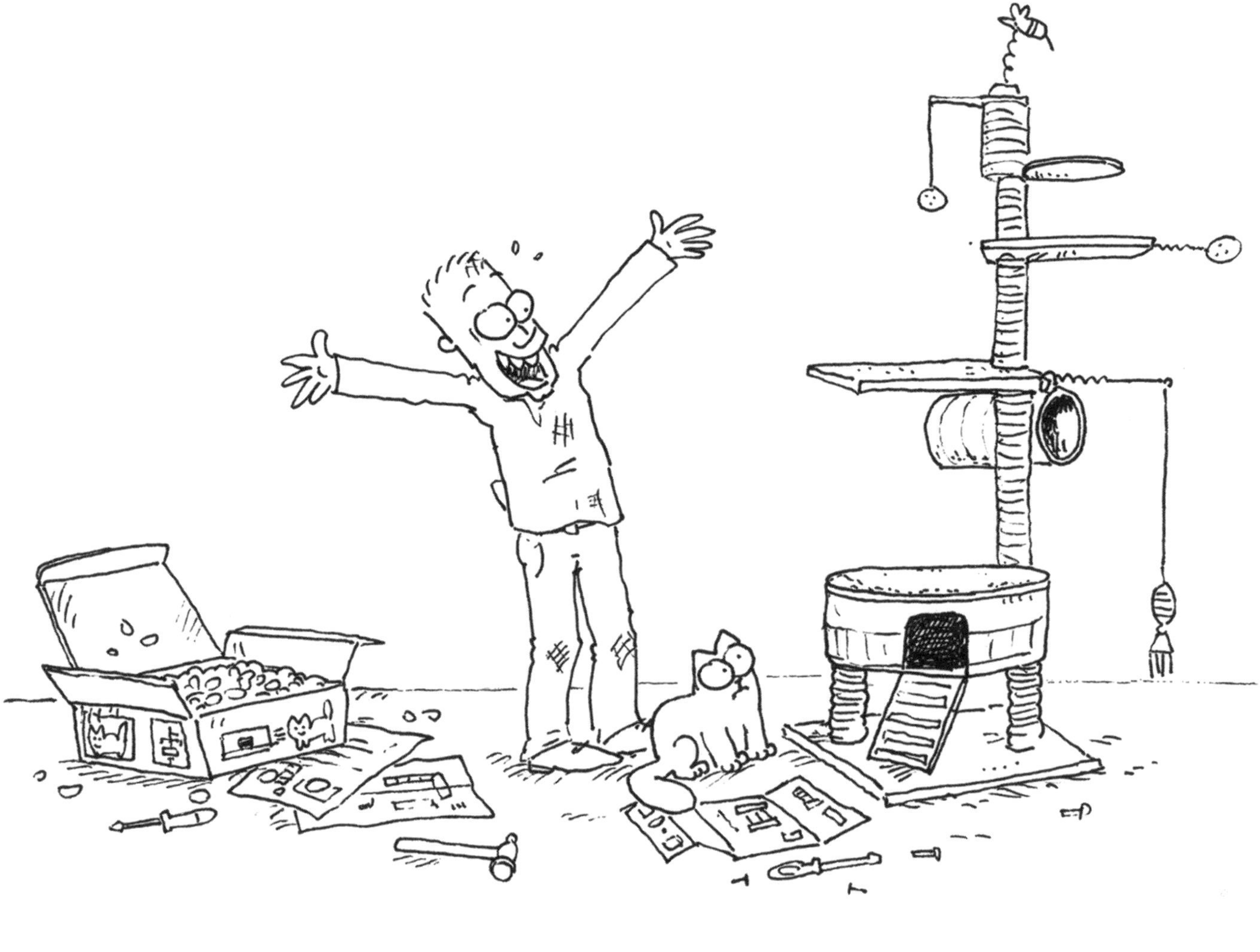

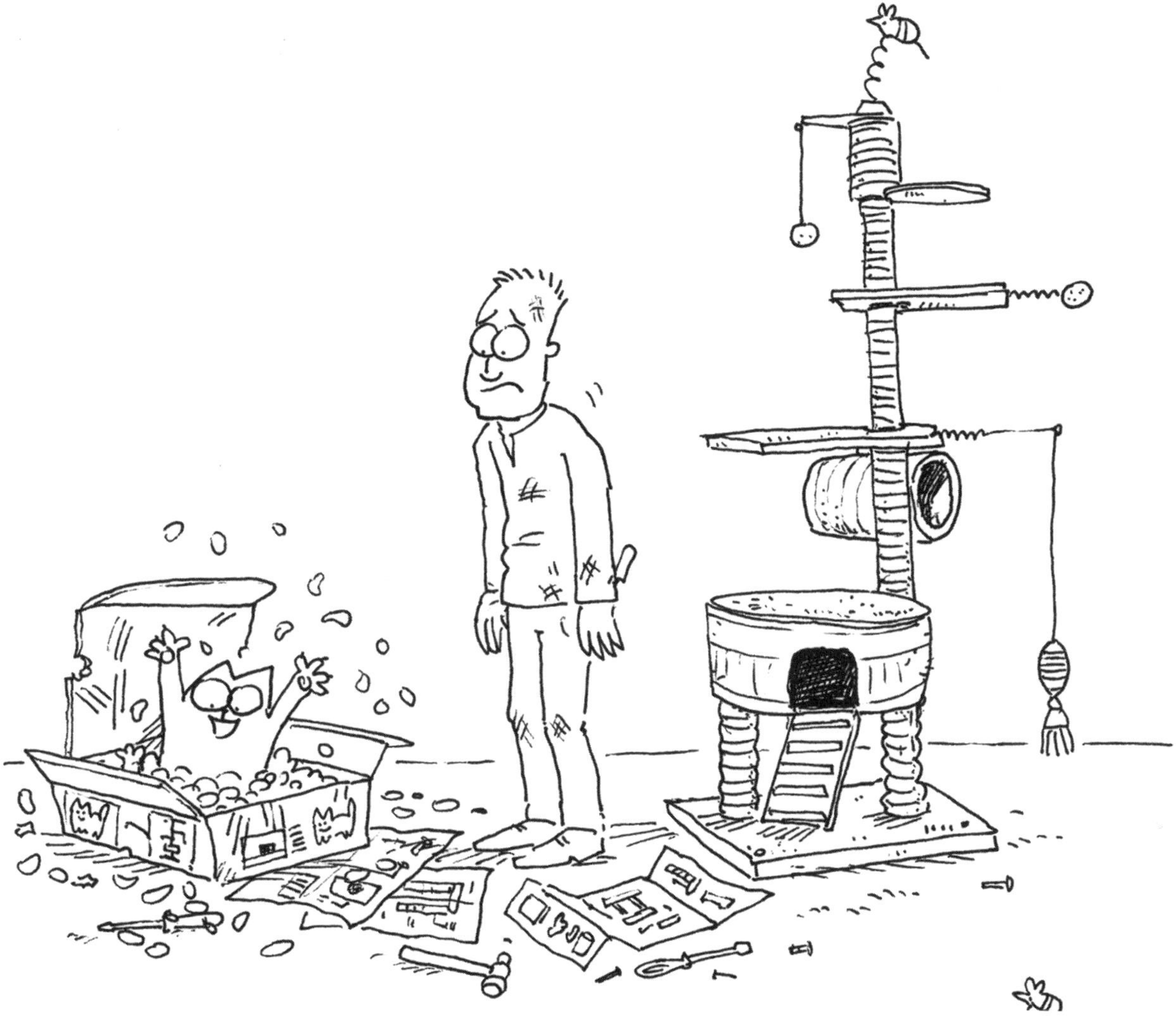

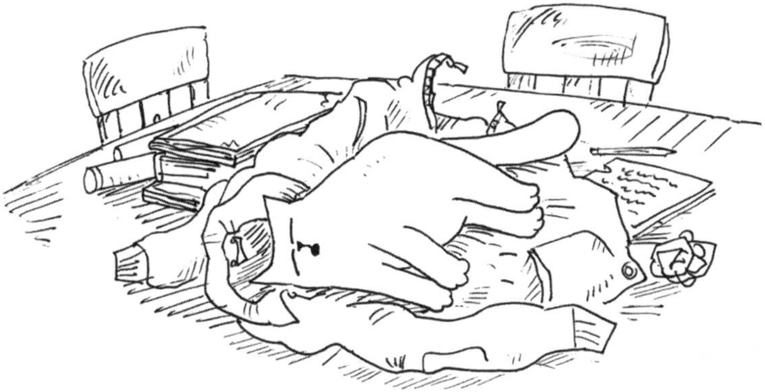

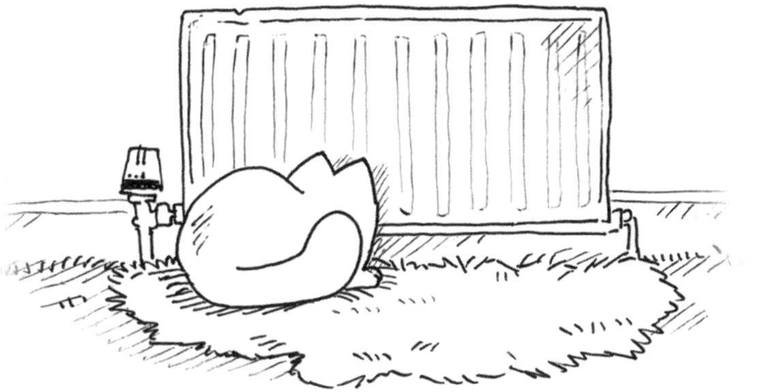

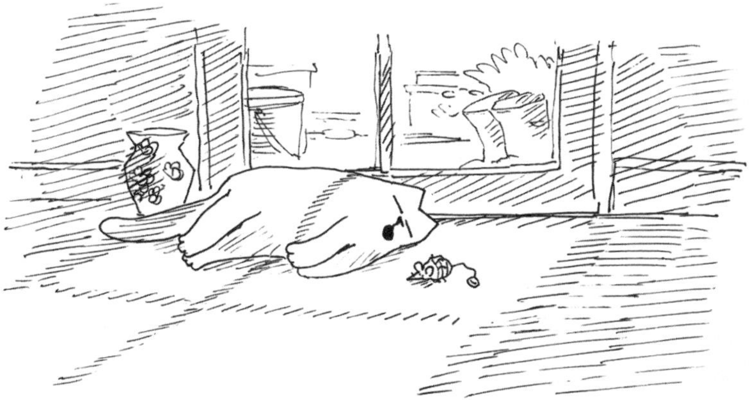

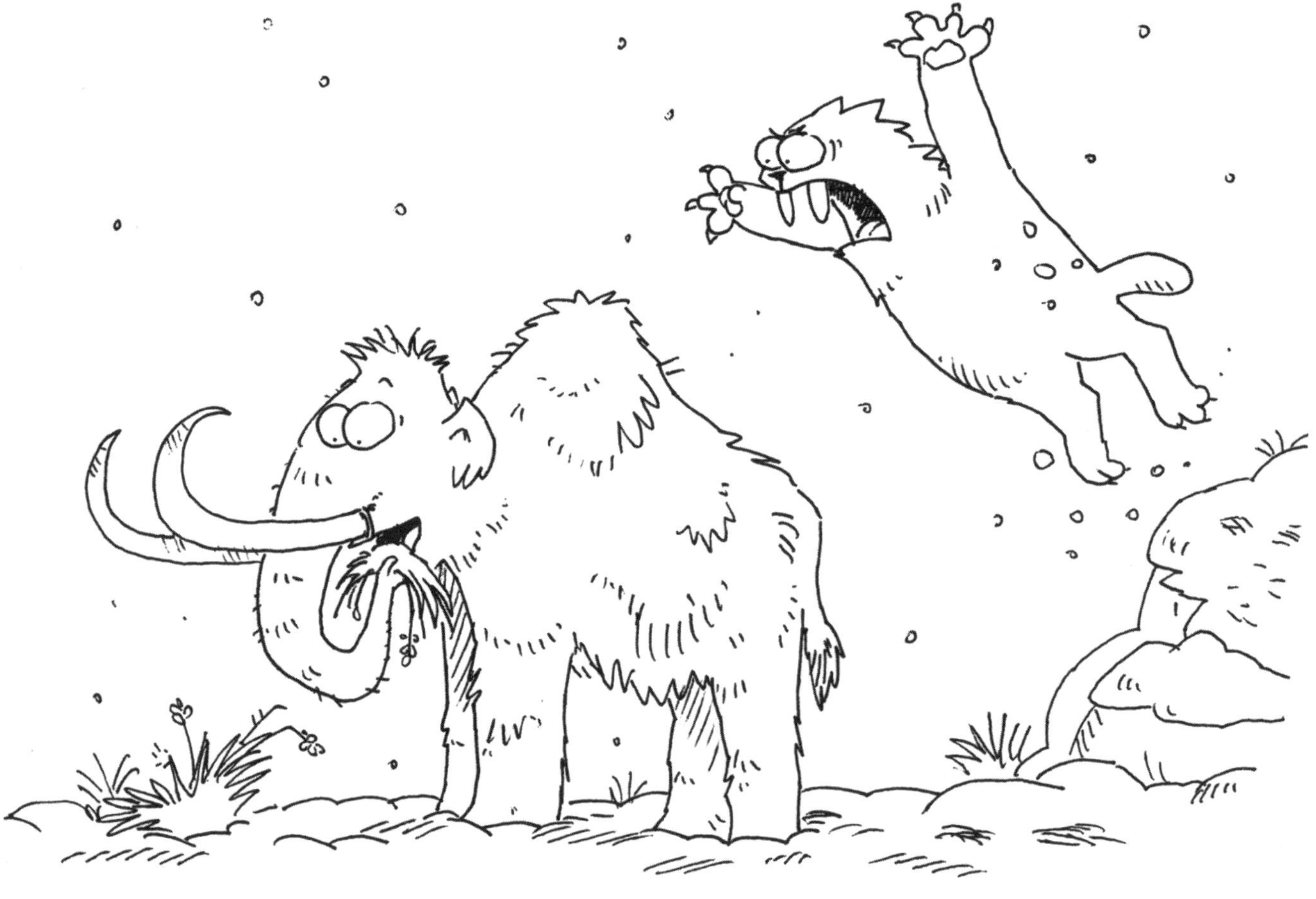

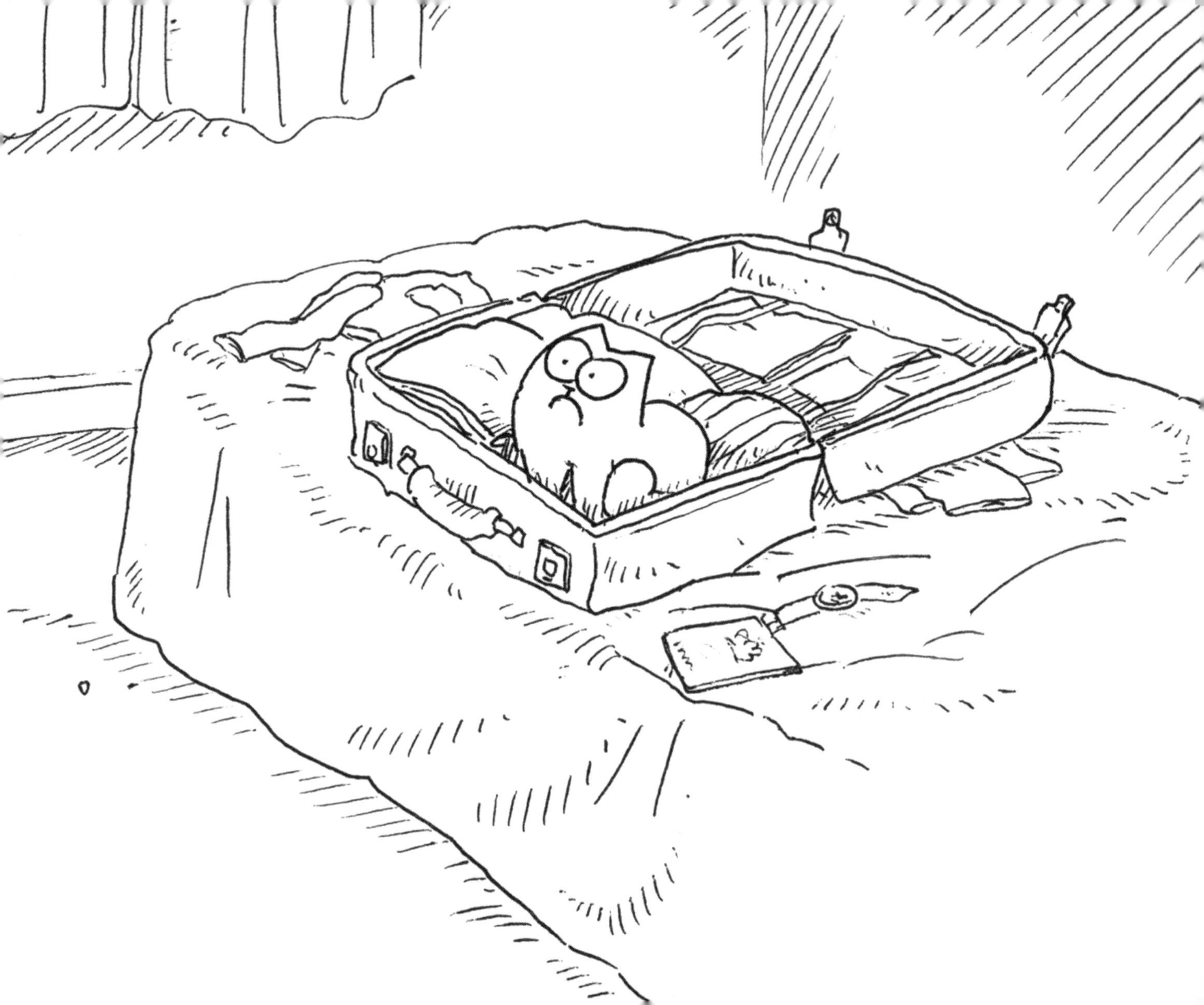

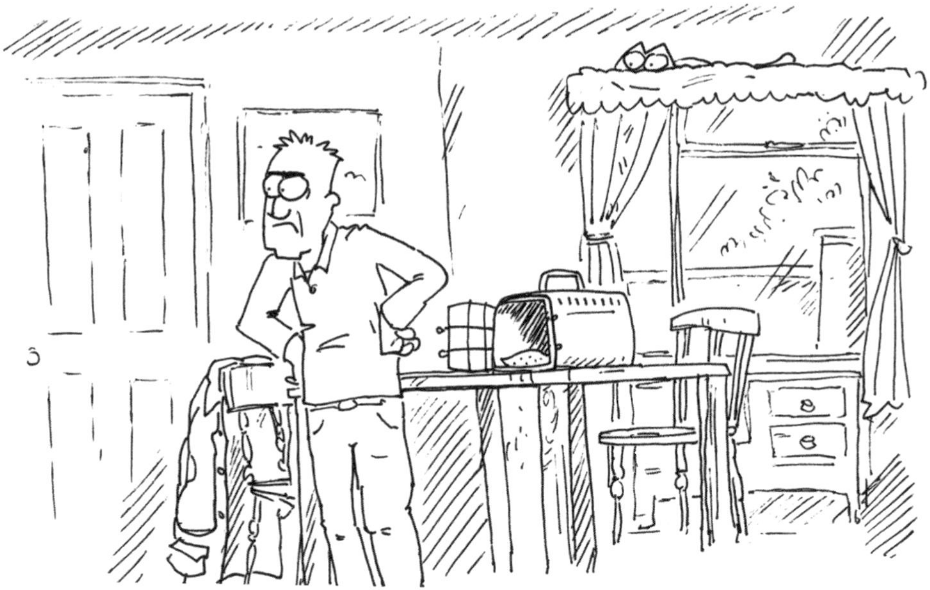

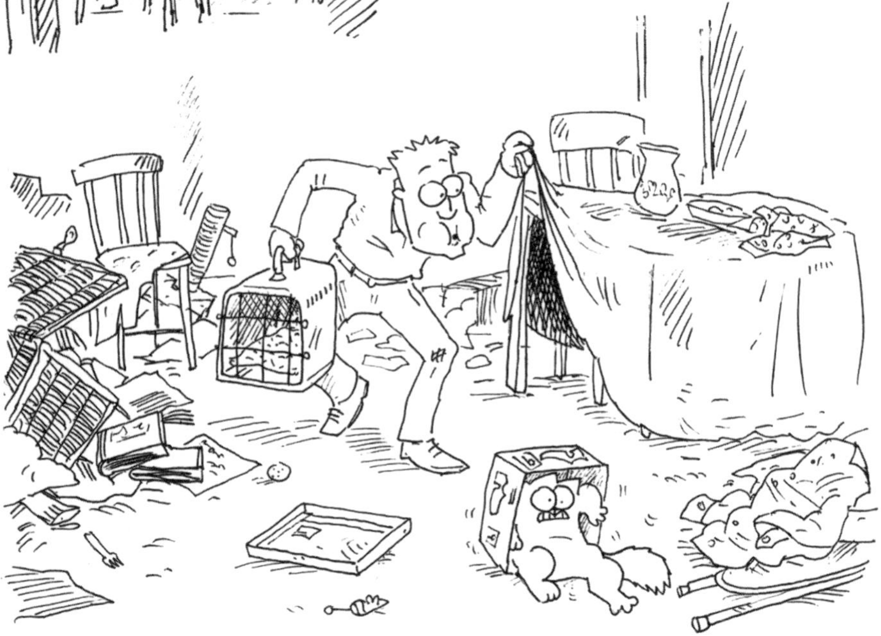

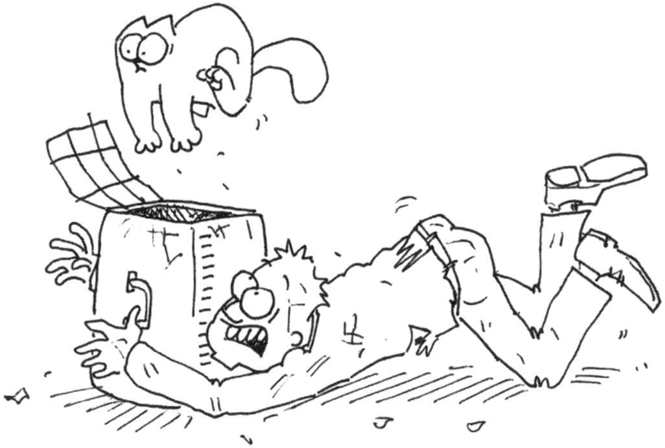

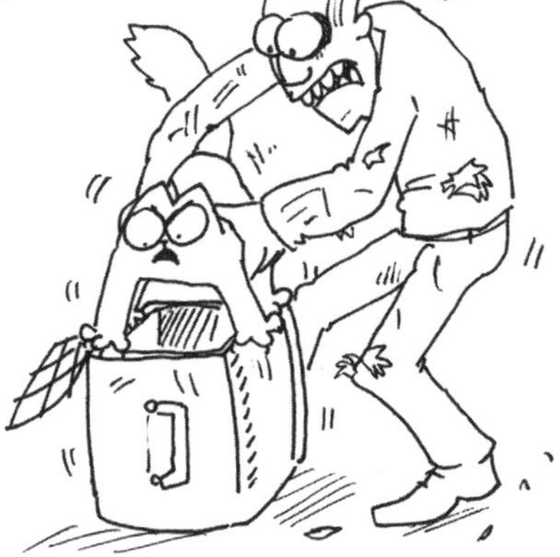

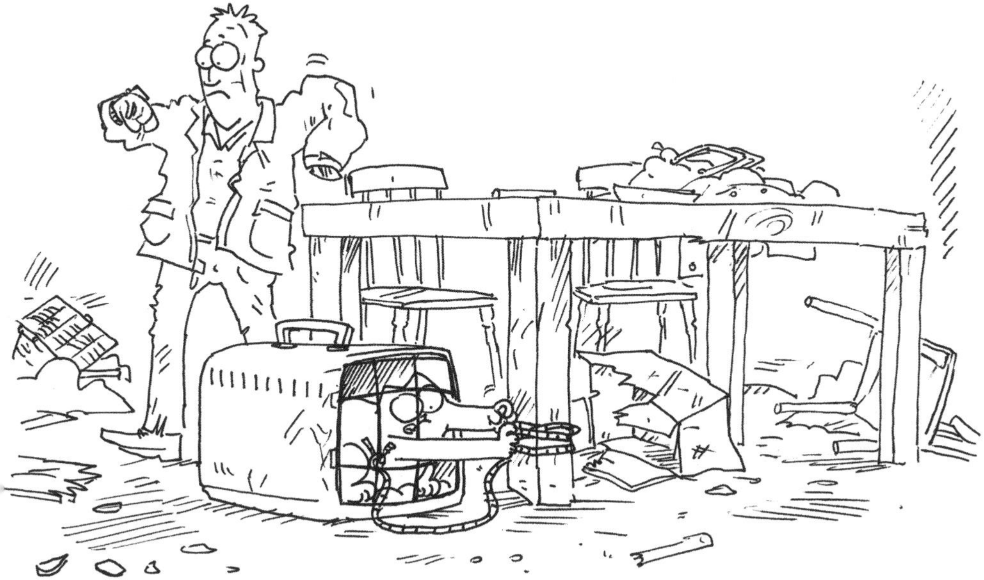

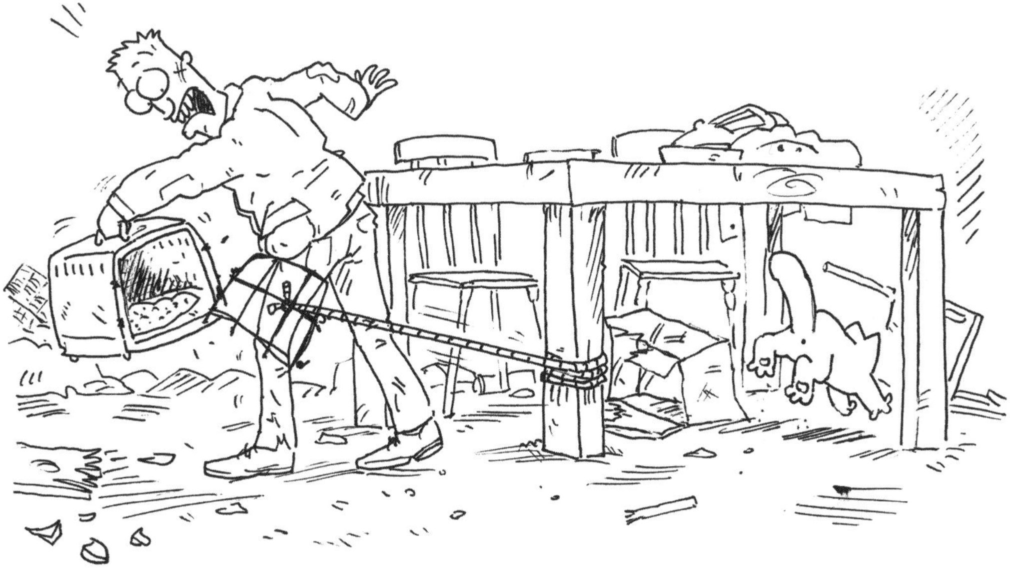

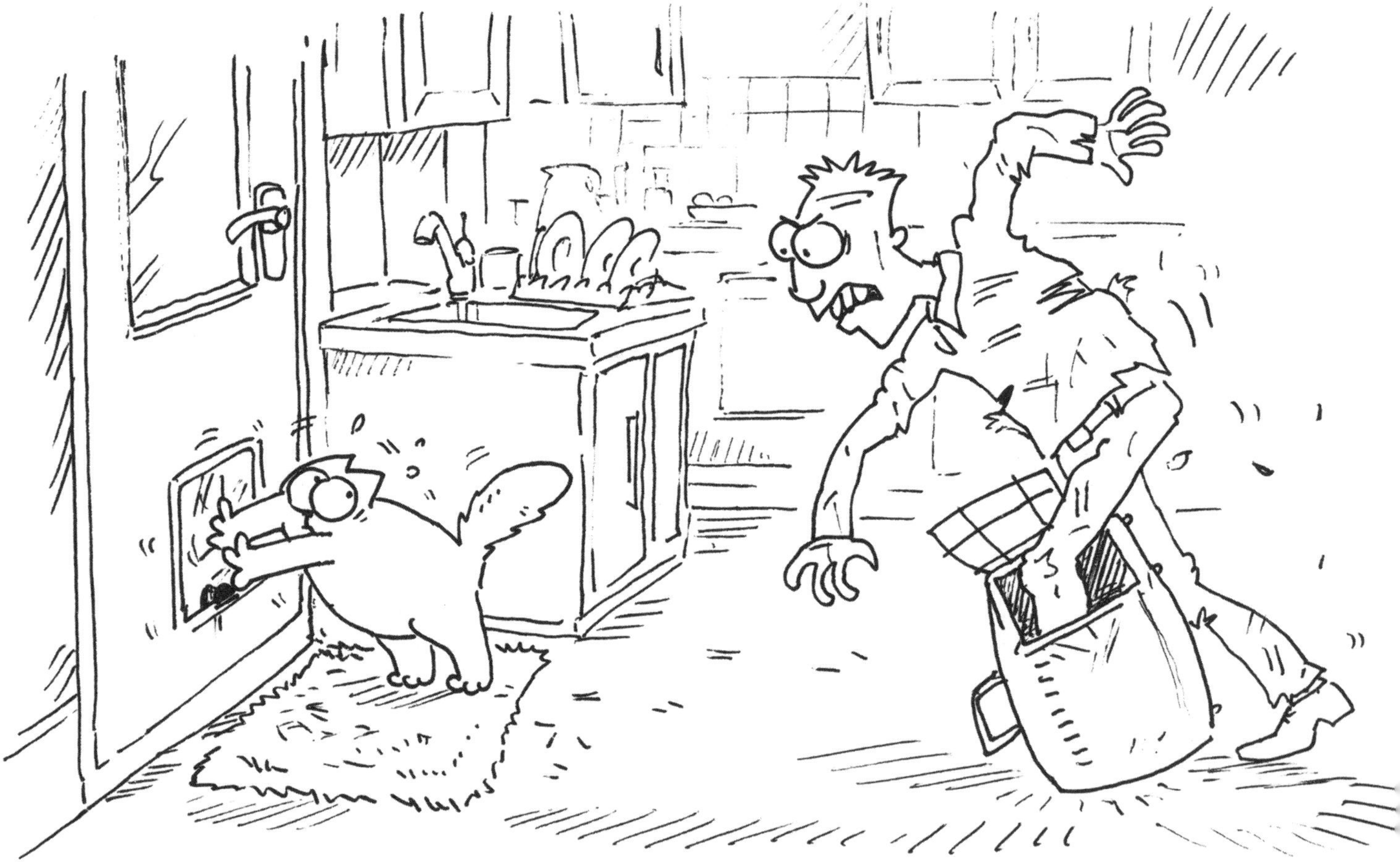

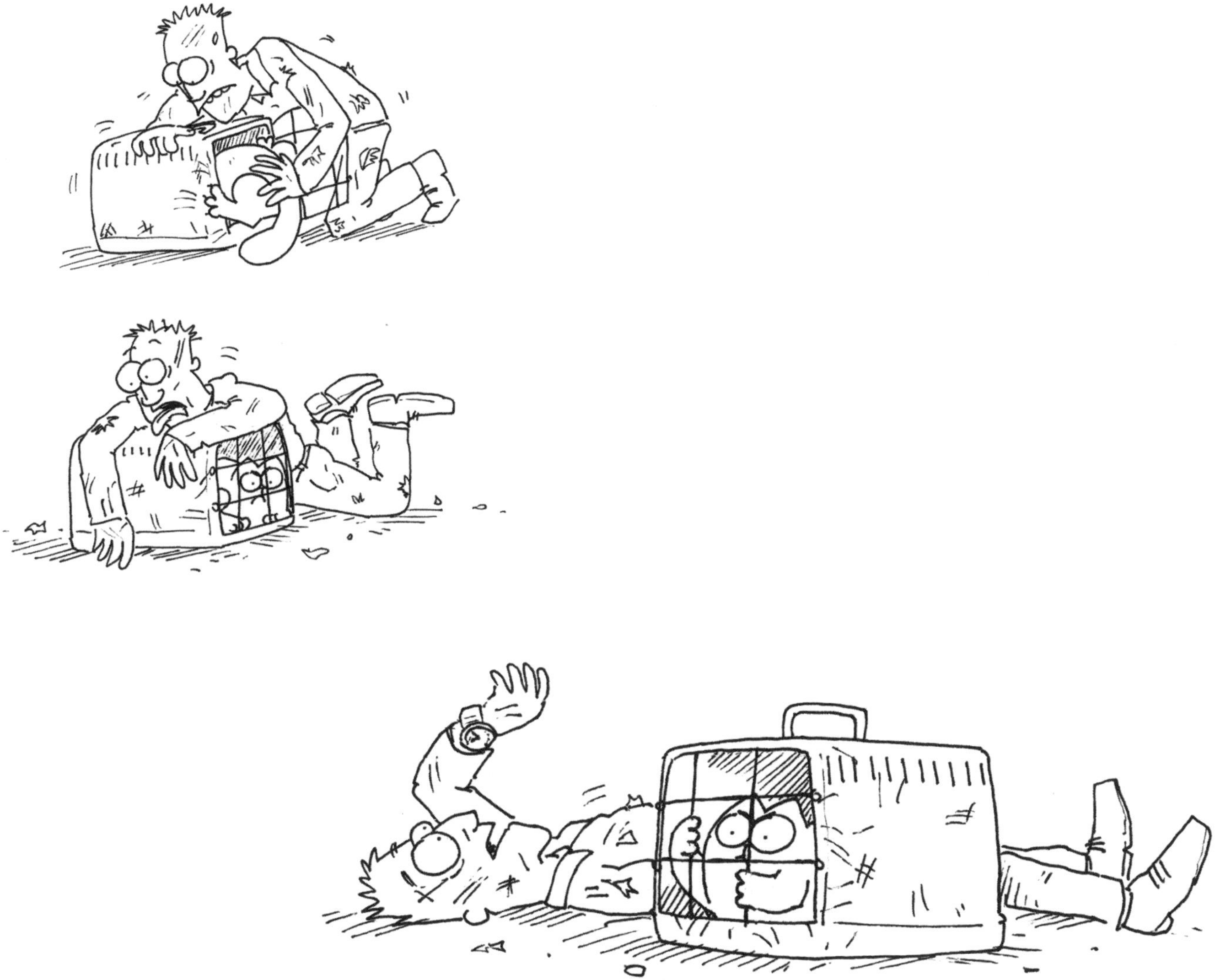

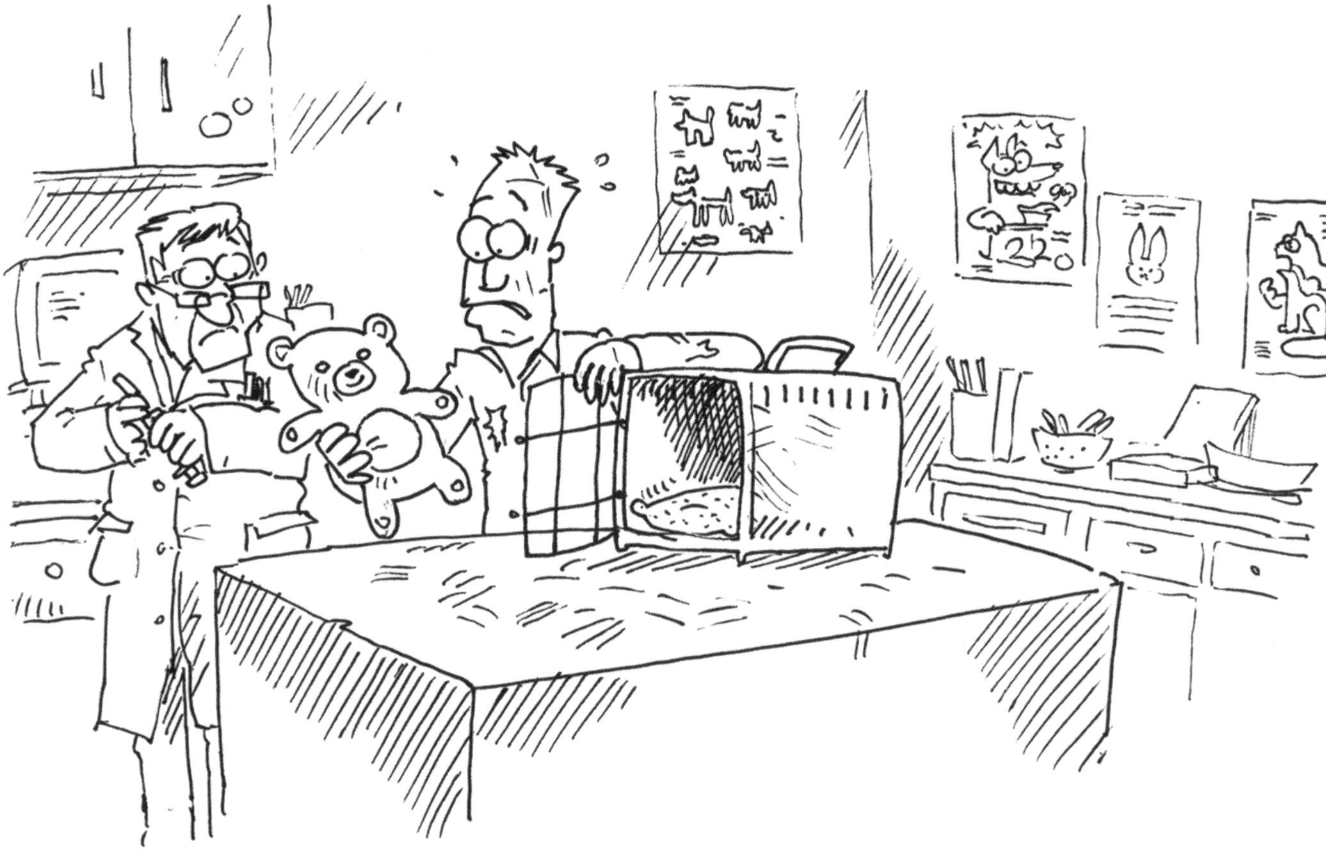

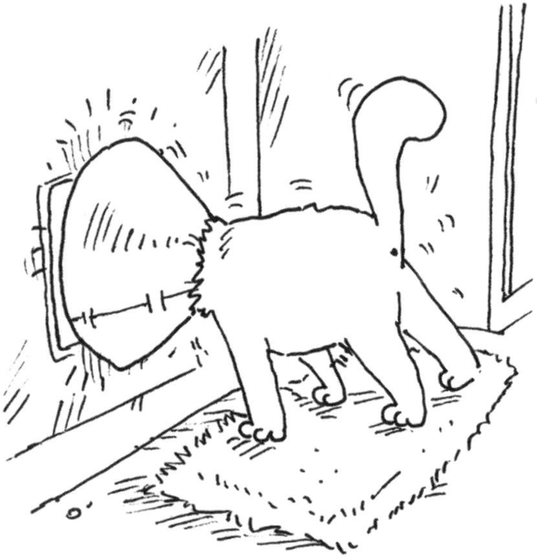

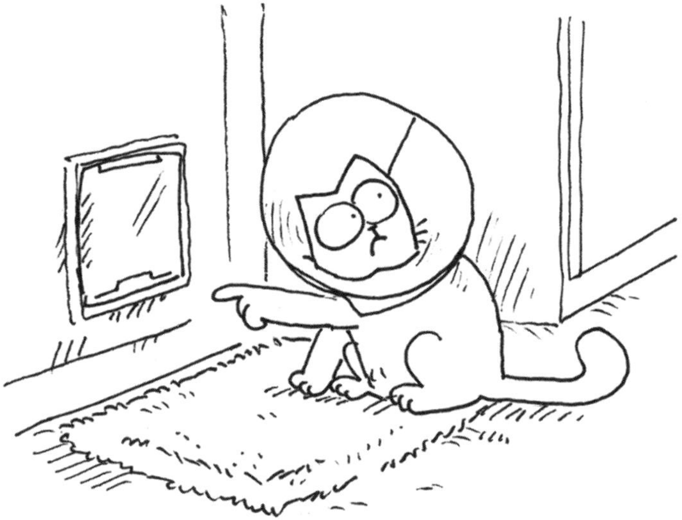

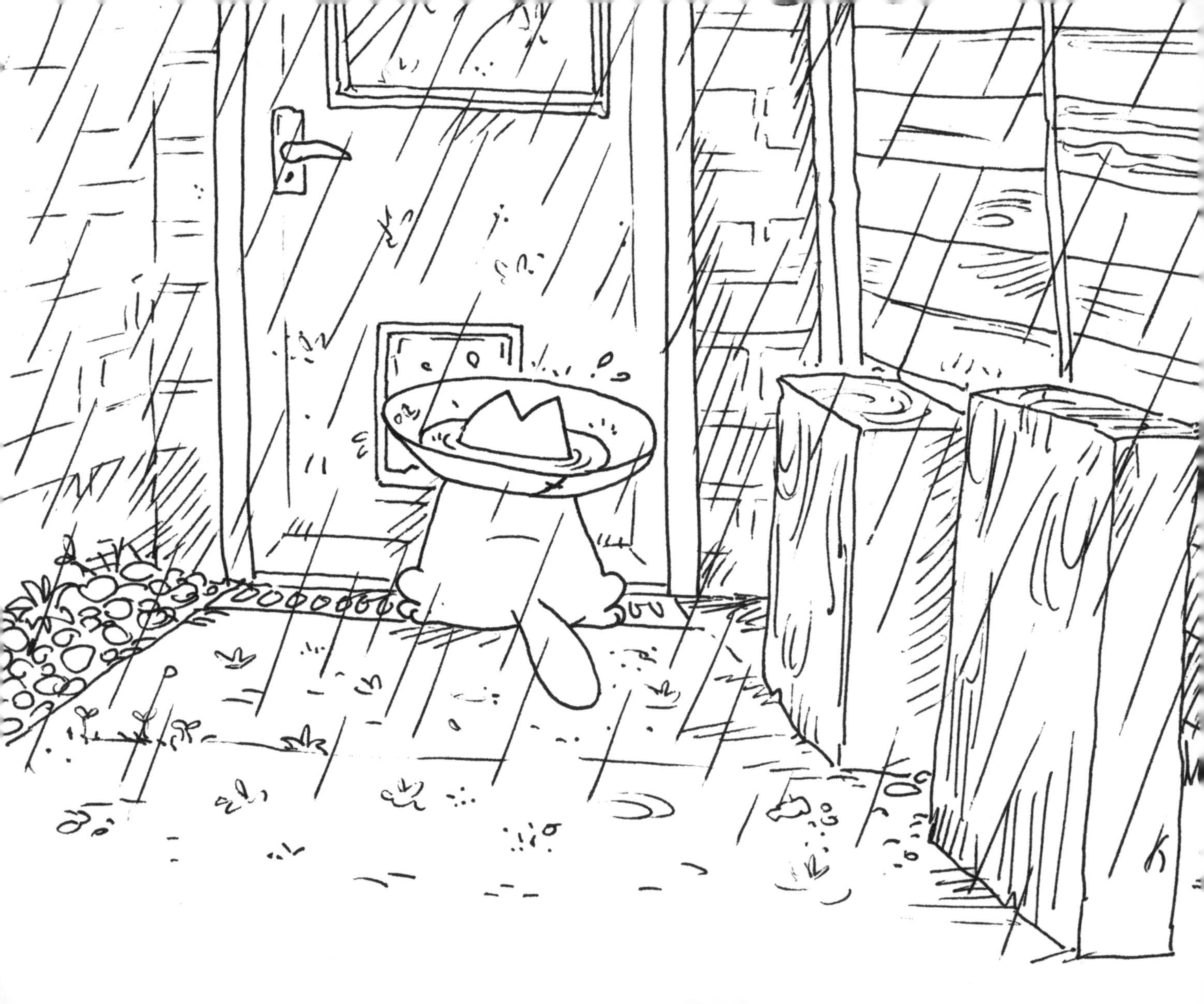

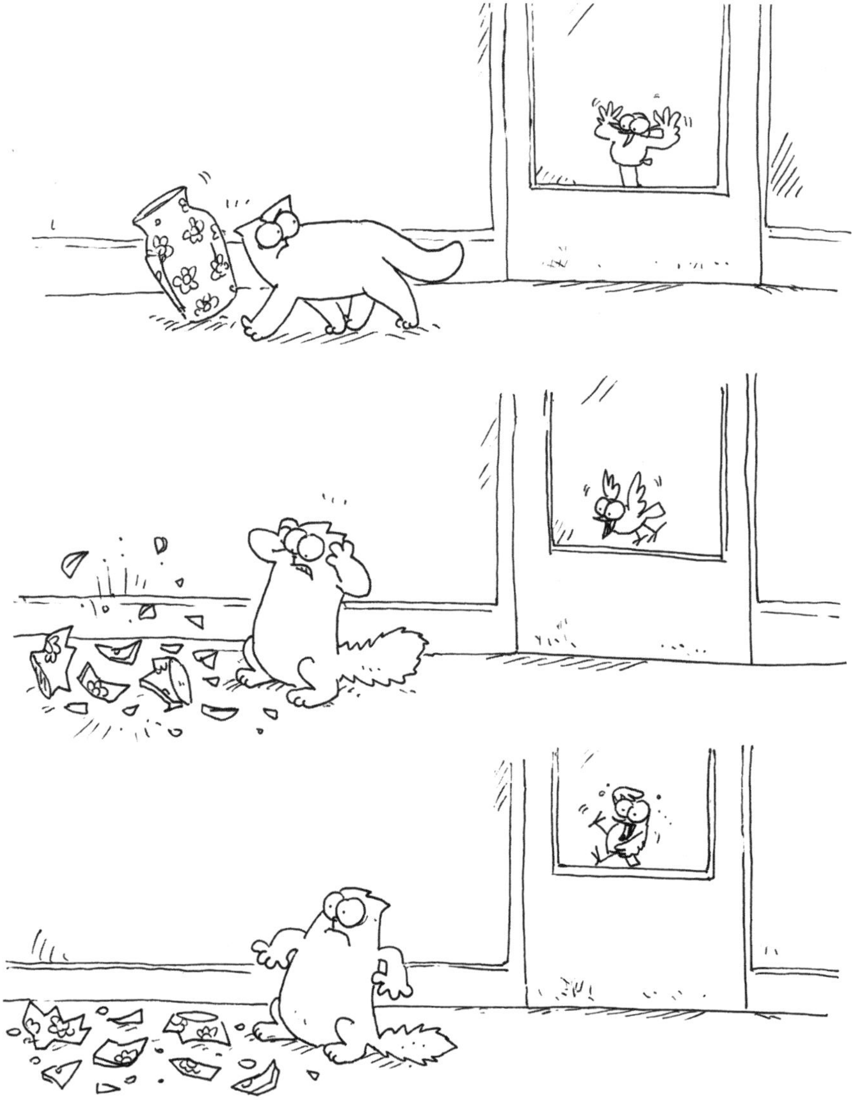

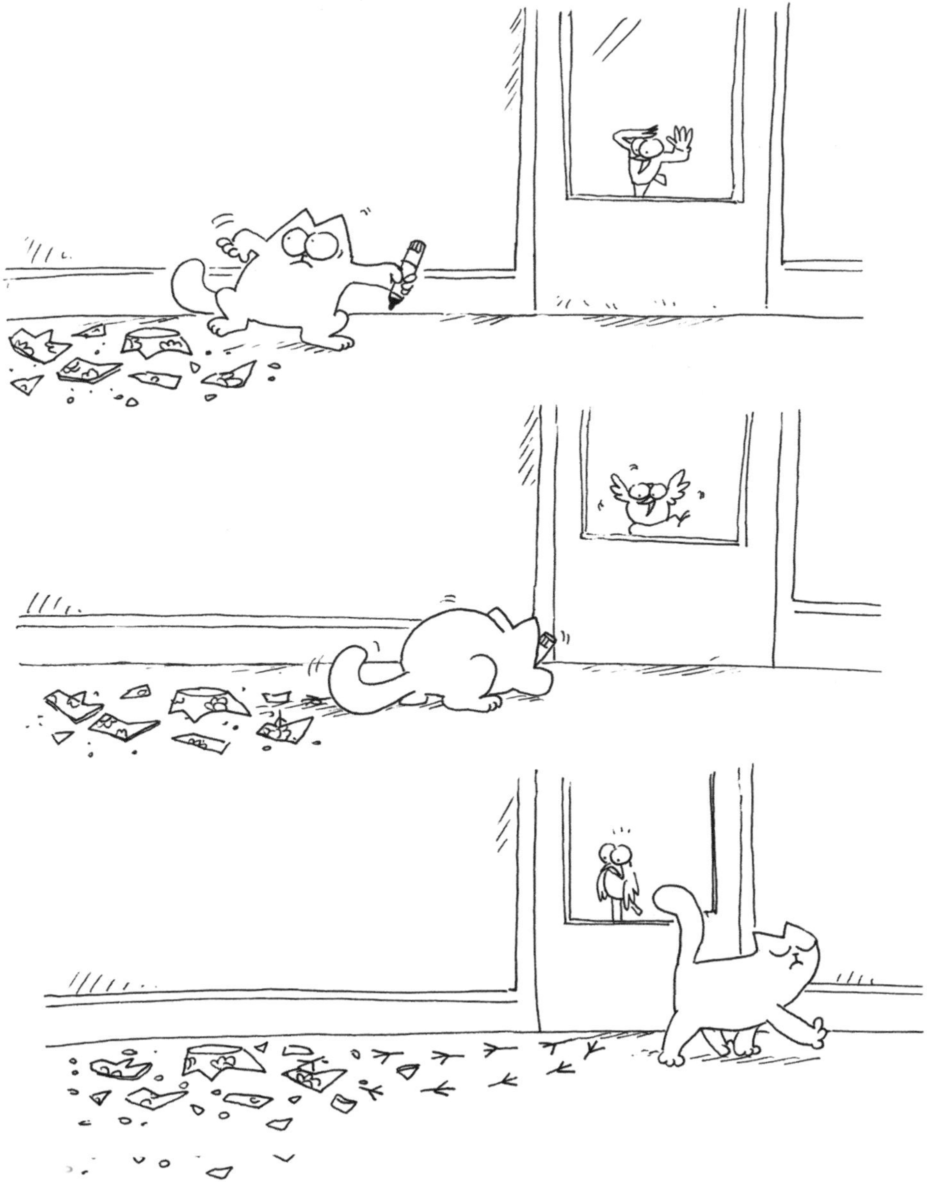

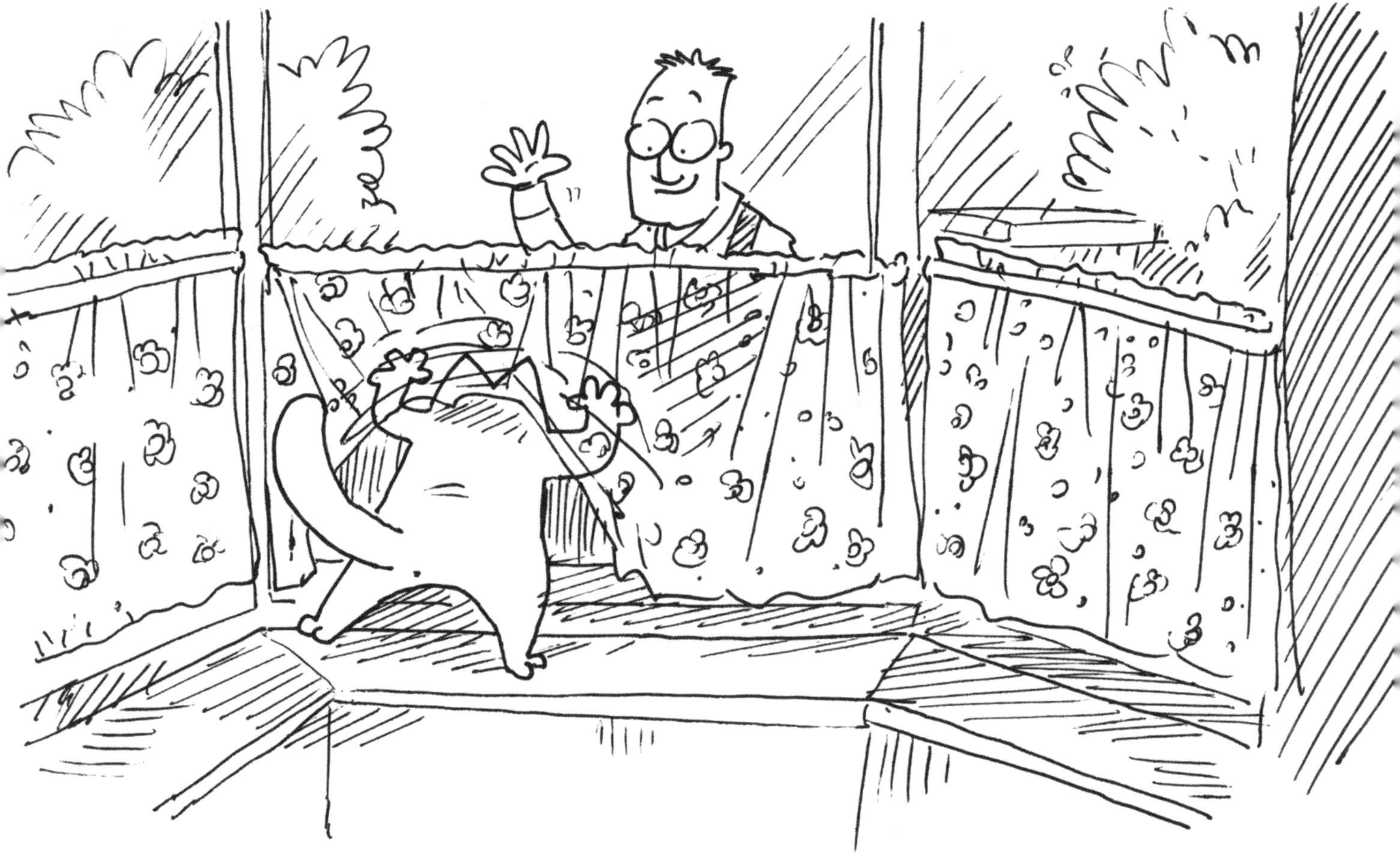

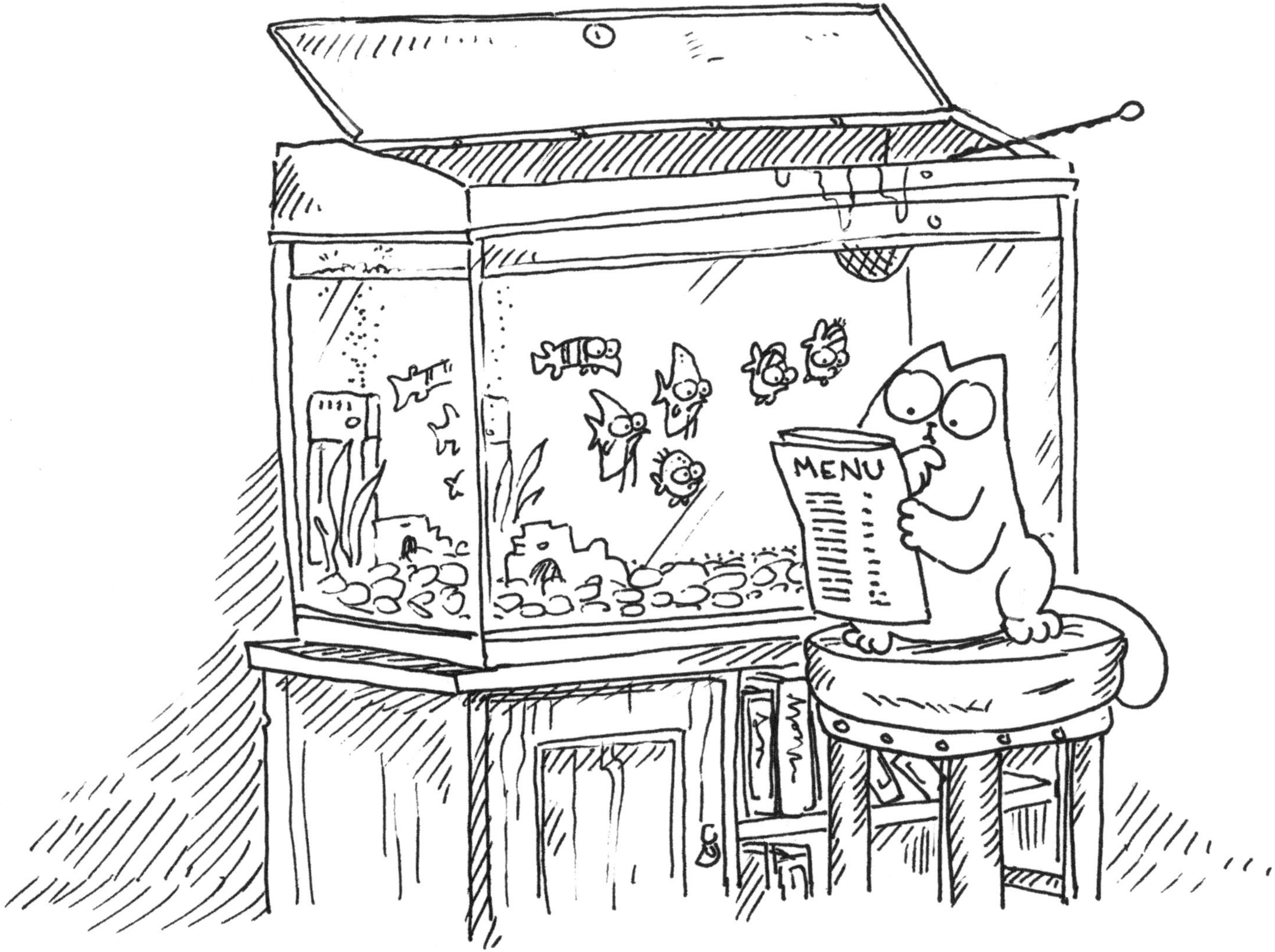
MENU

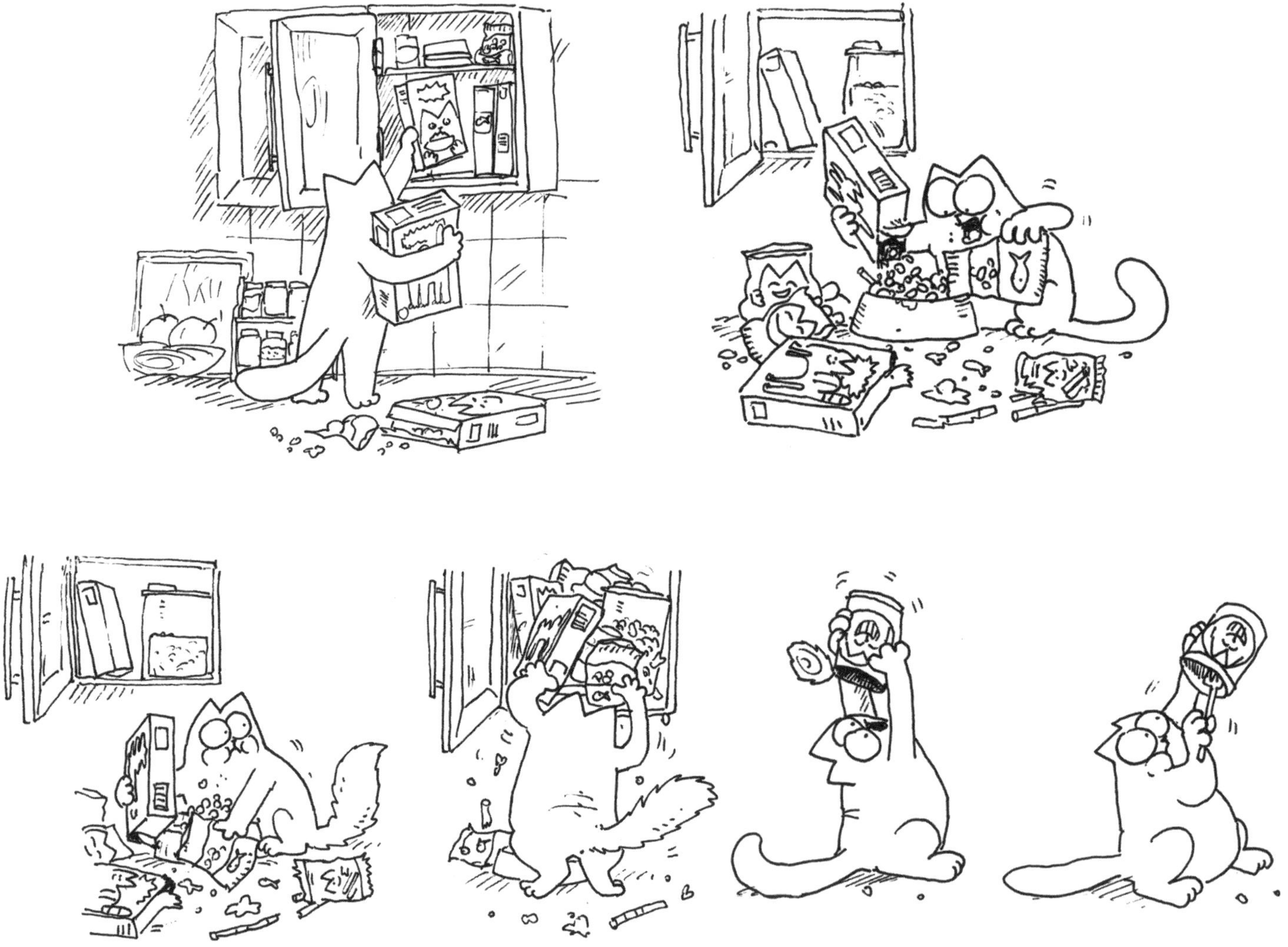

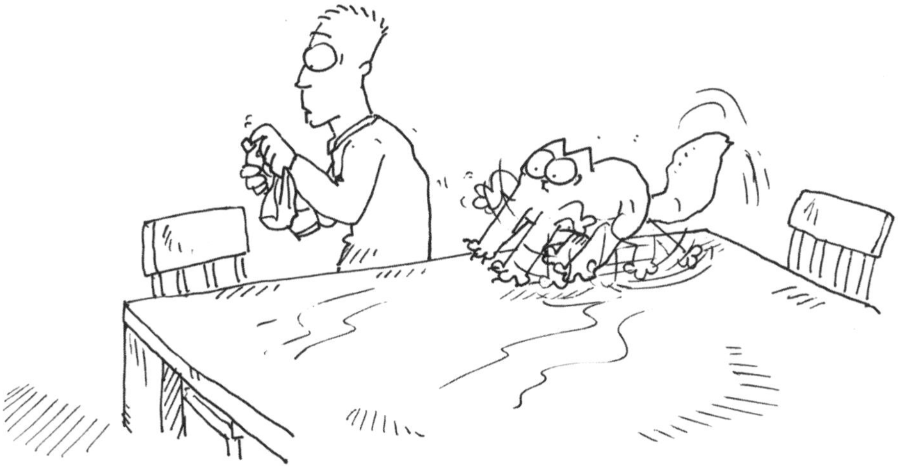

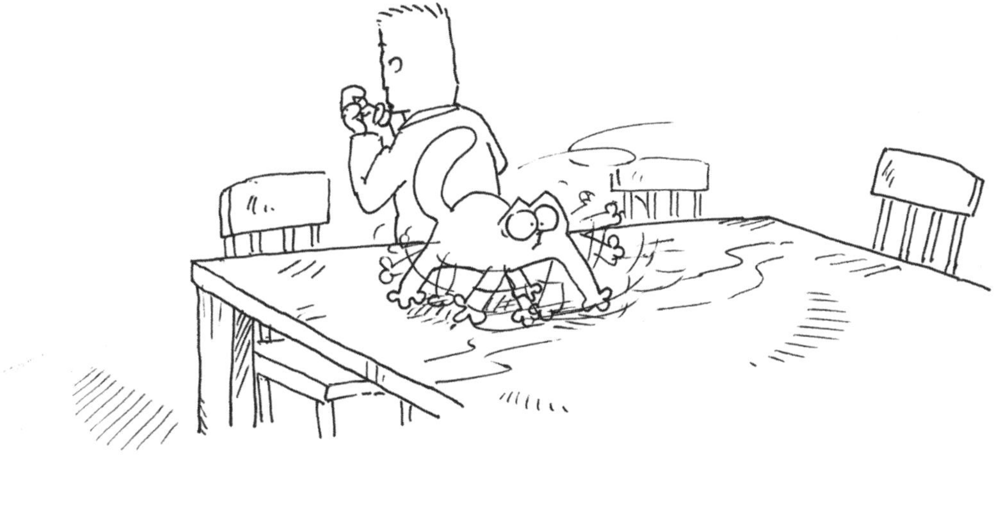

77

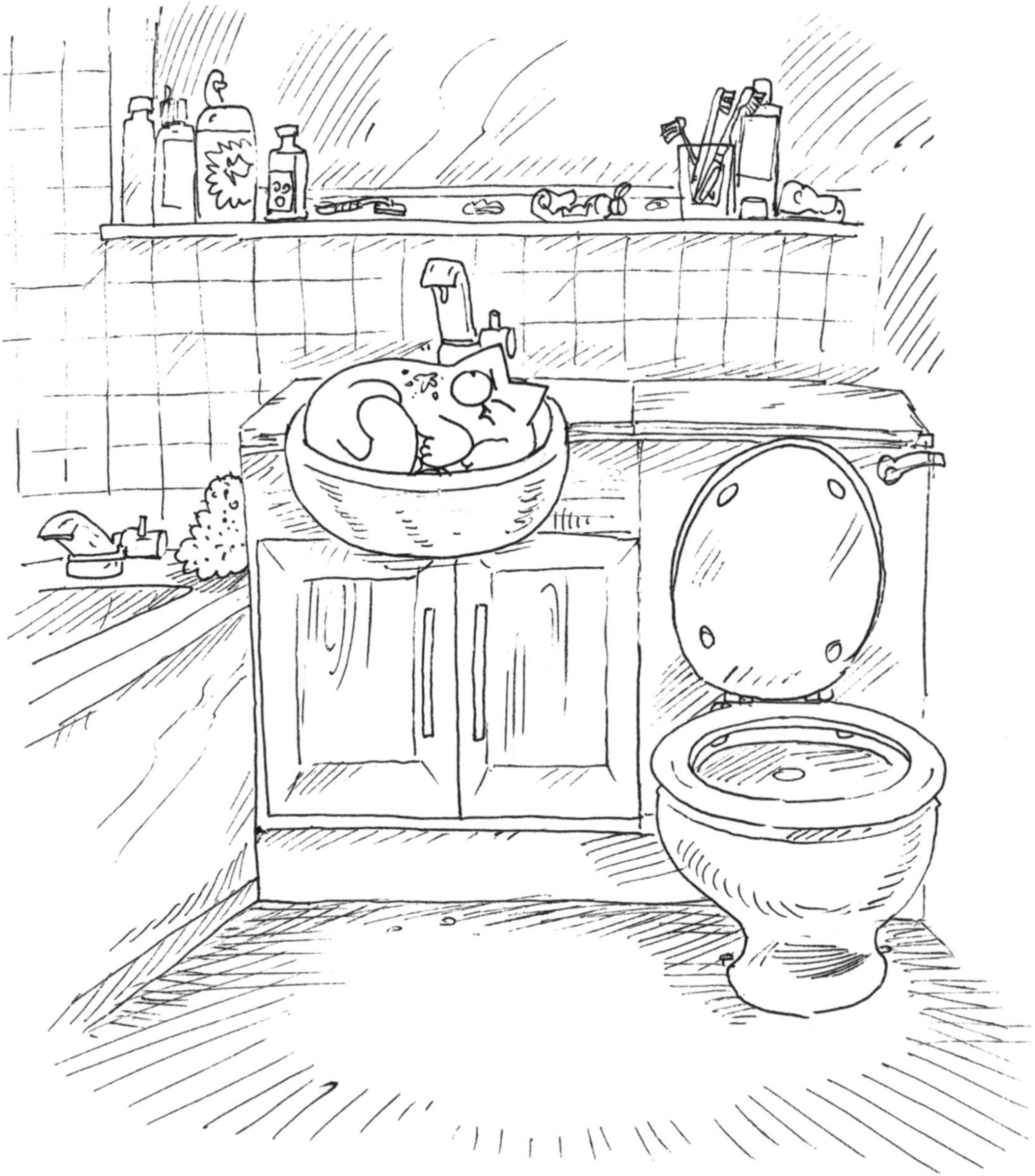

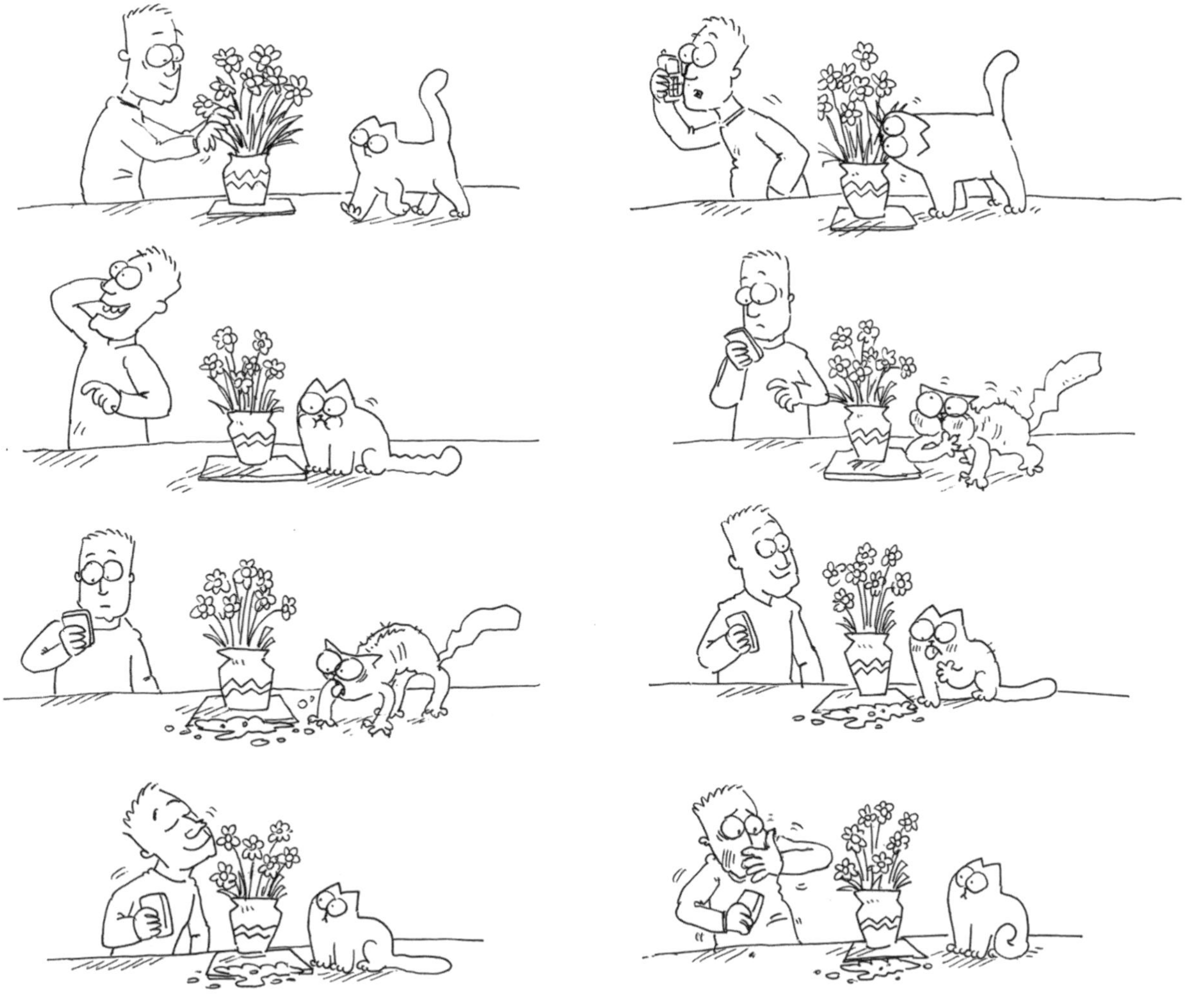

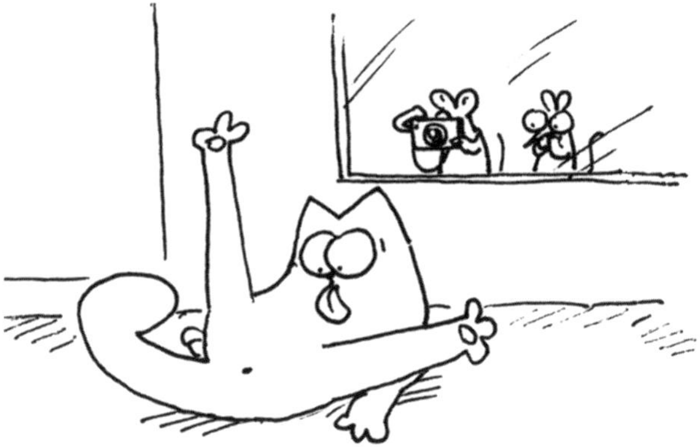

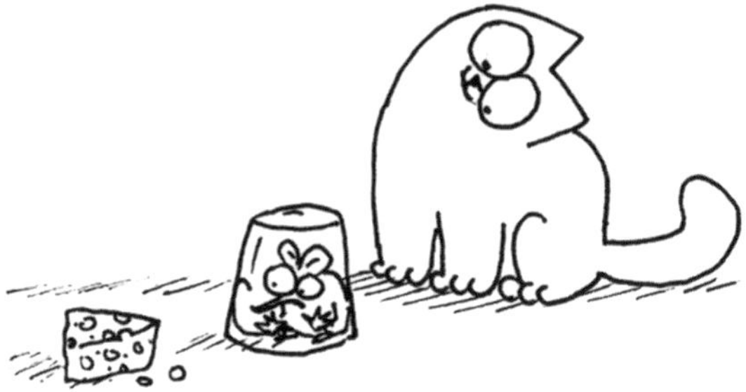

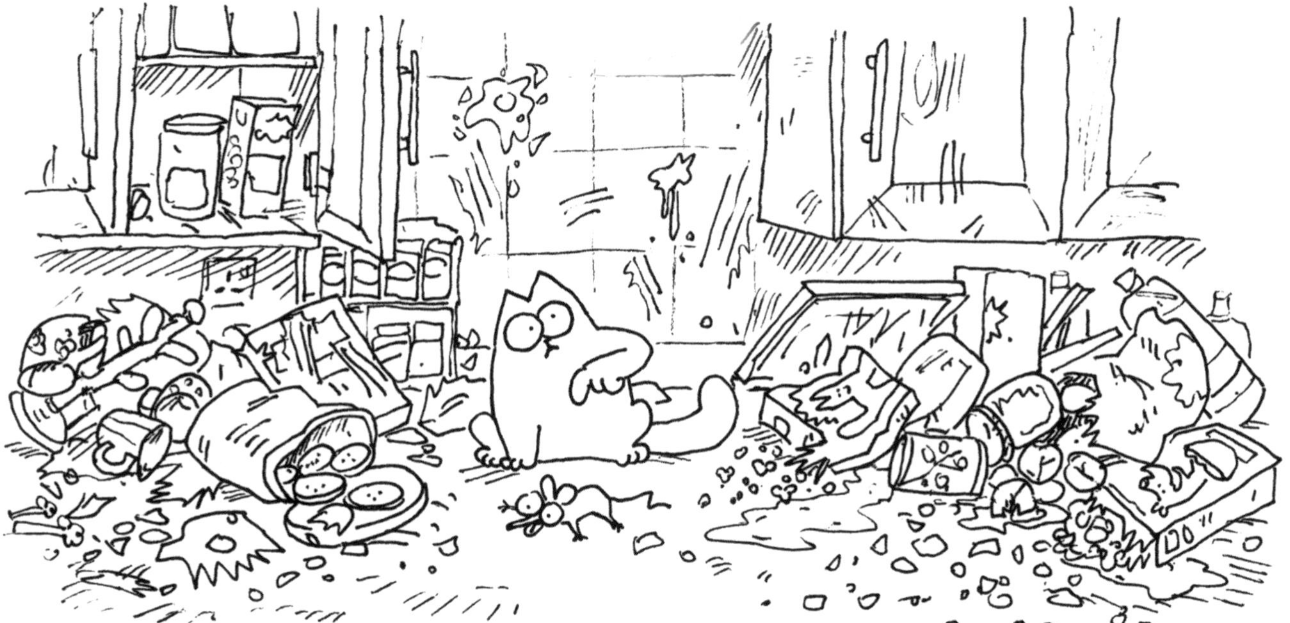

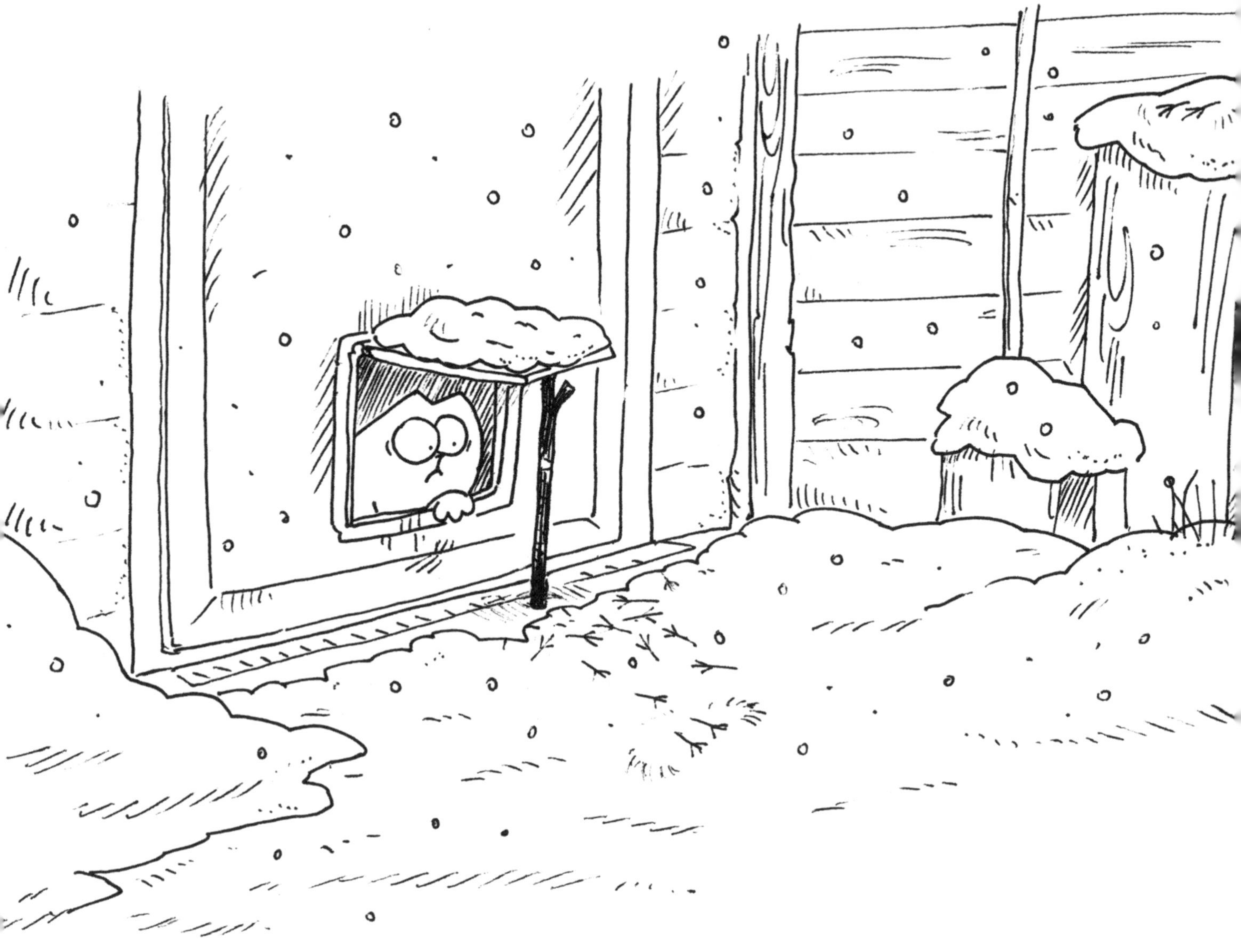

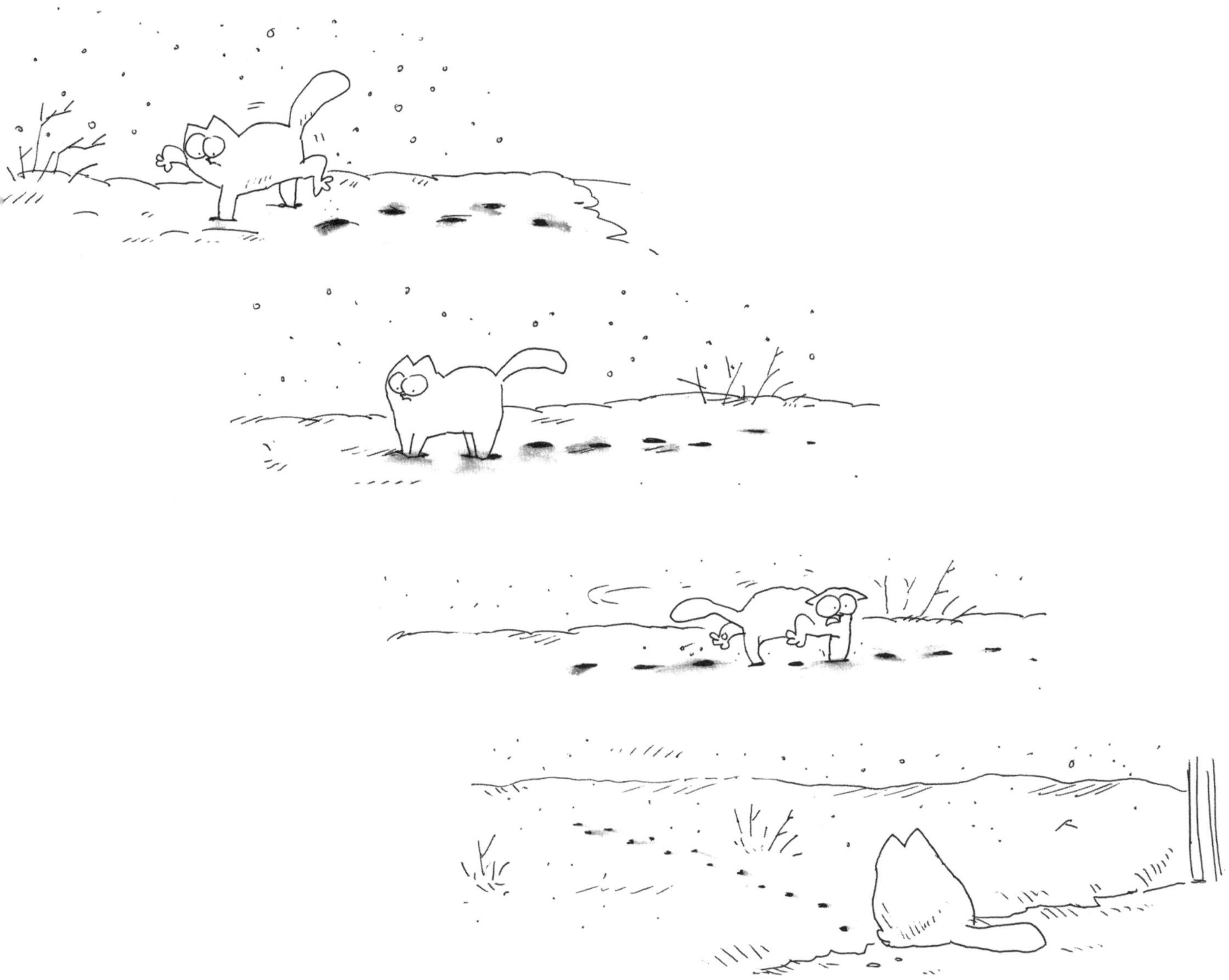

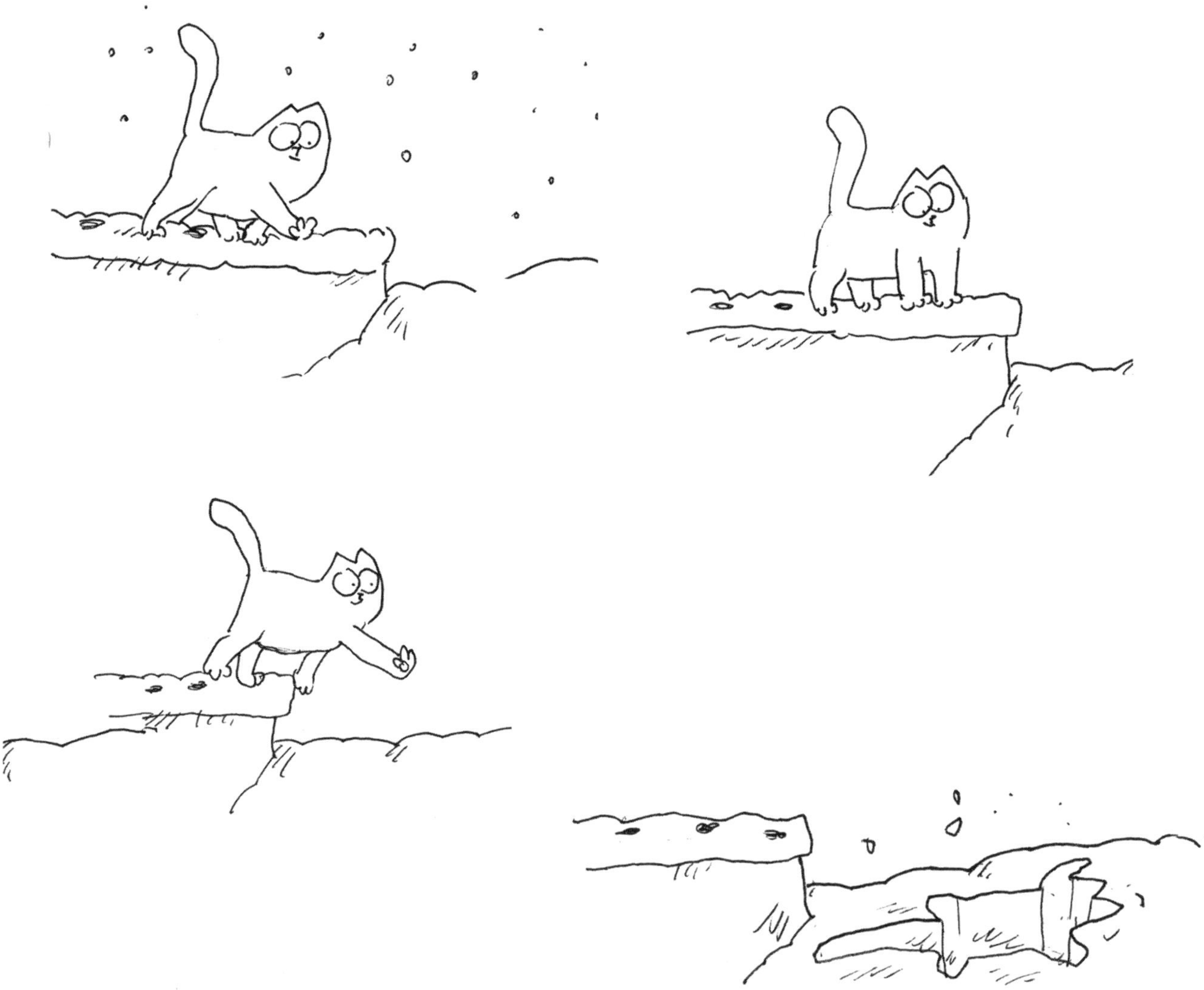

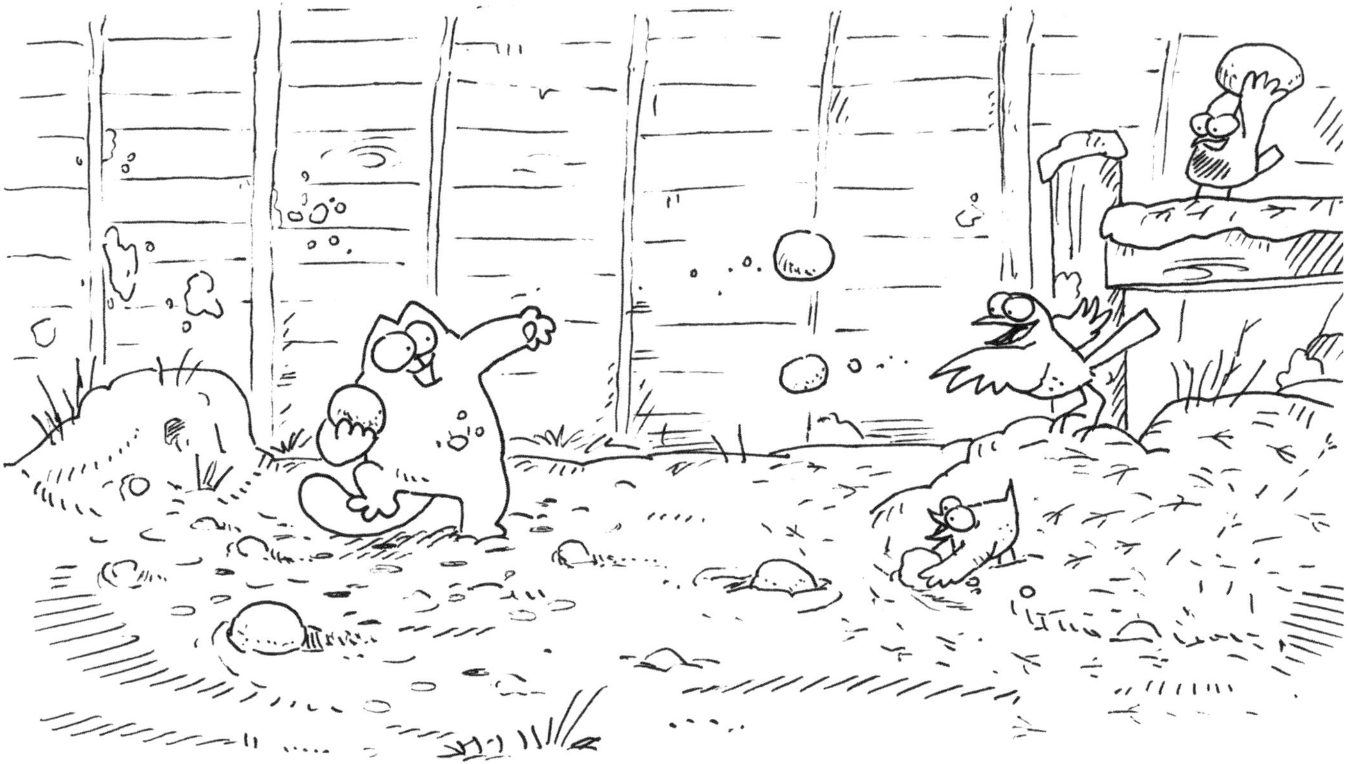

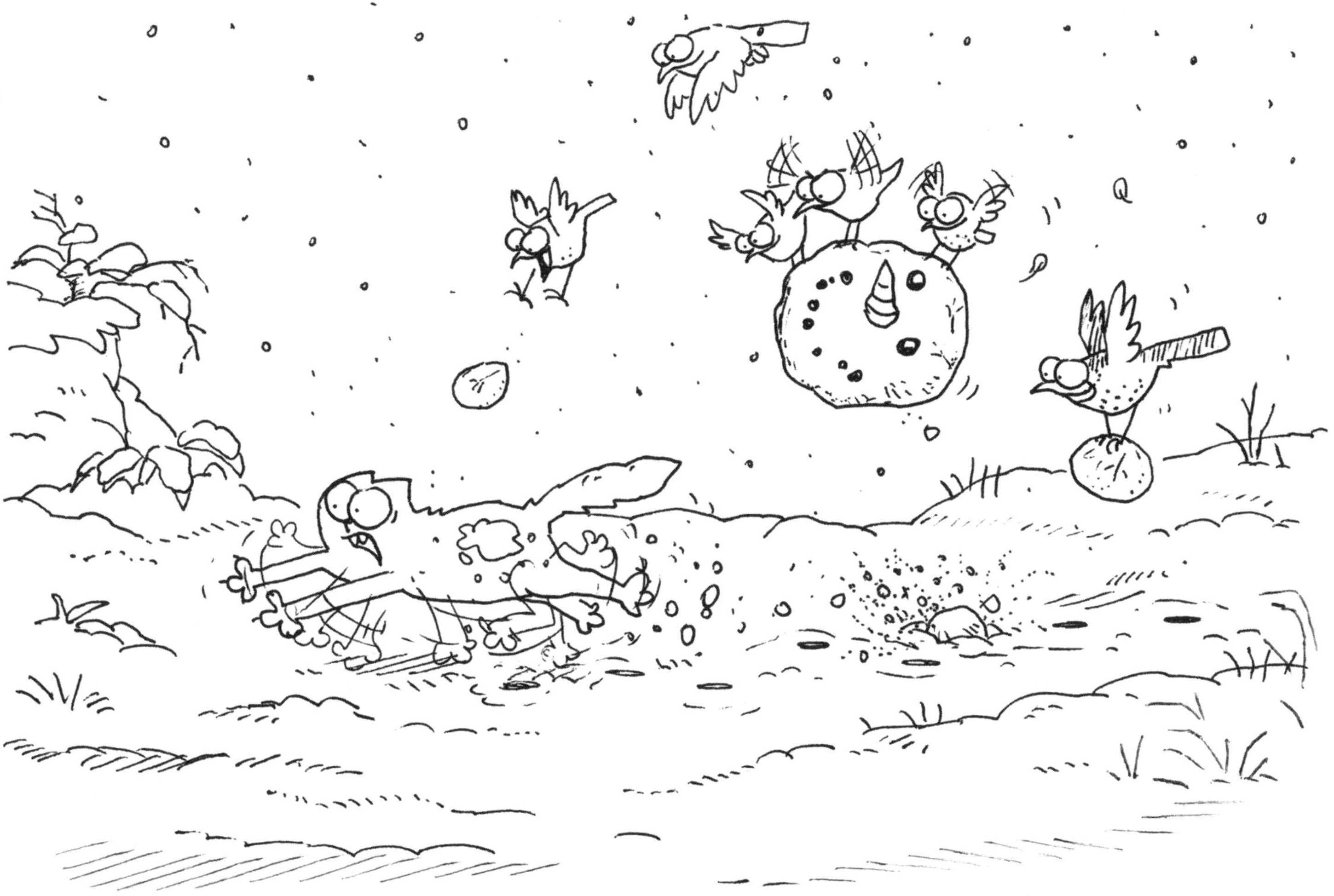

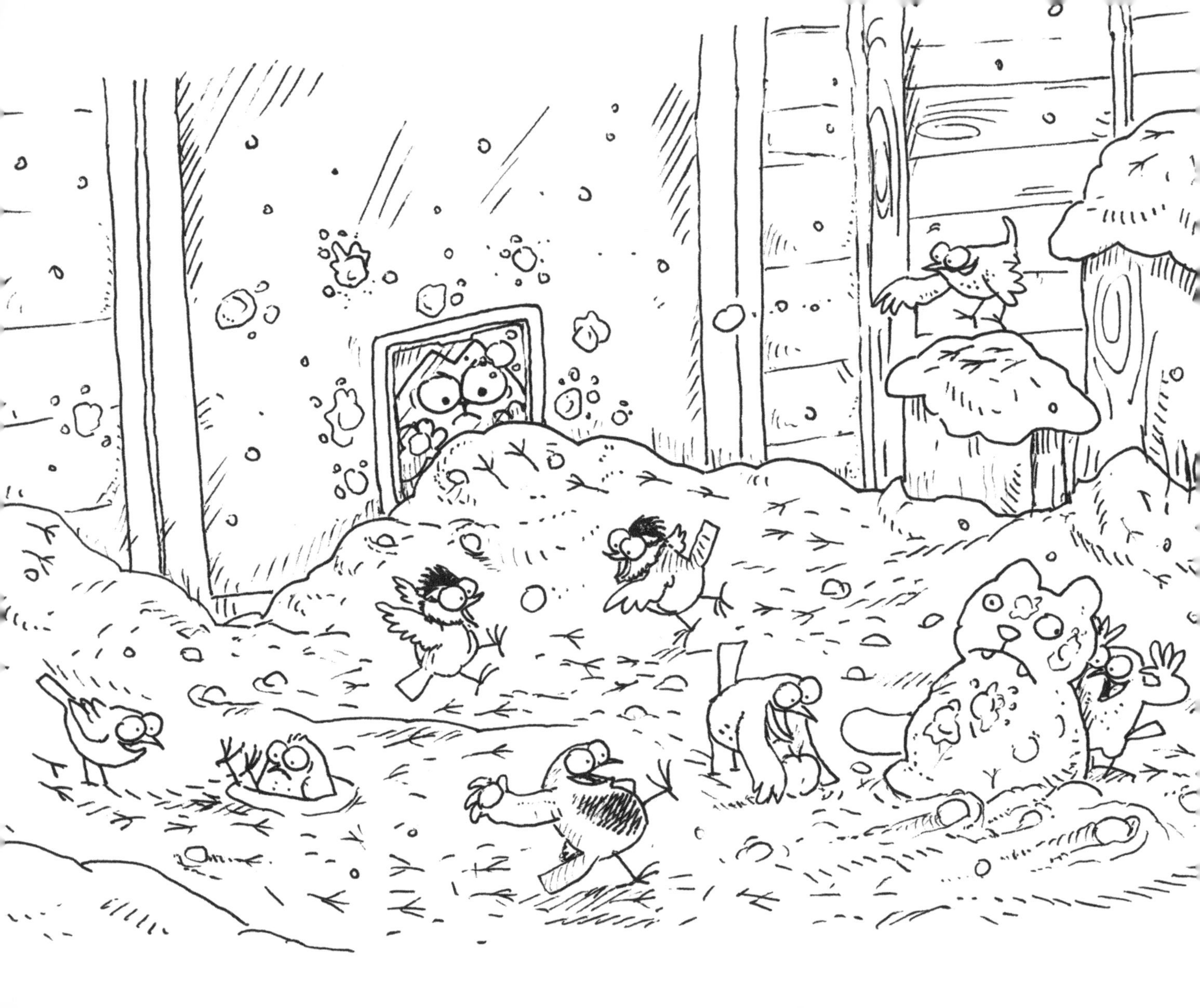

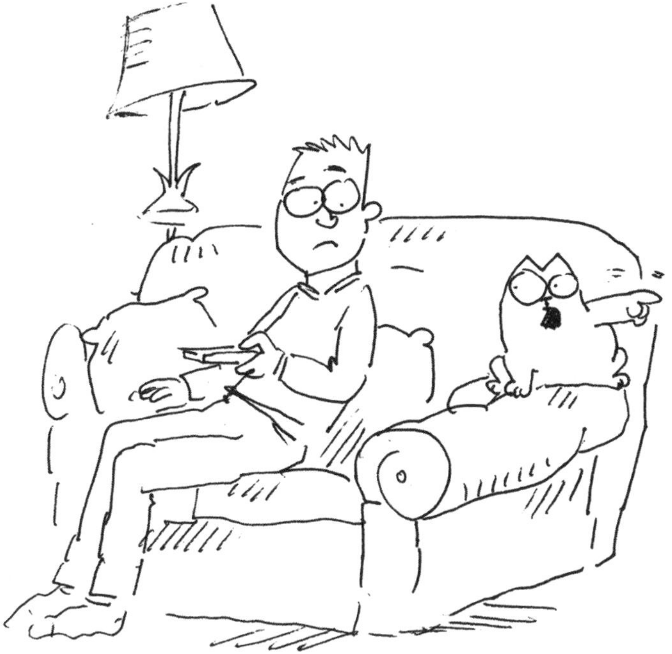

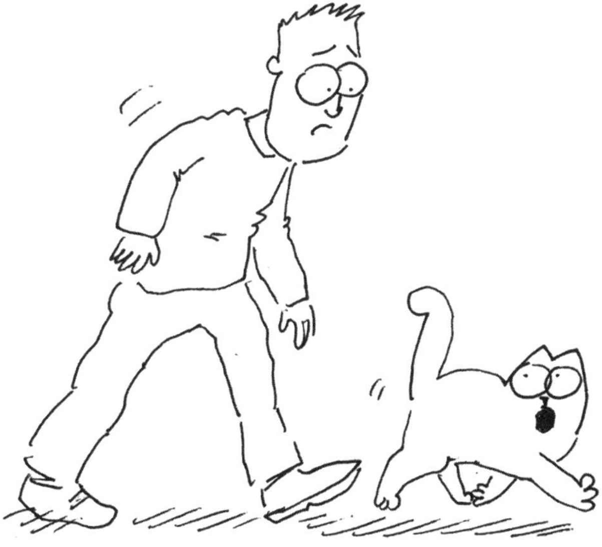

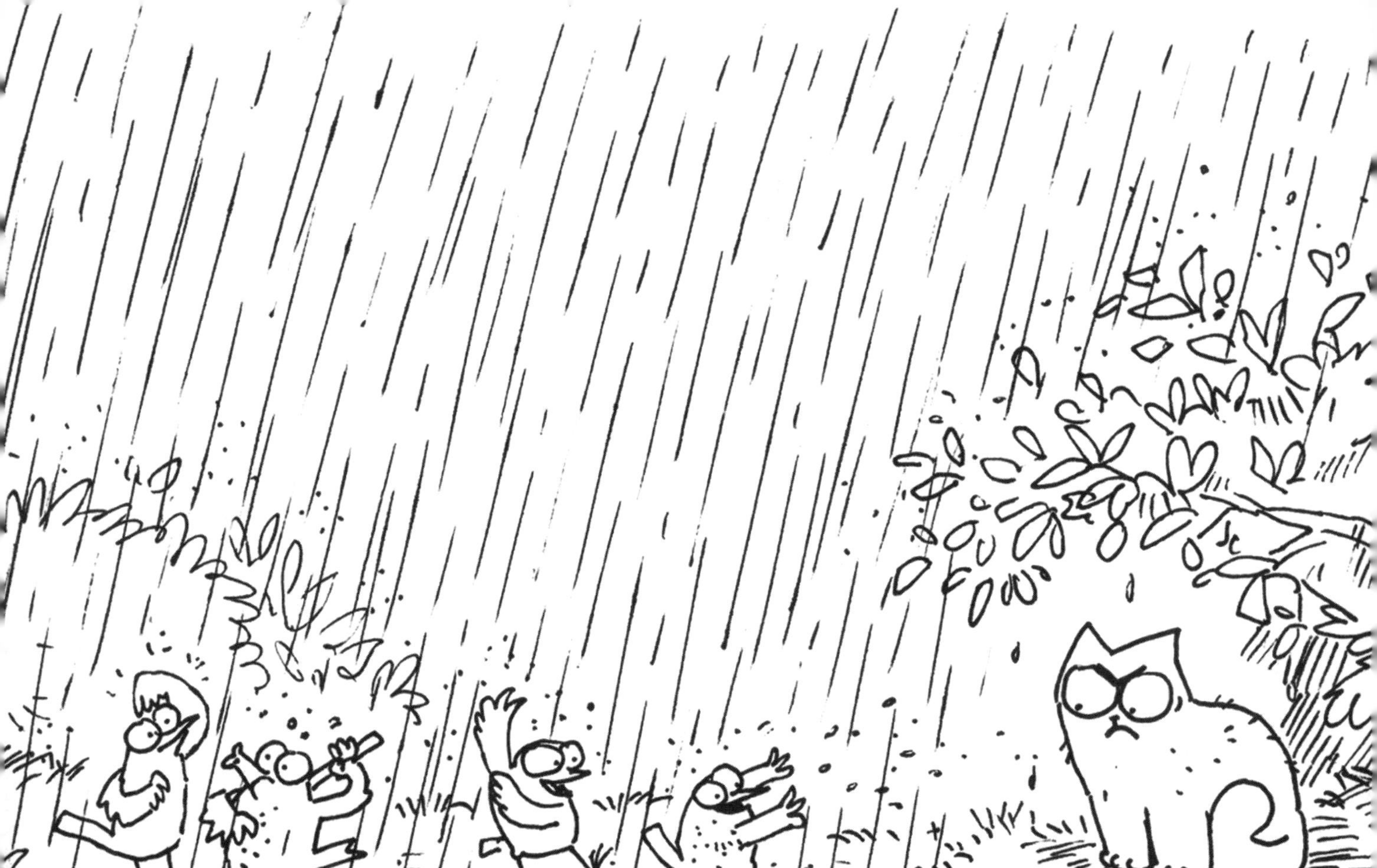

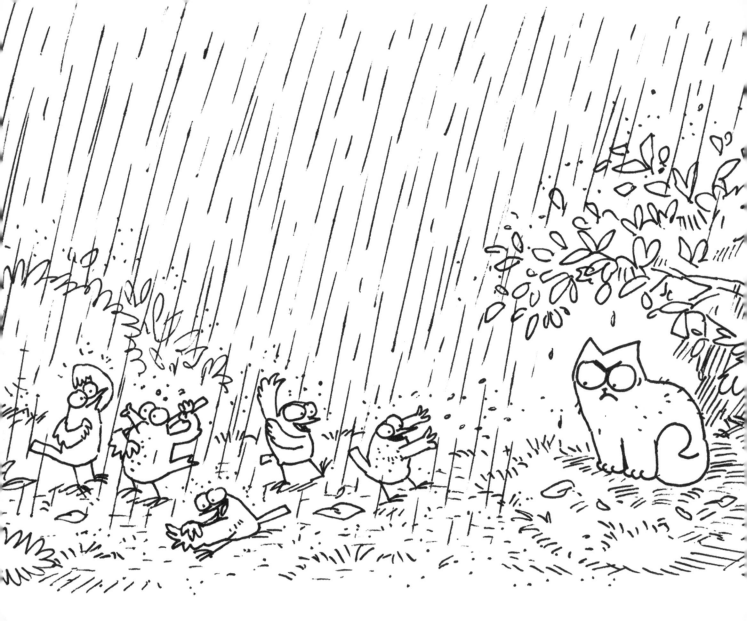

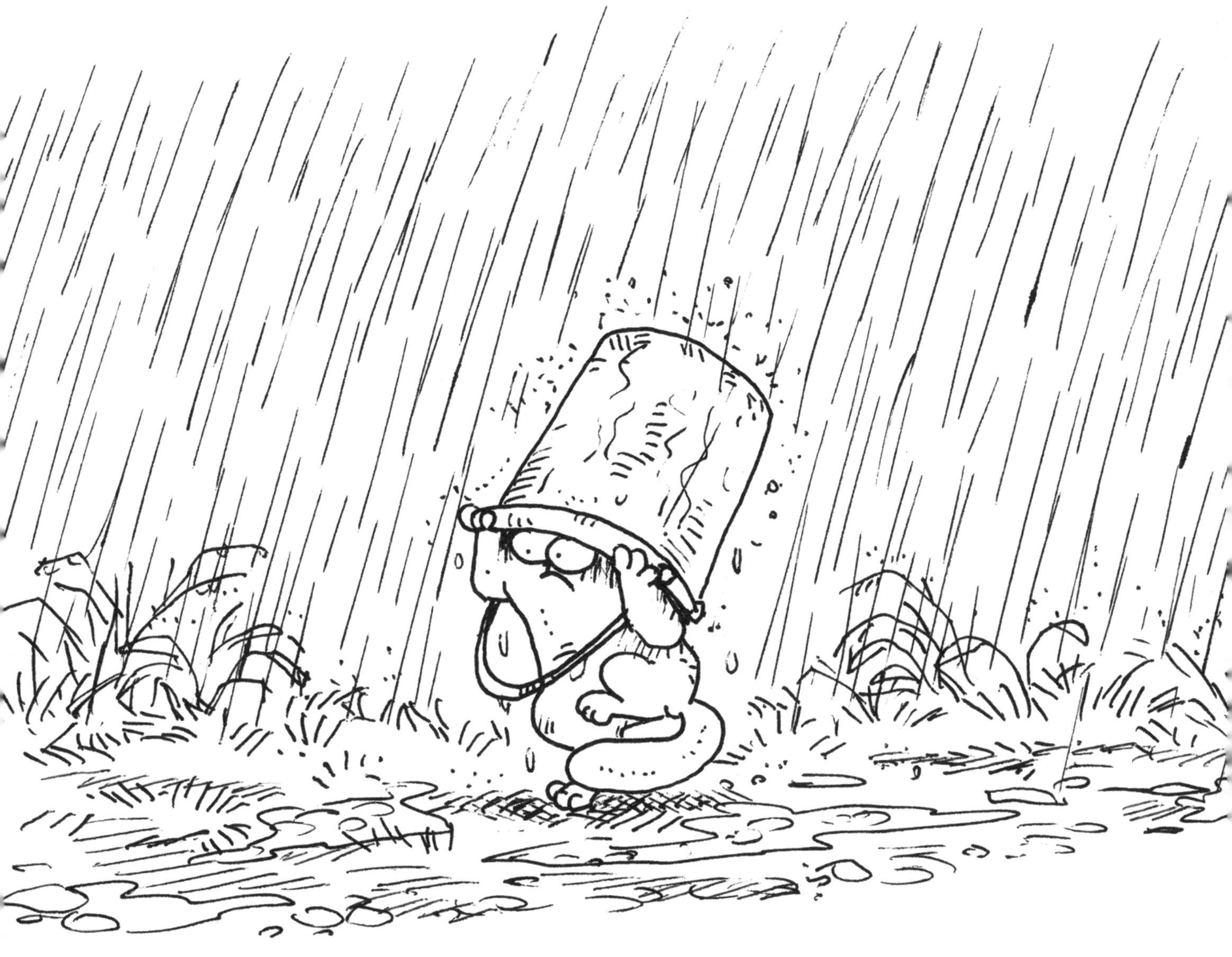

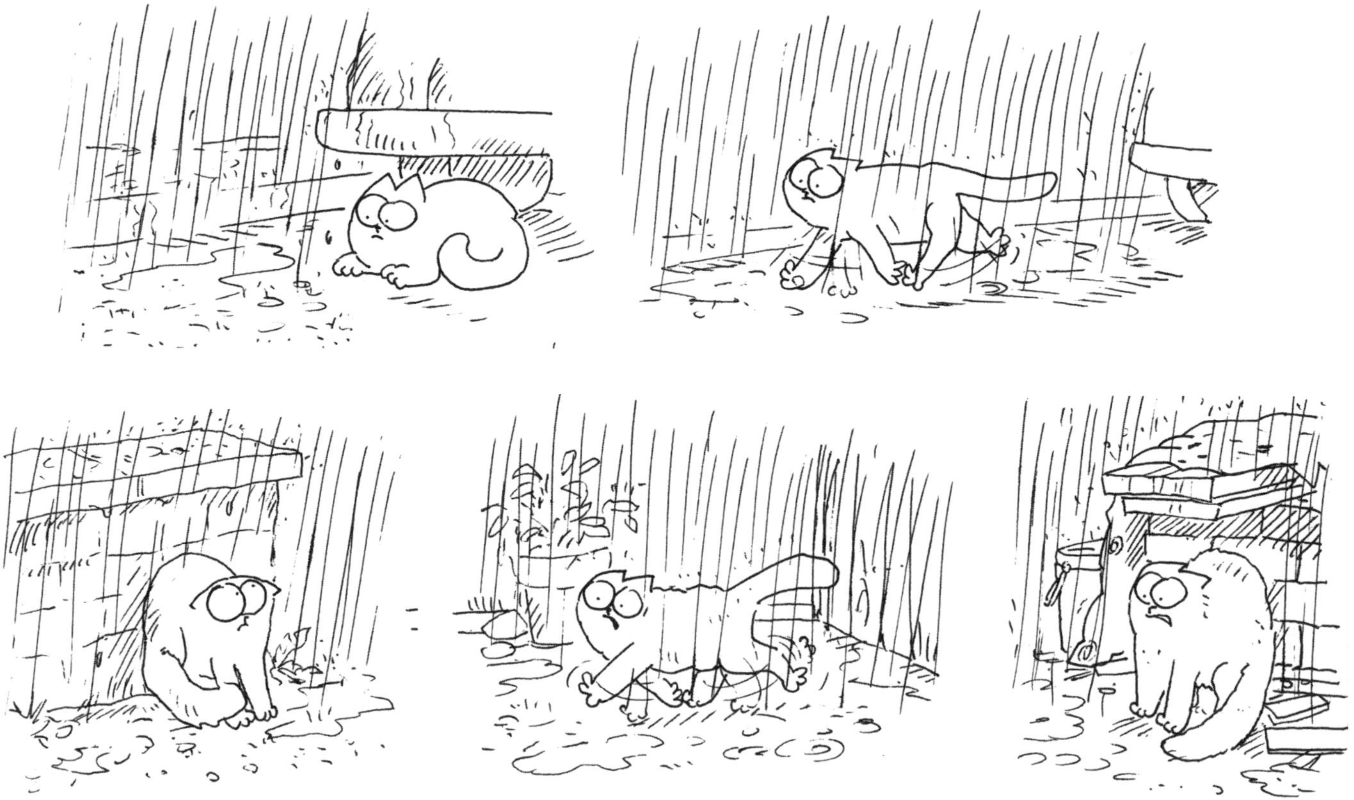

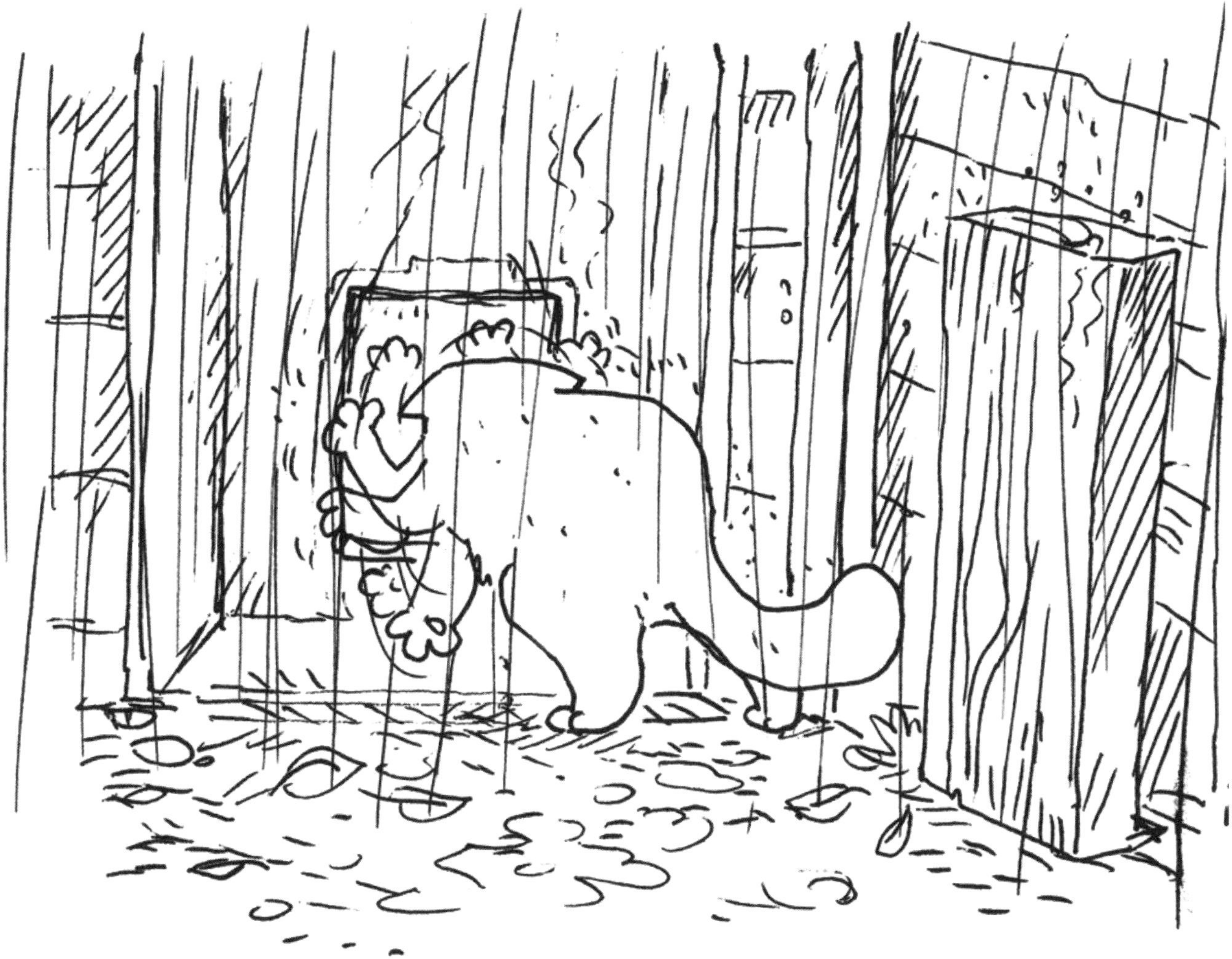

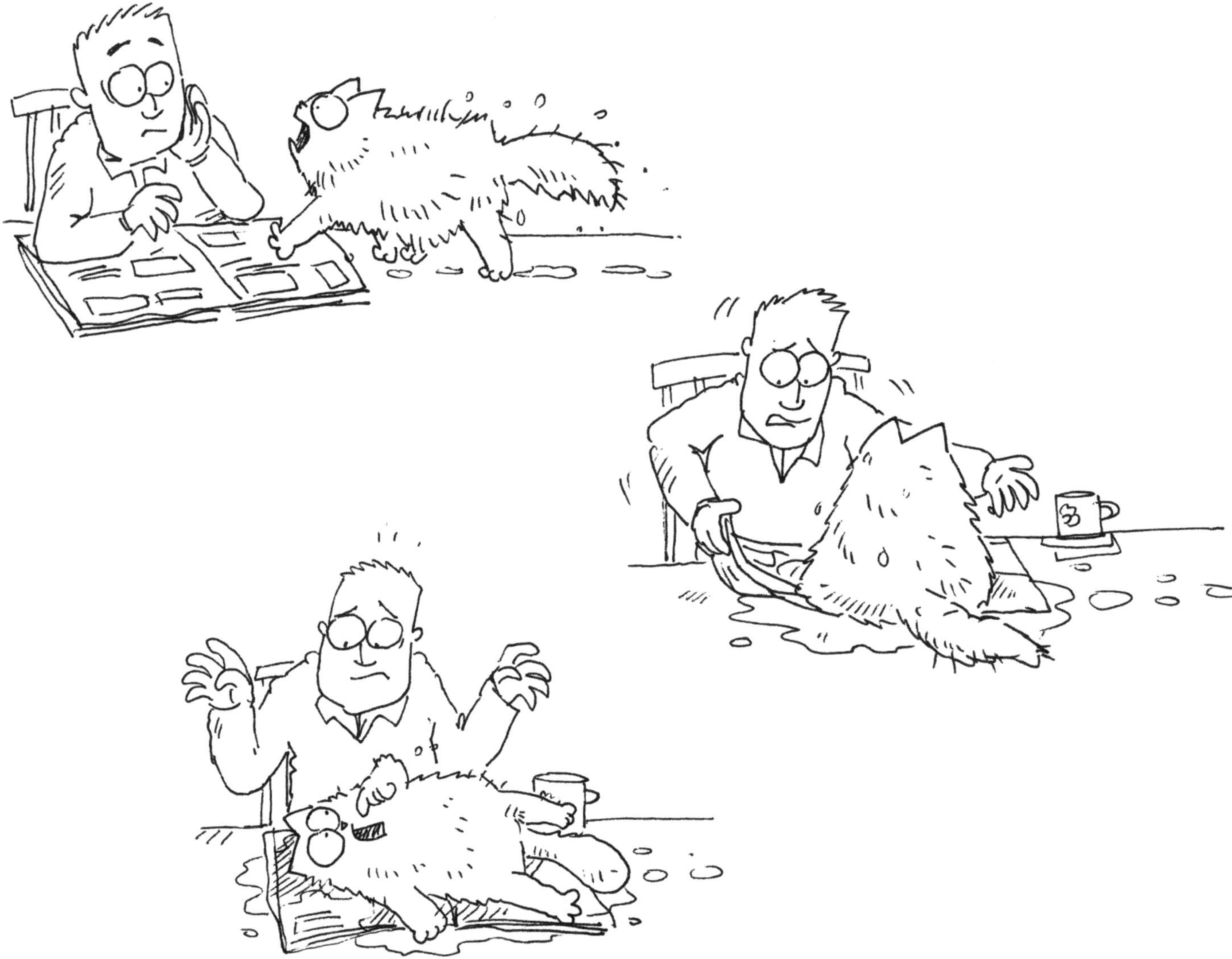

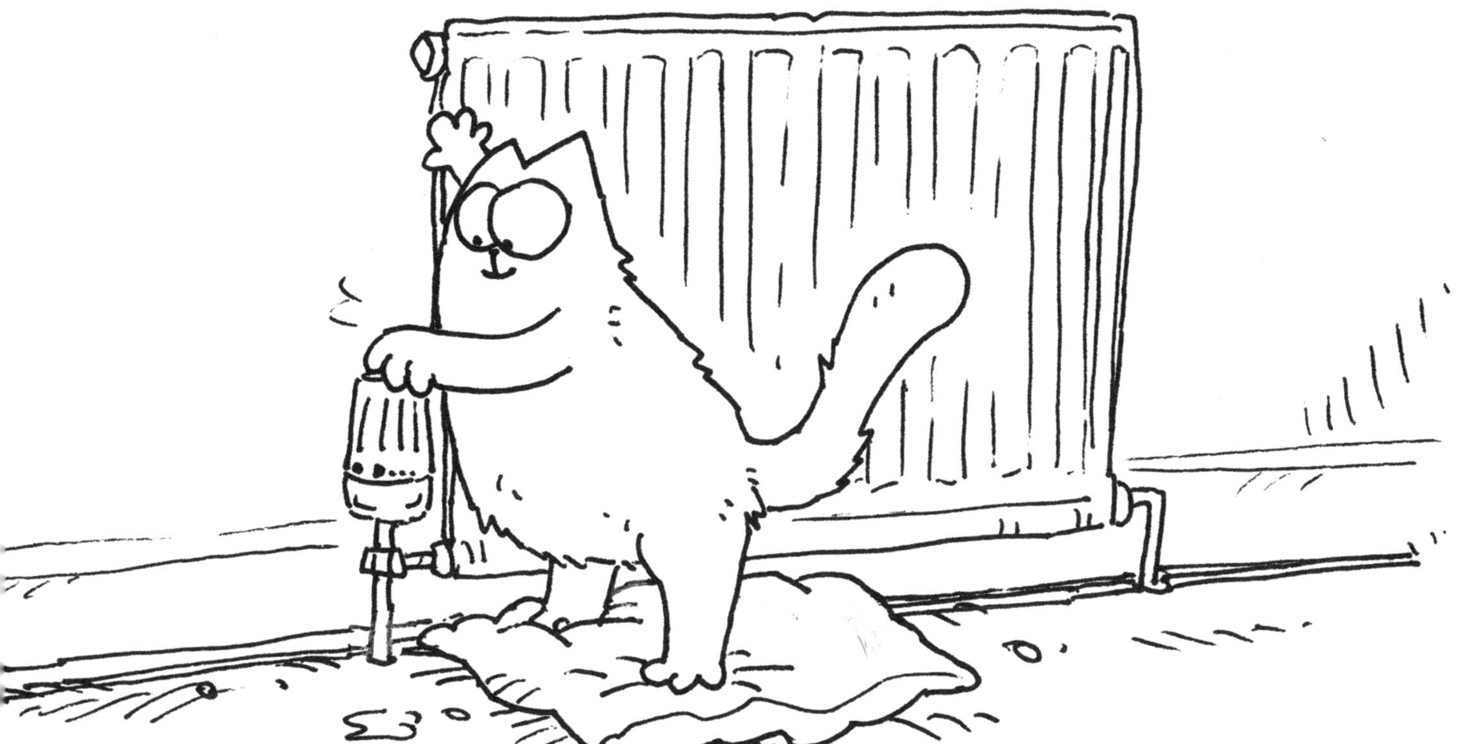

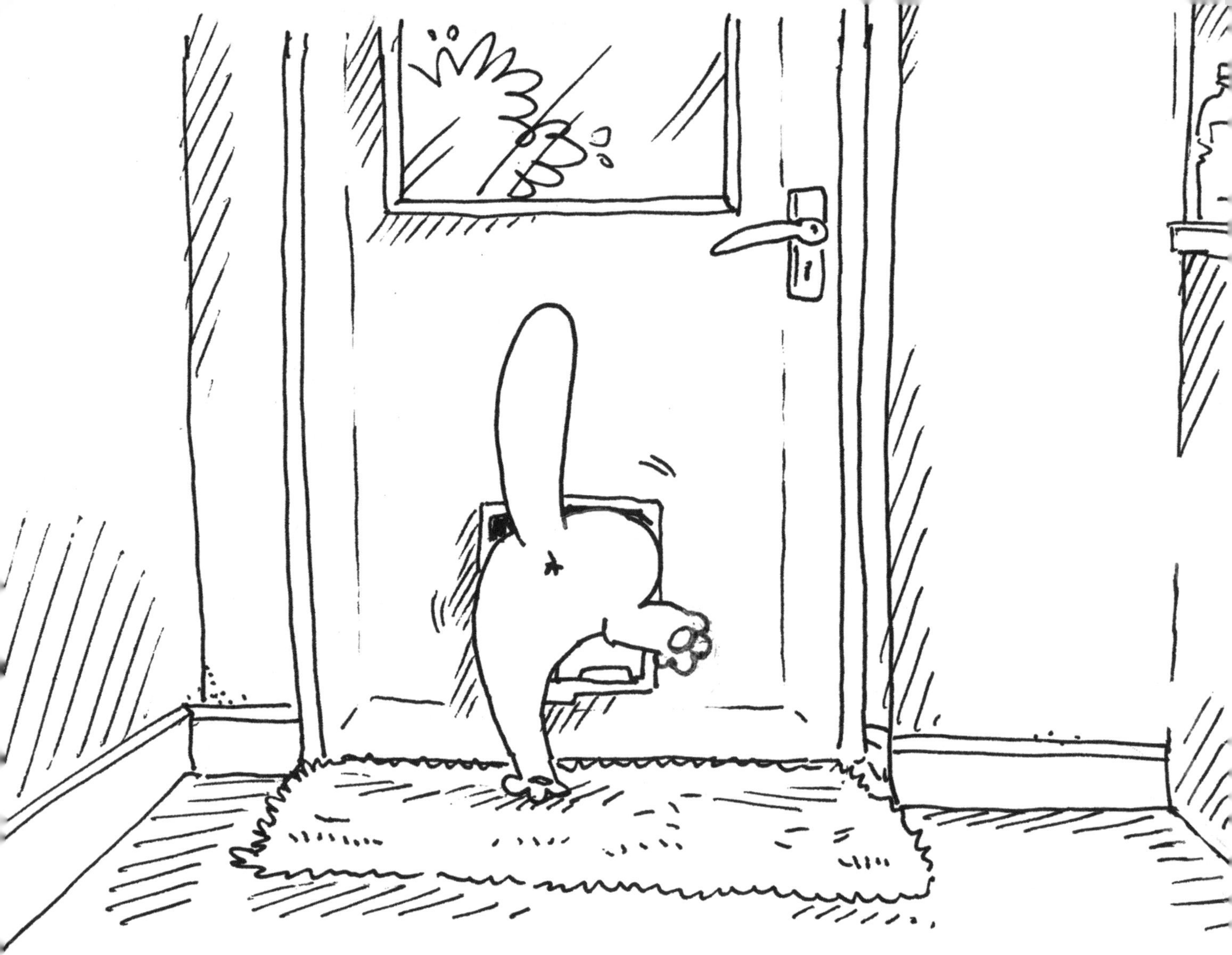

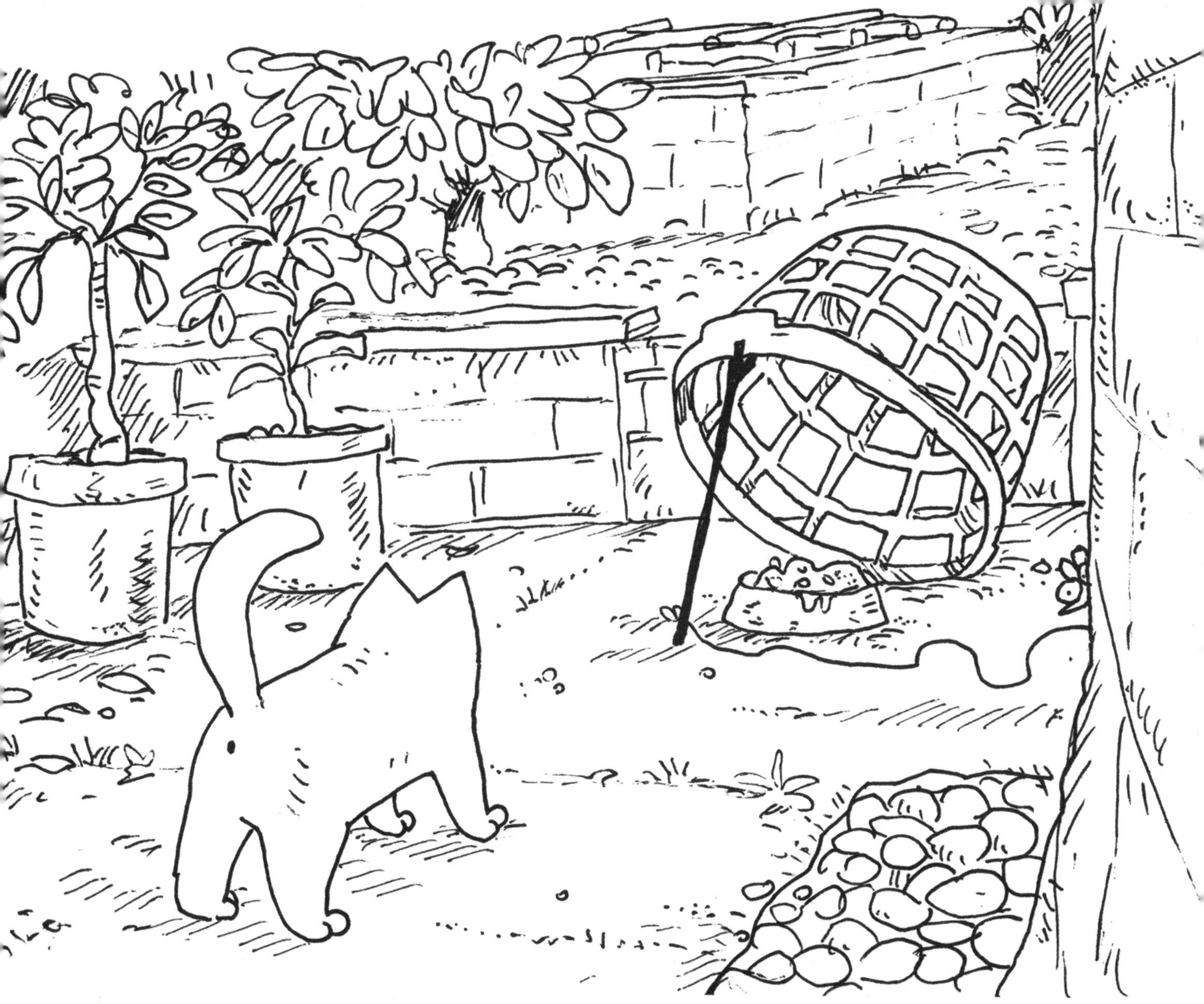

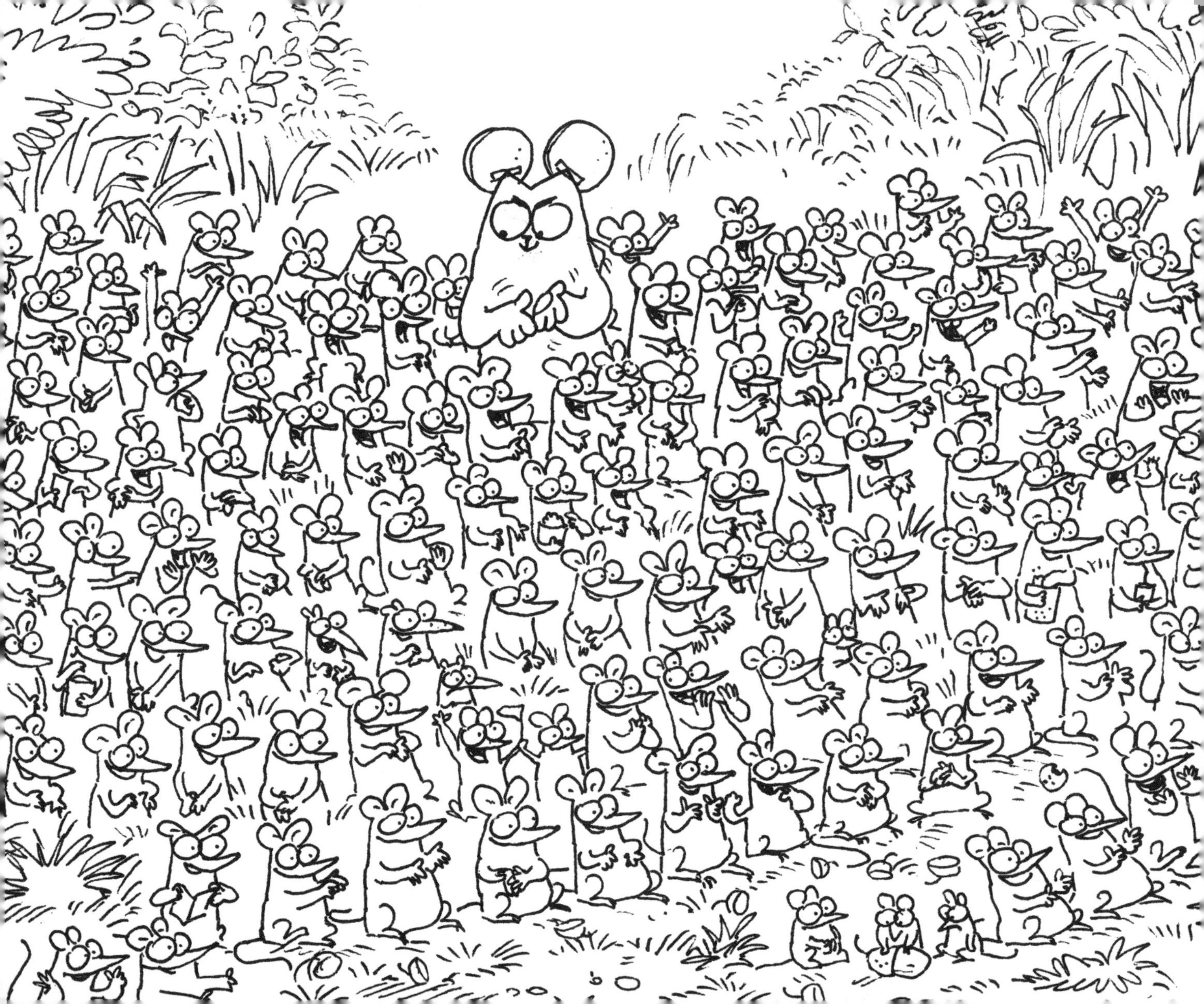

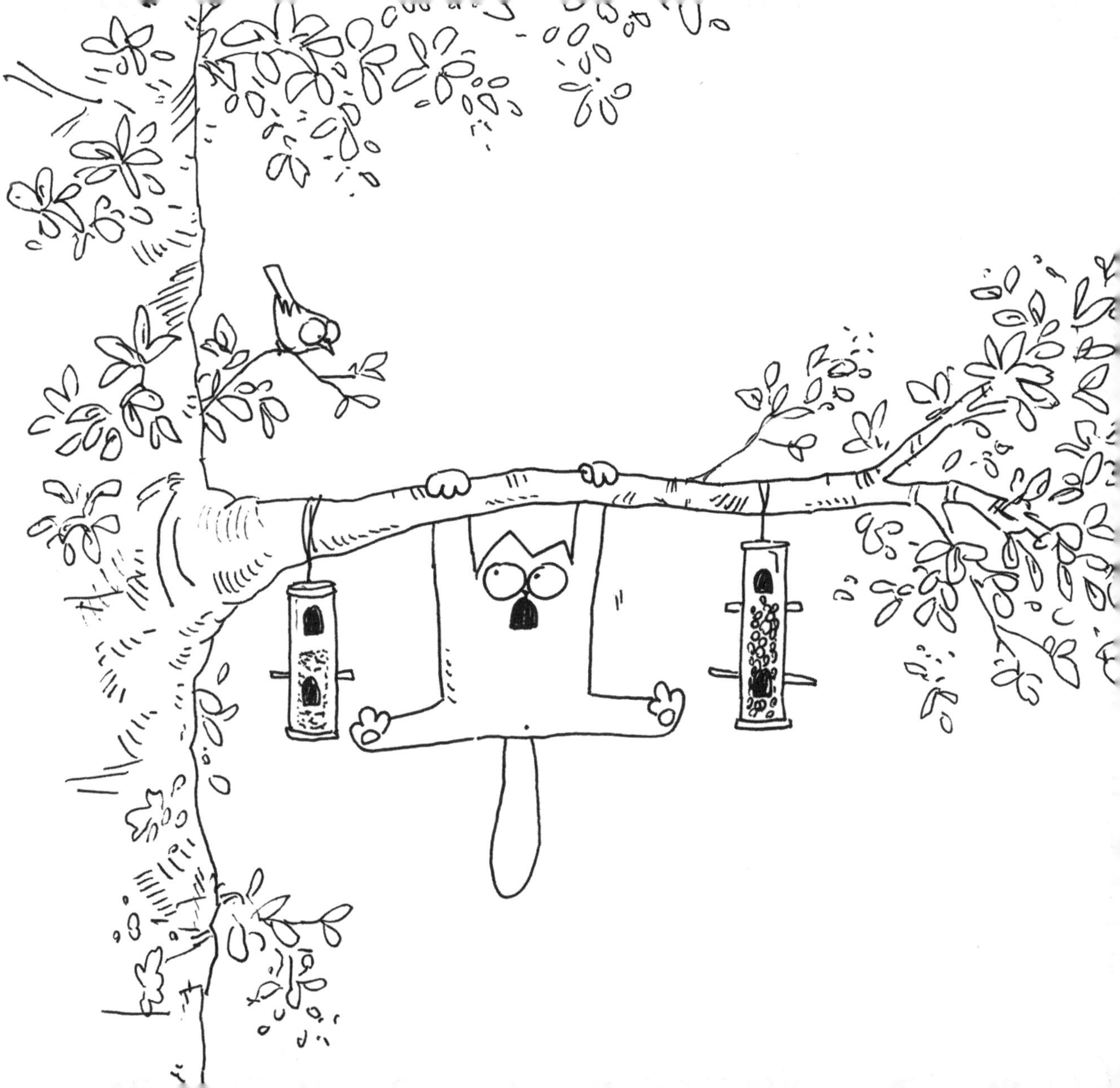

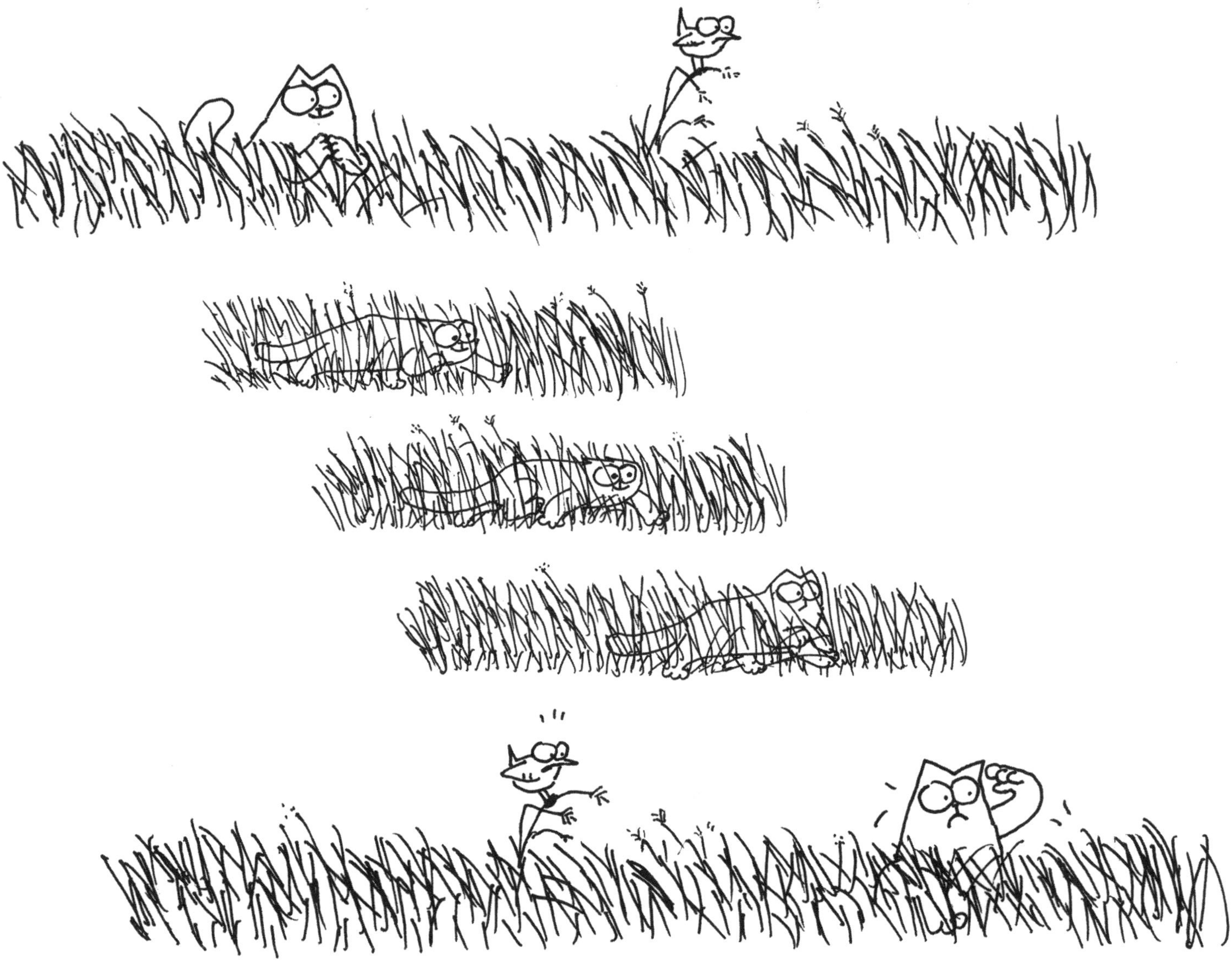

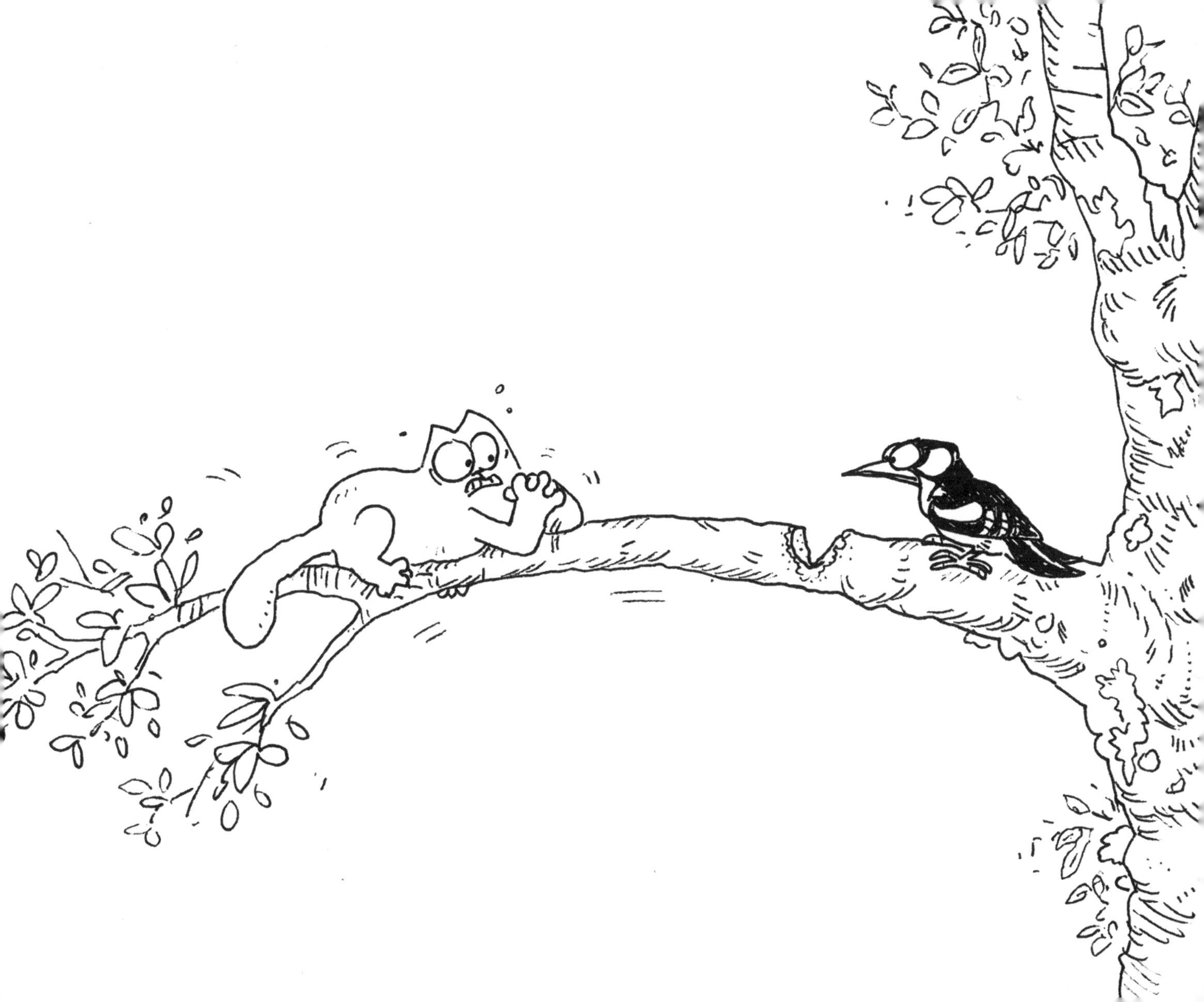

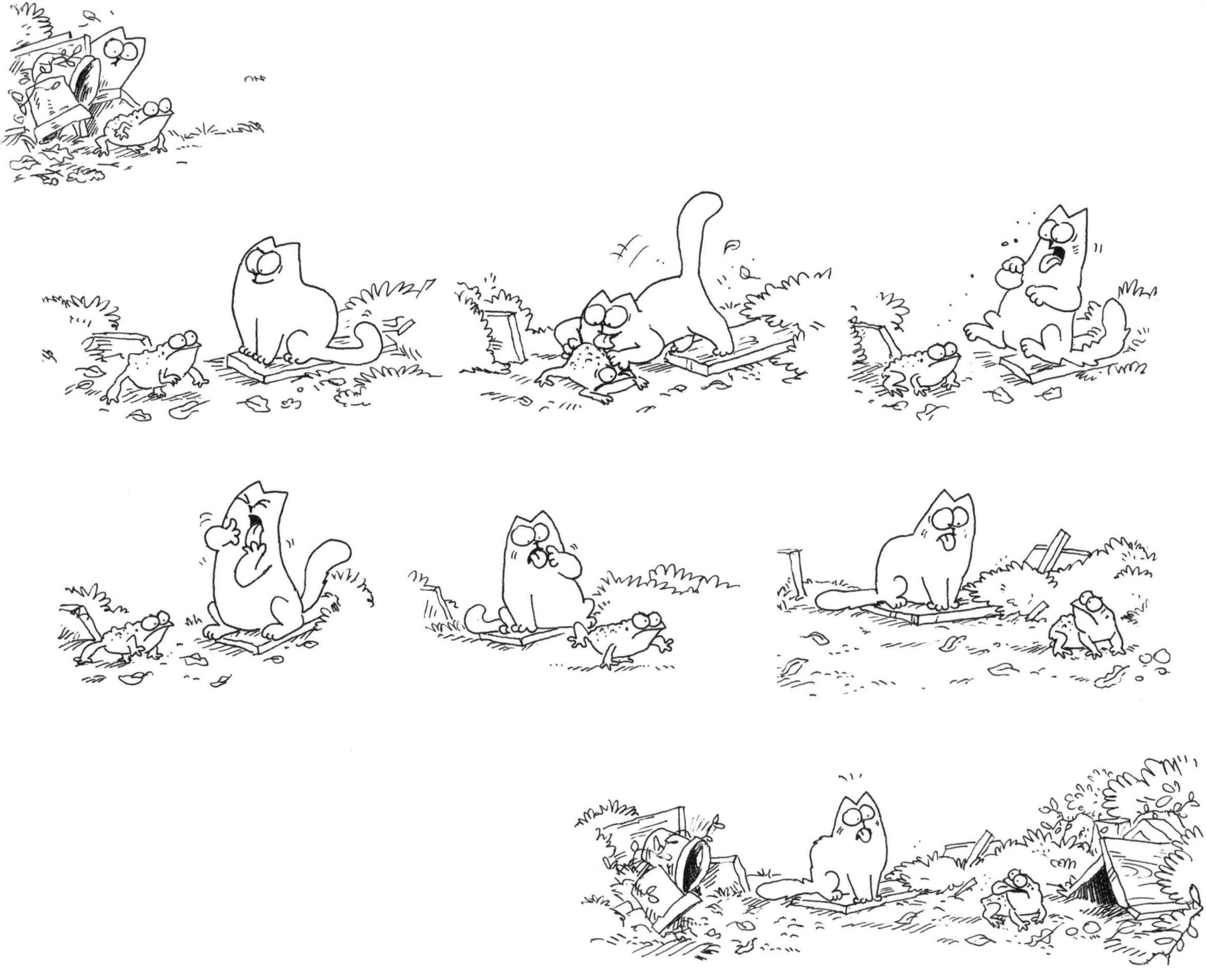

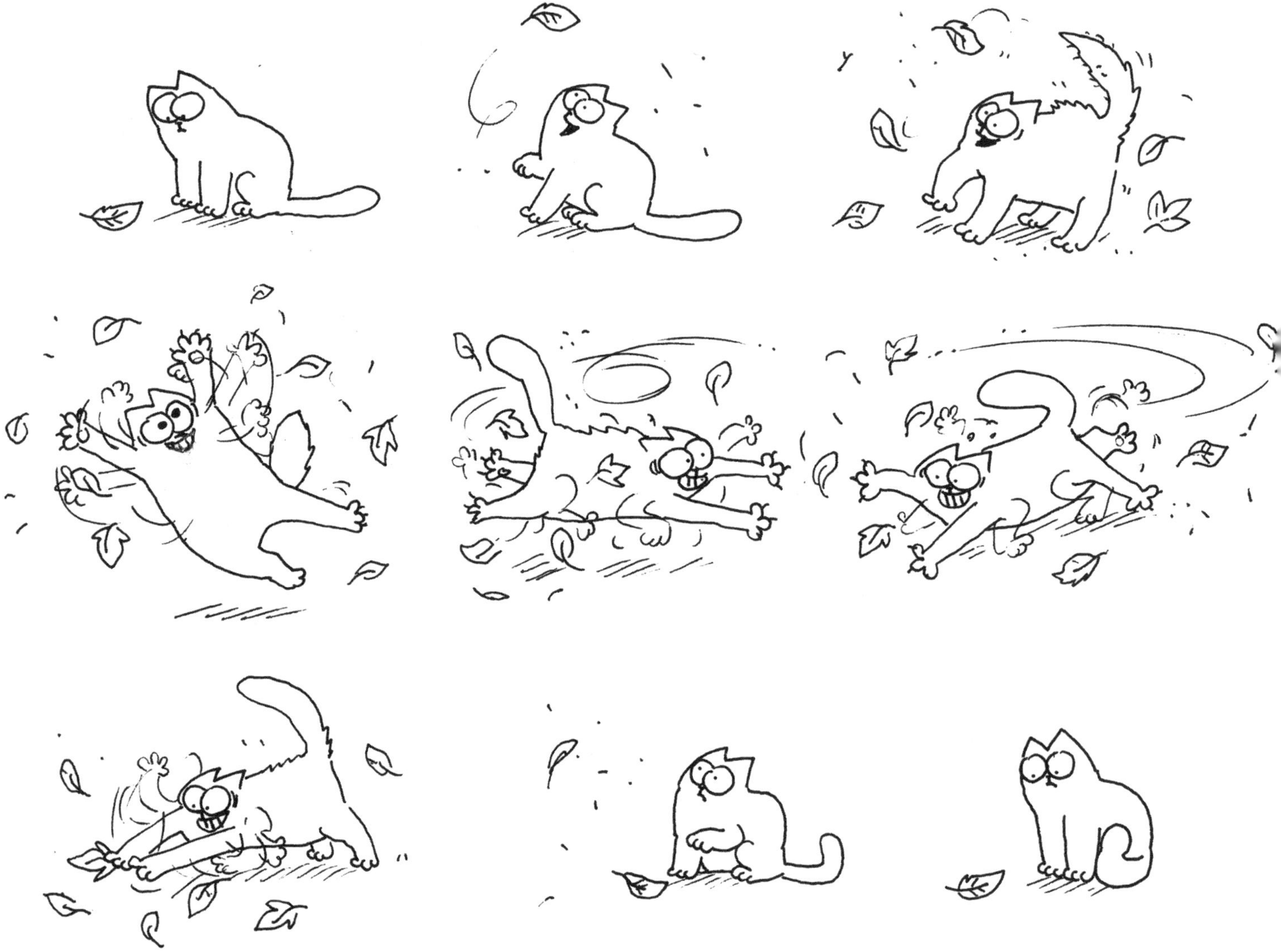

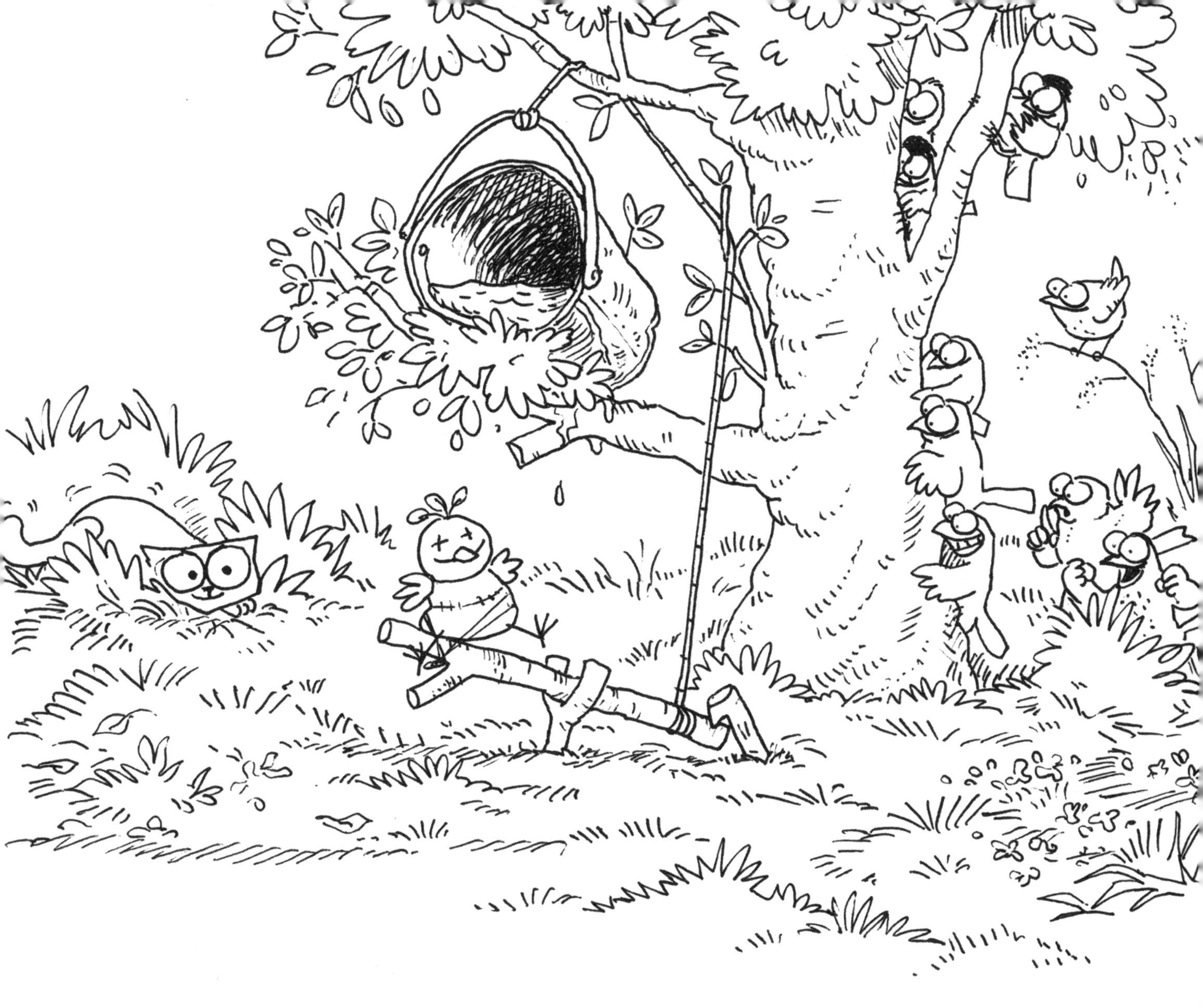

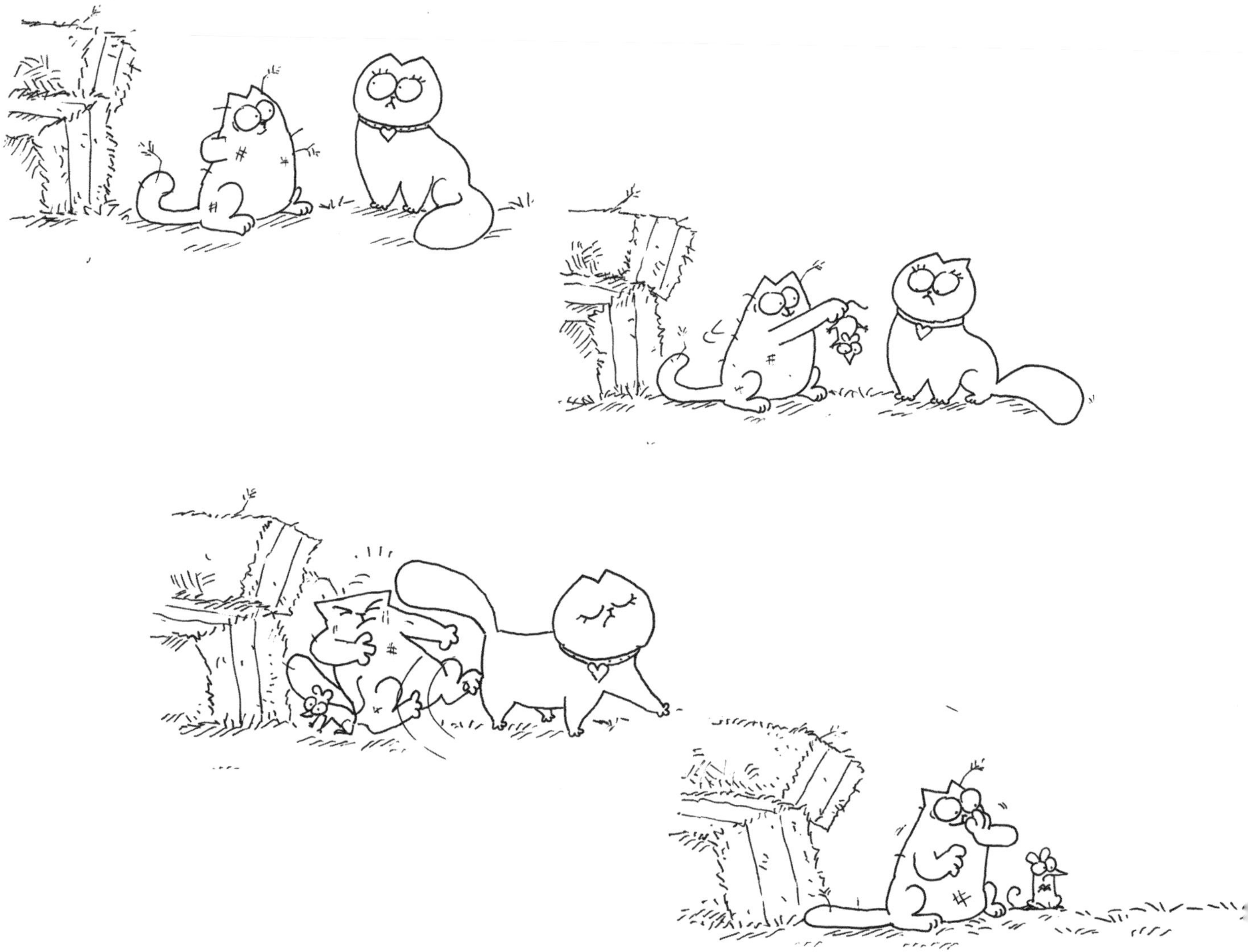

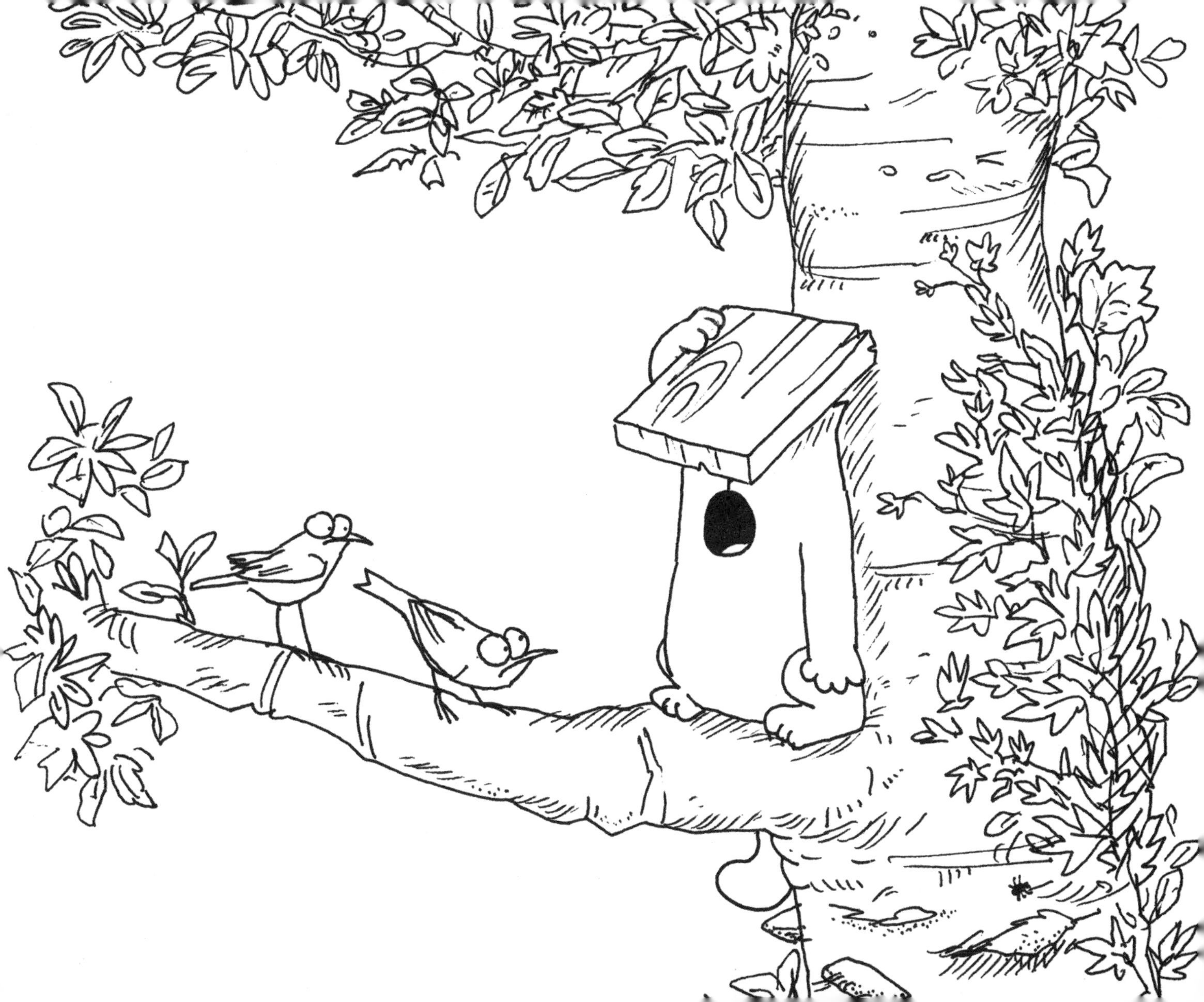

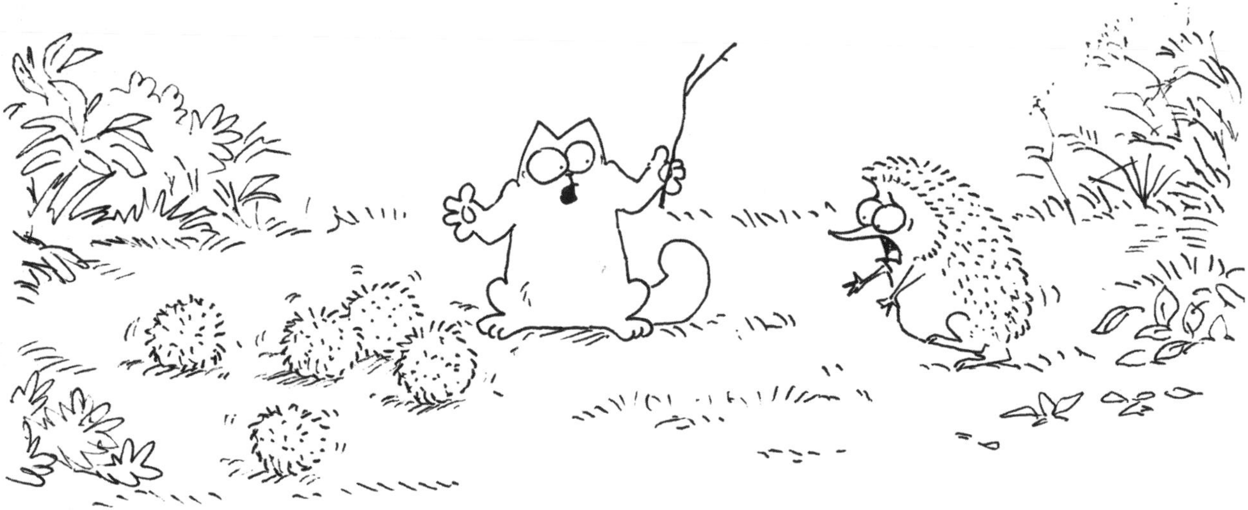

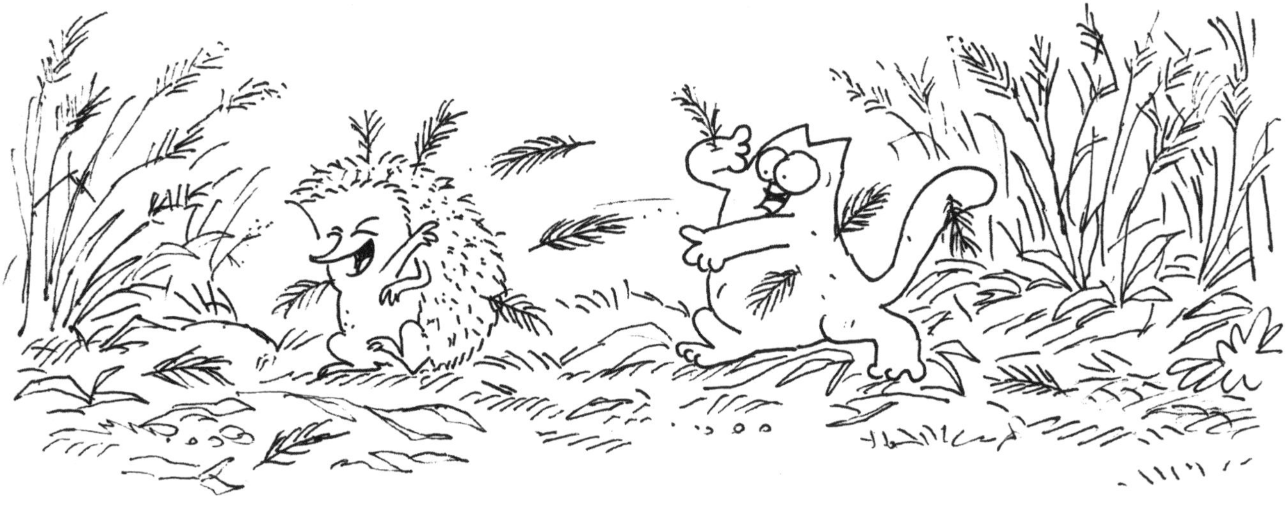

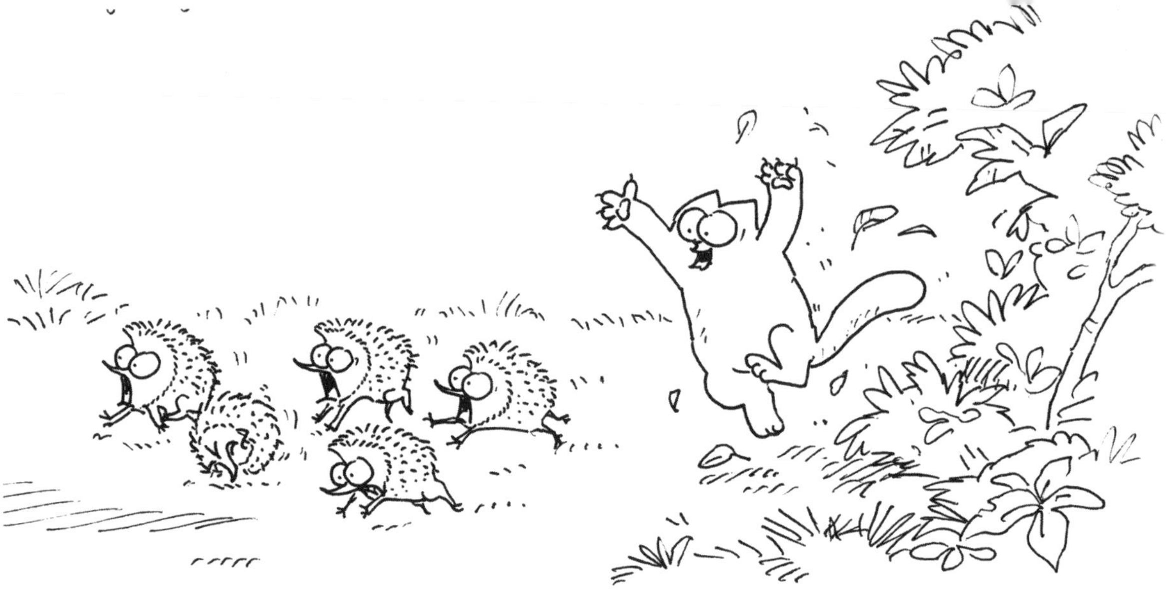

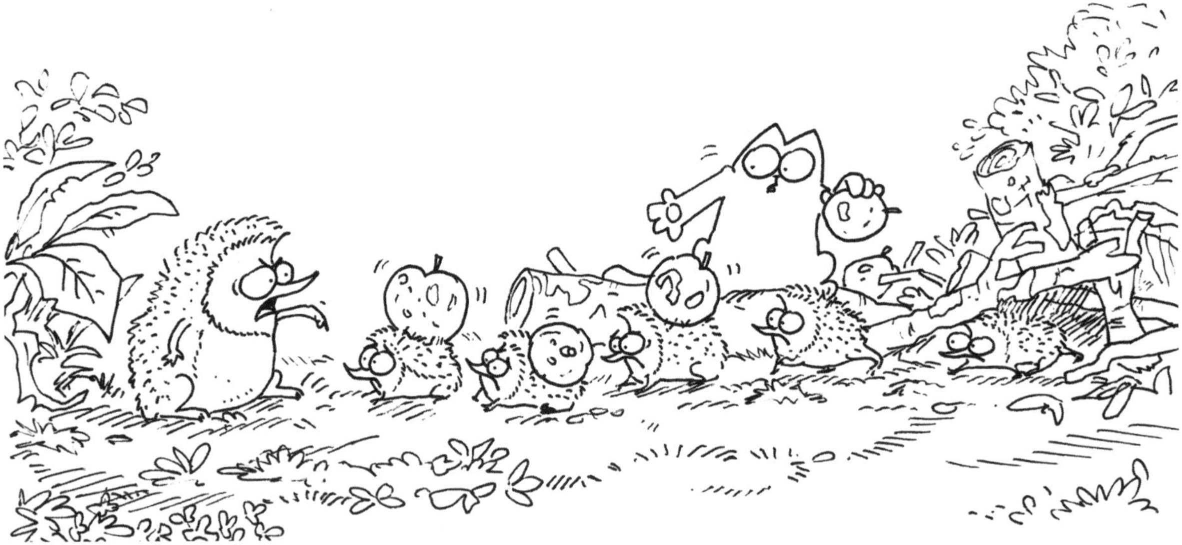

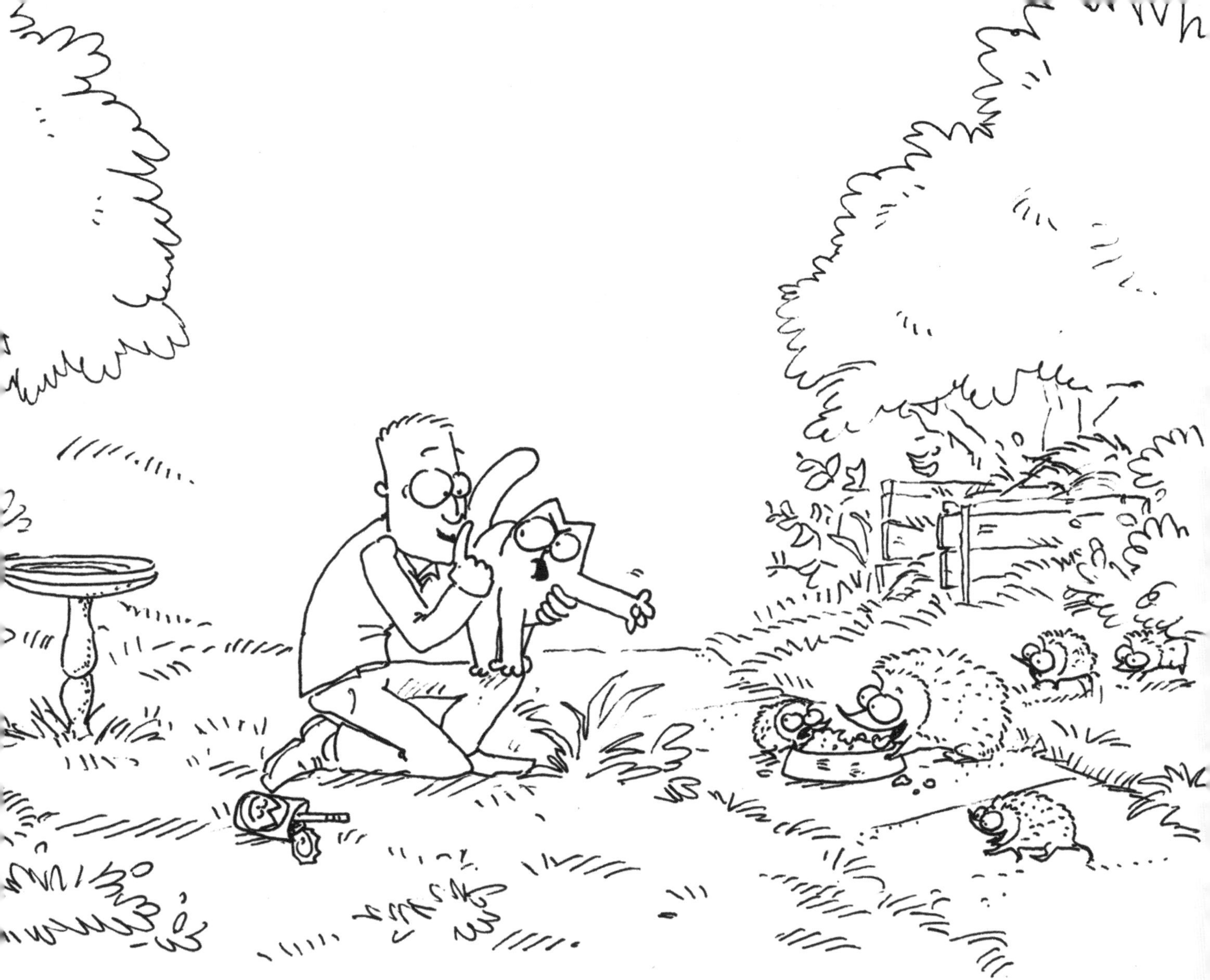

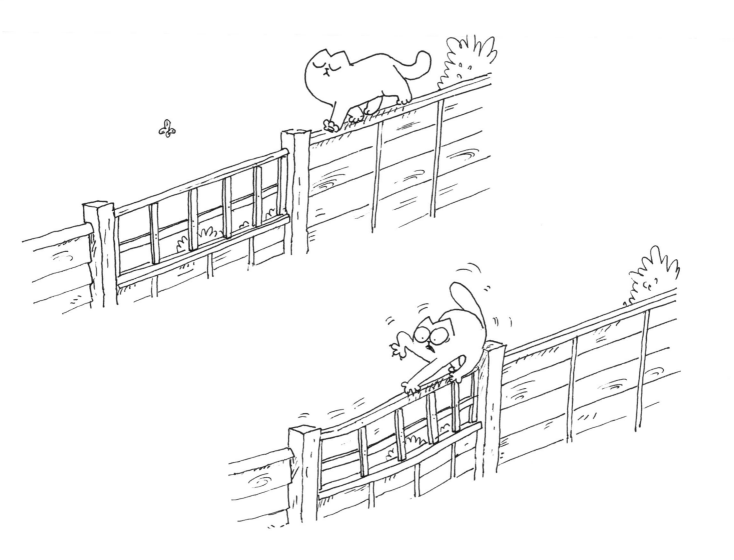

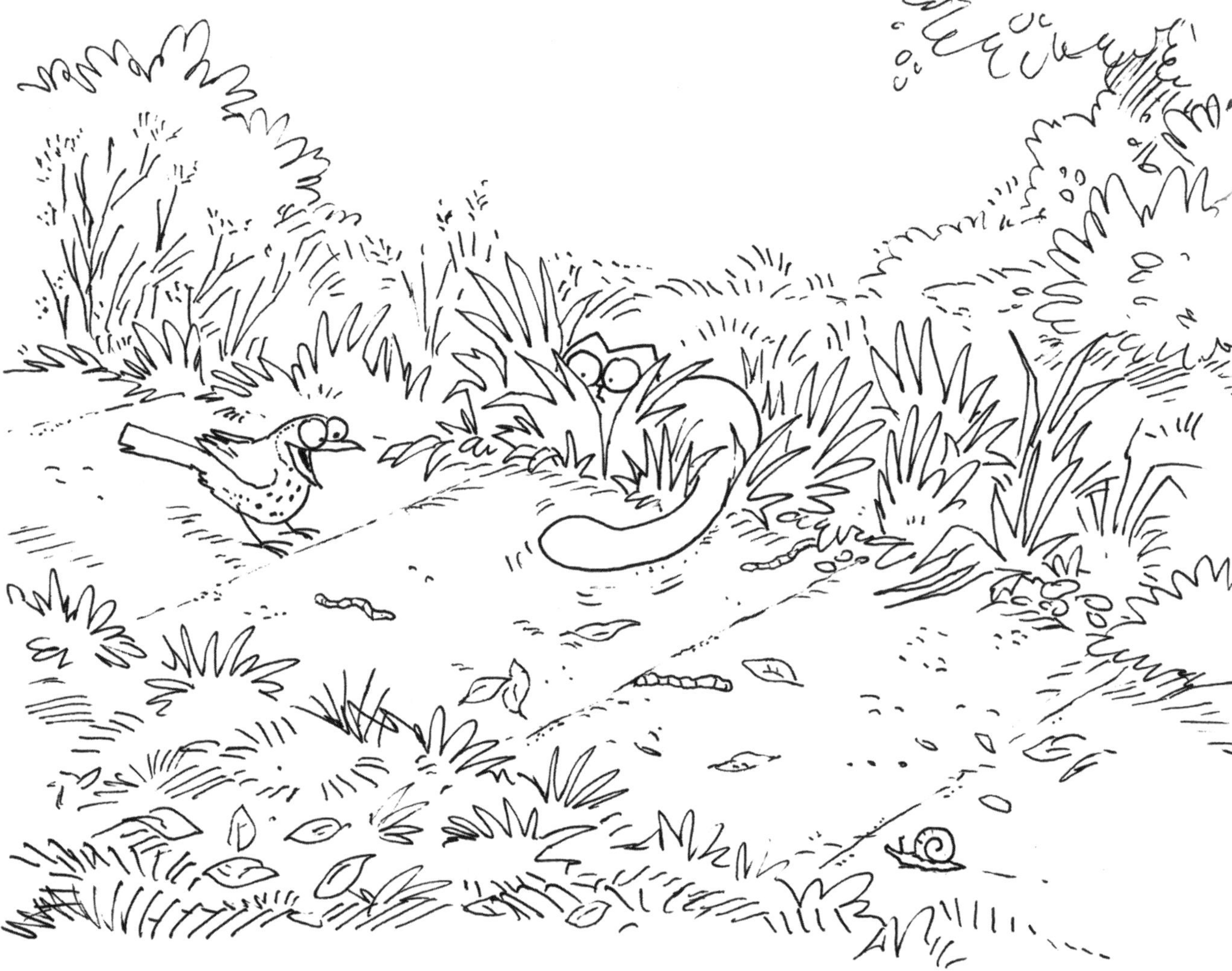

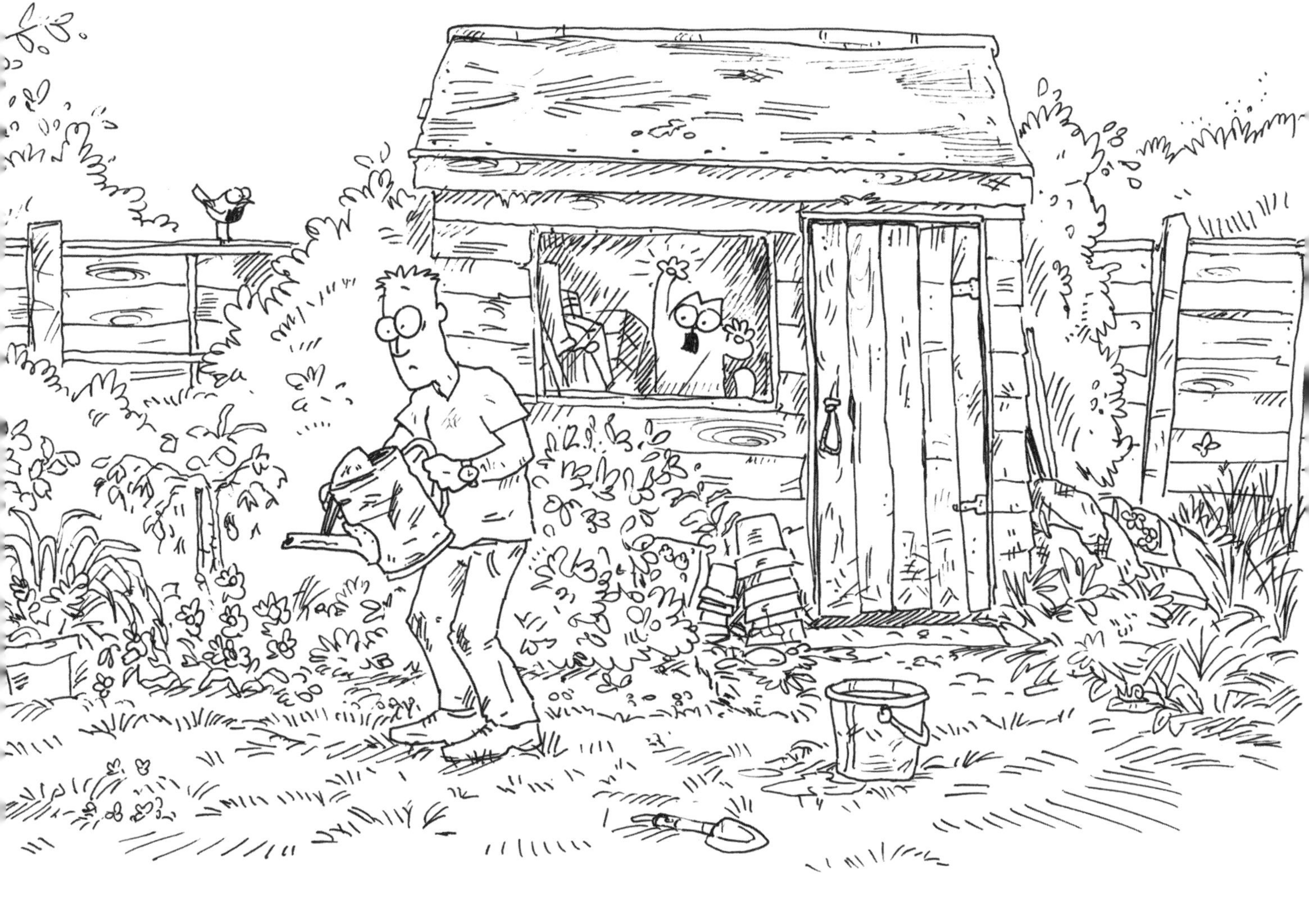

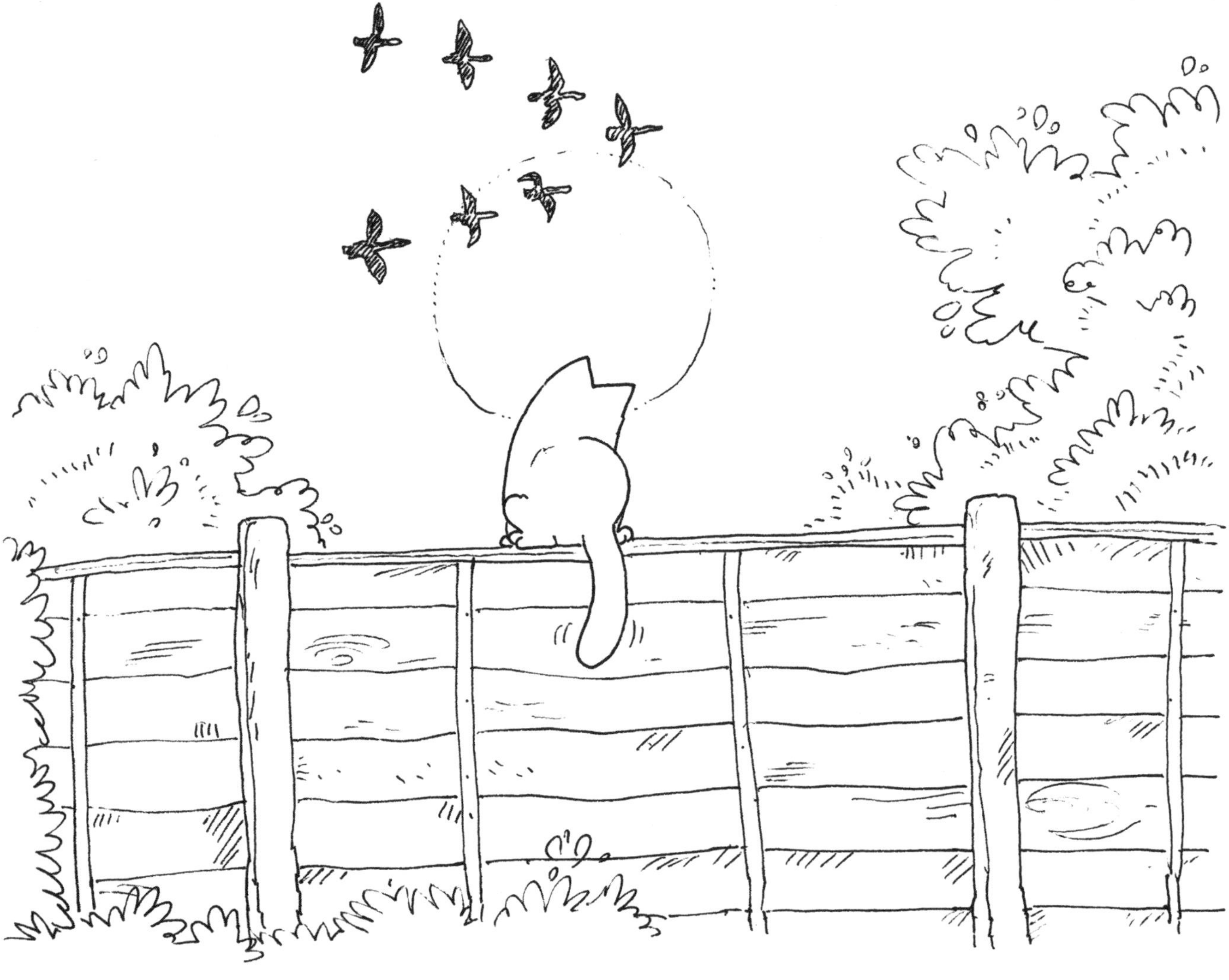

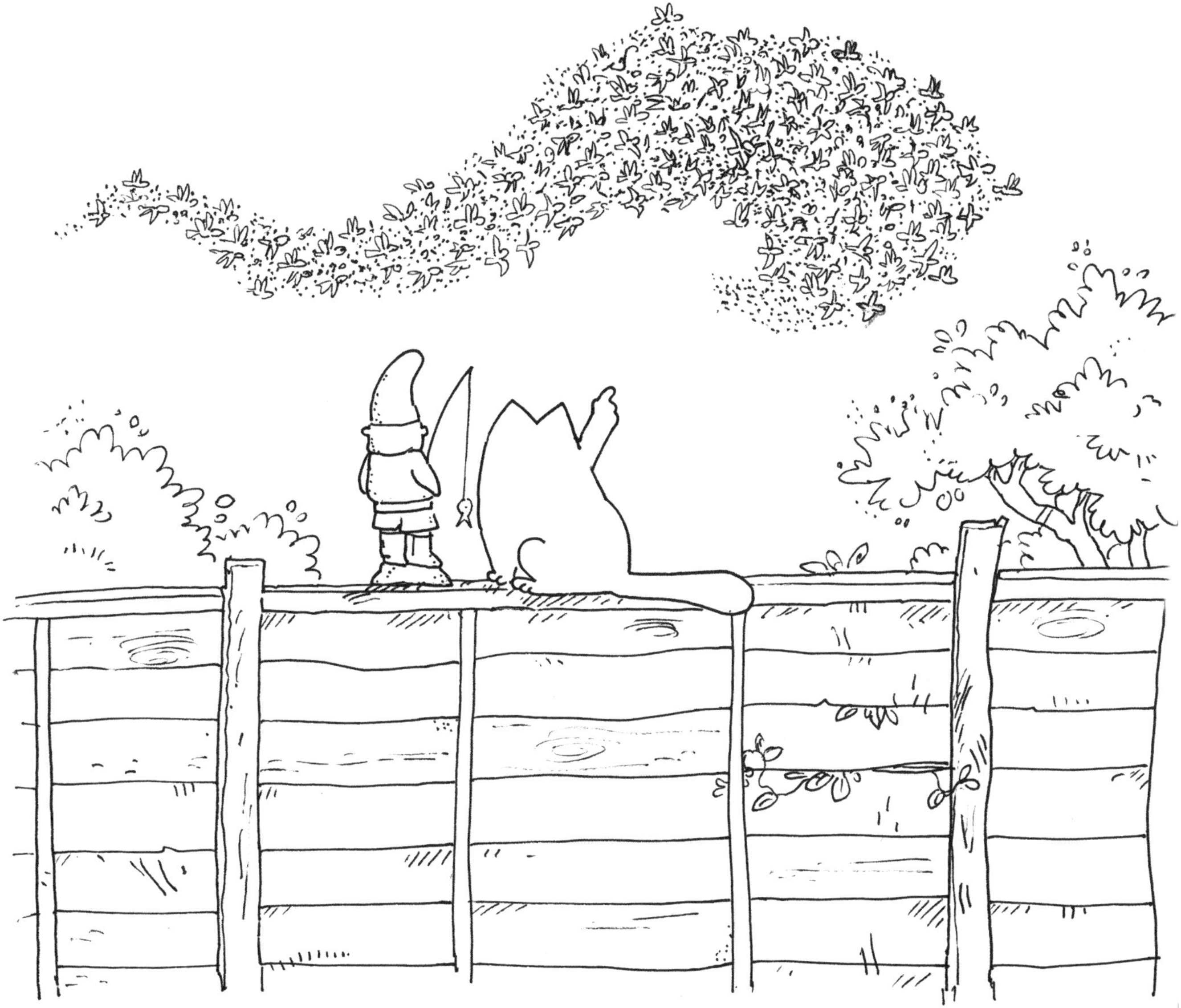

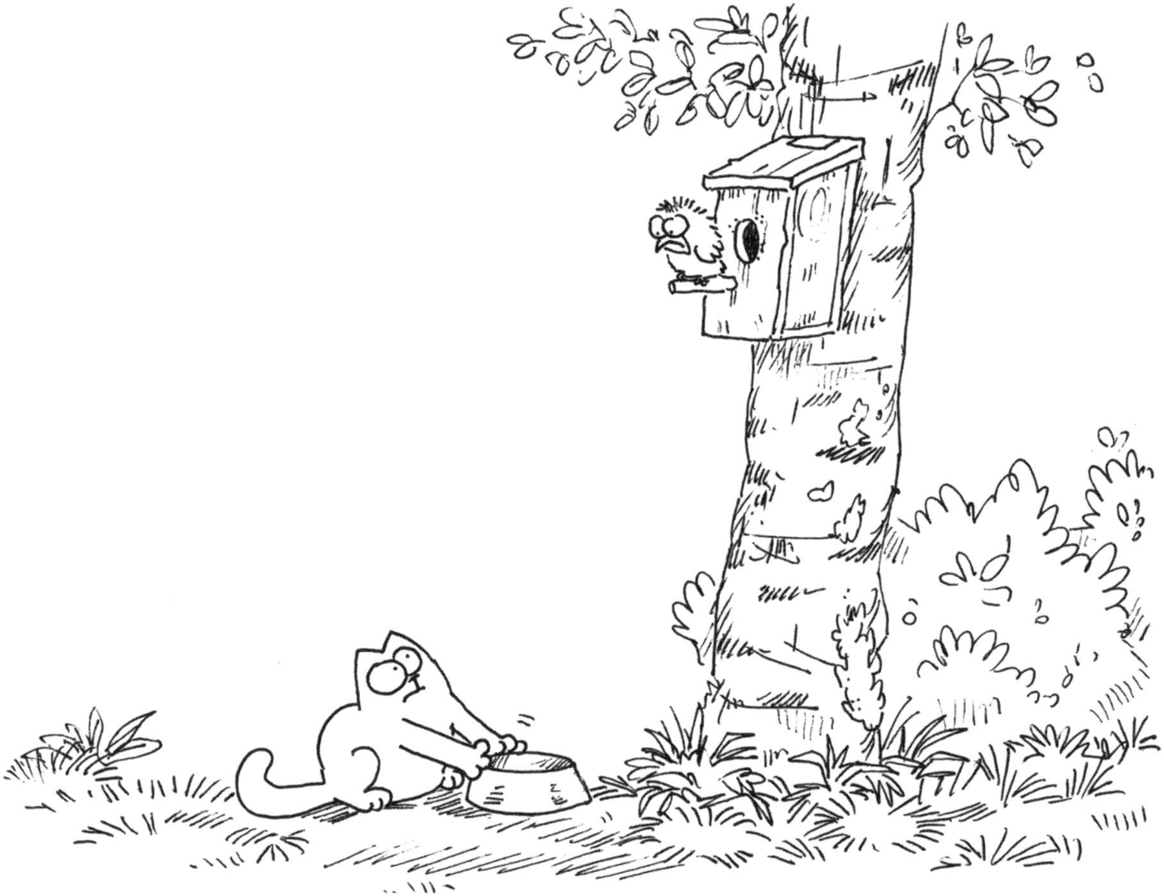

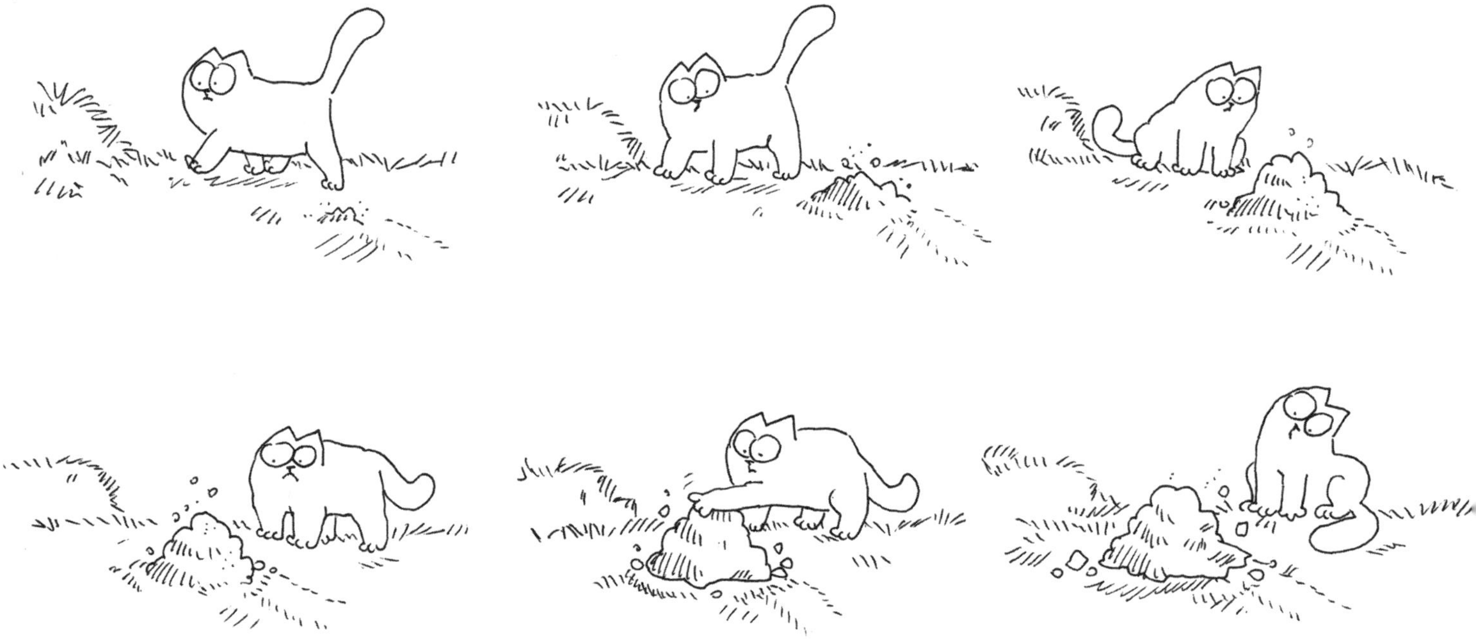

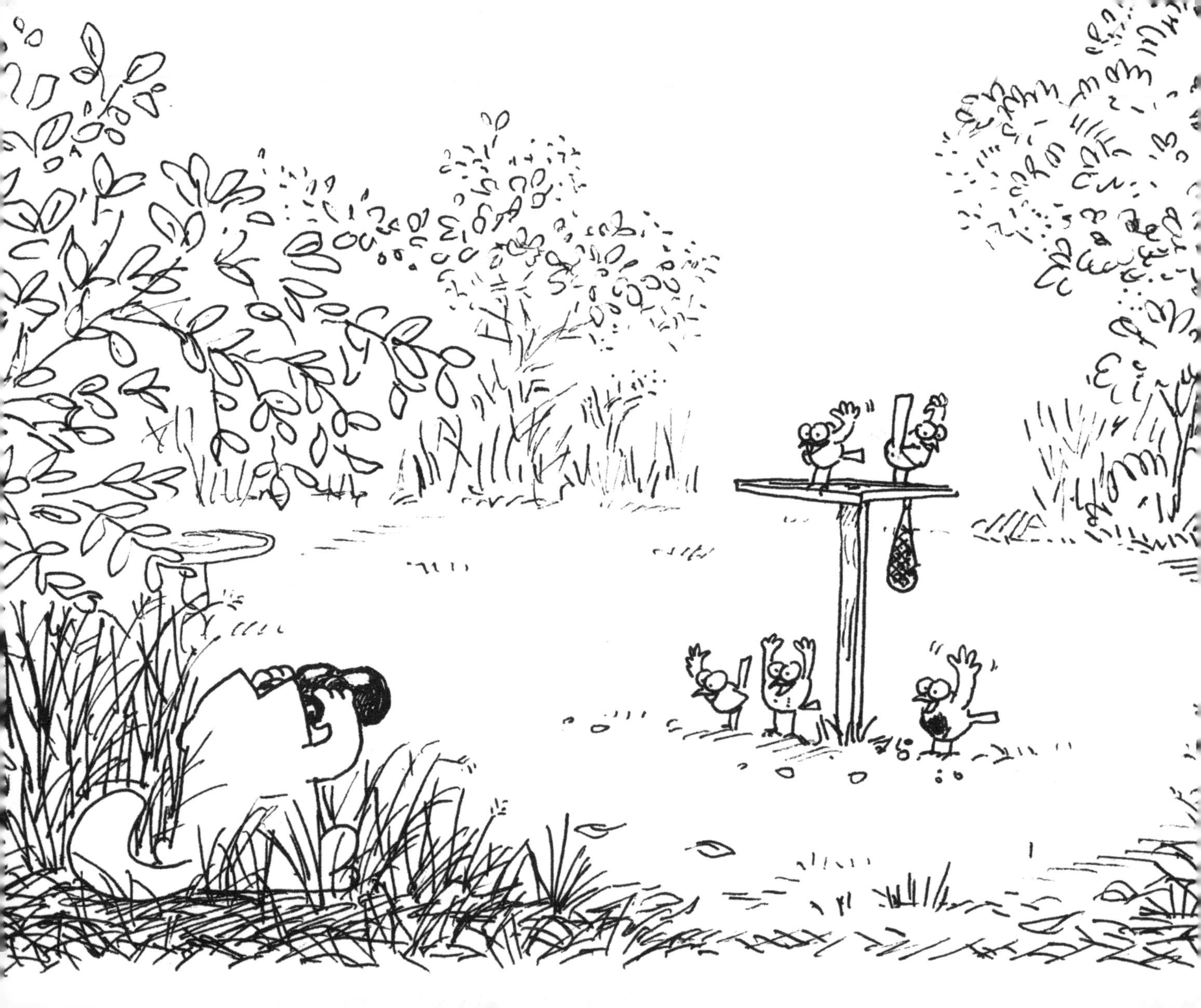

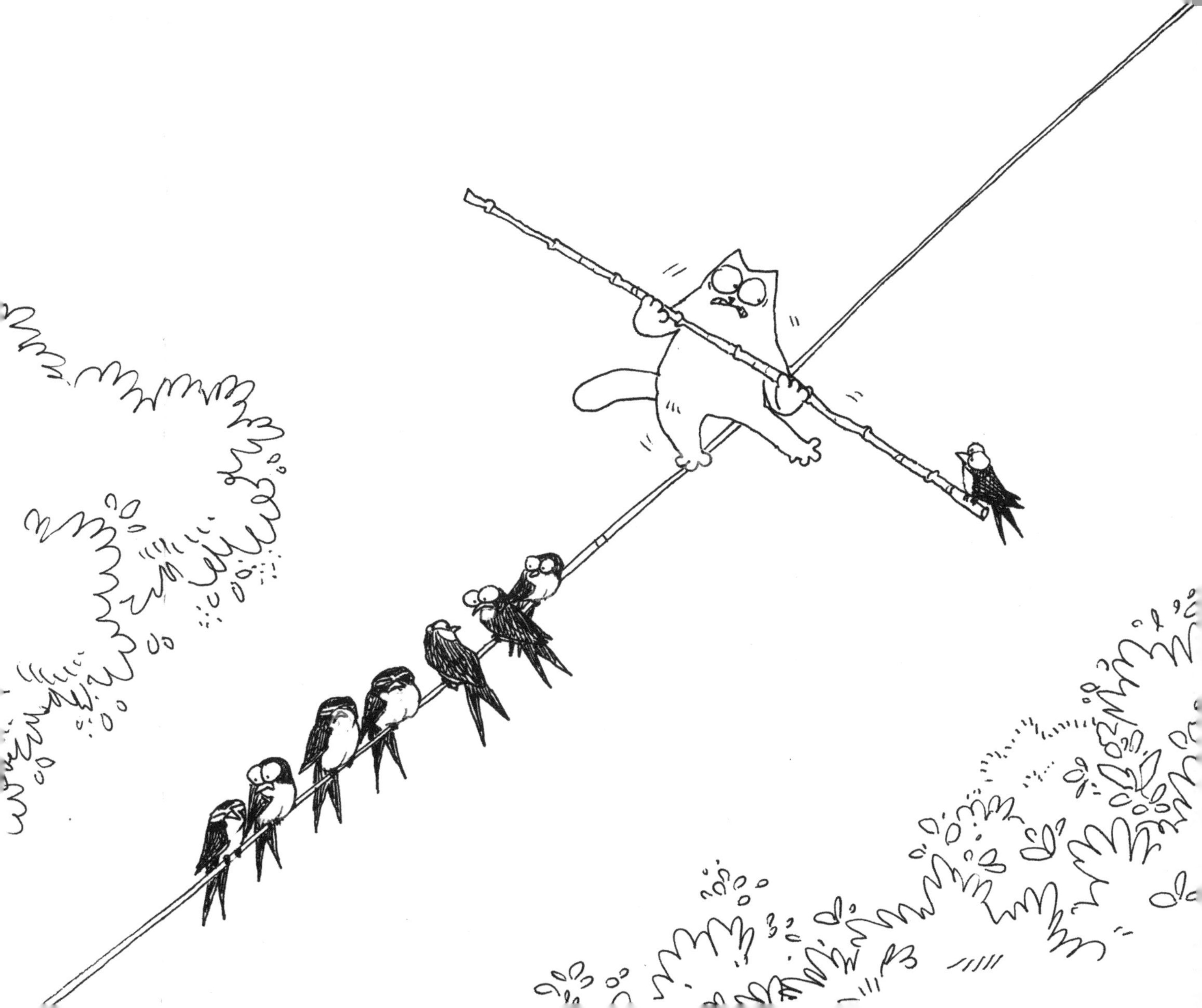

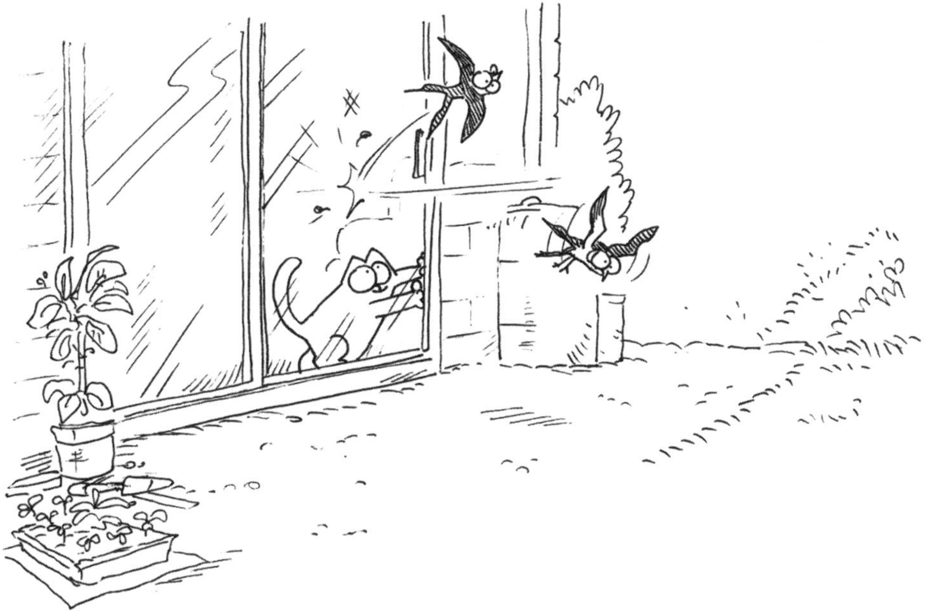

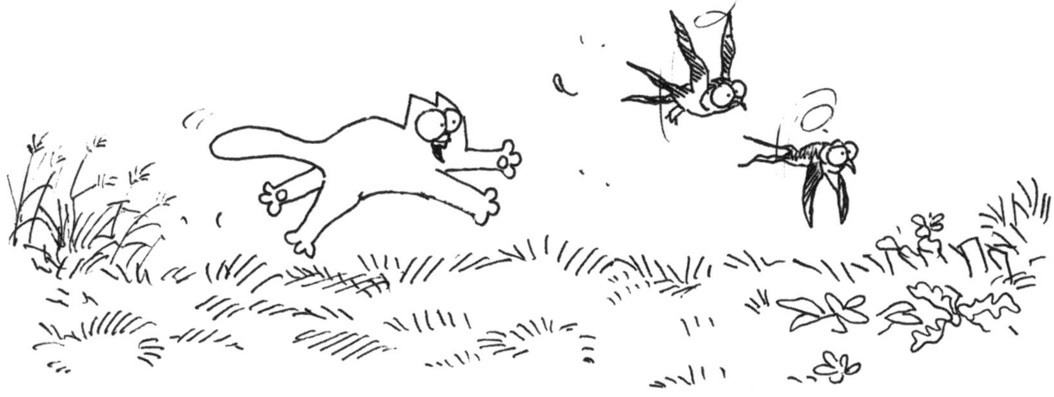

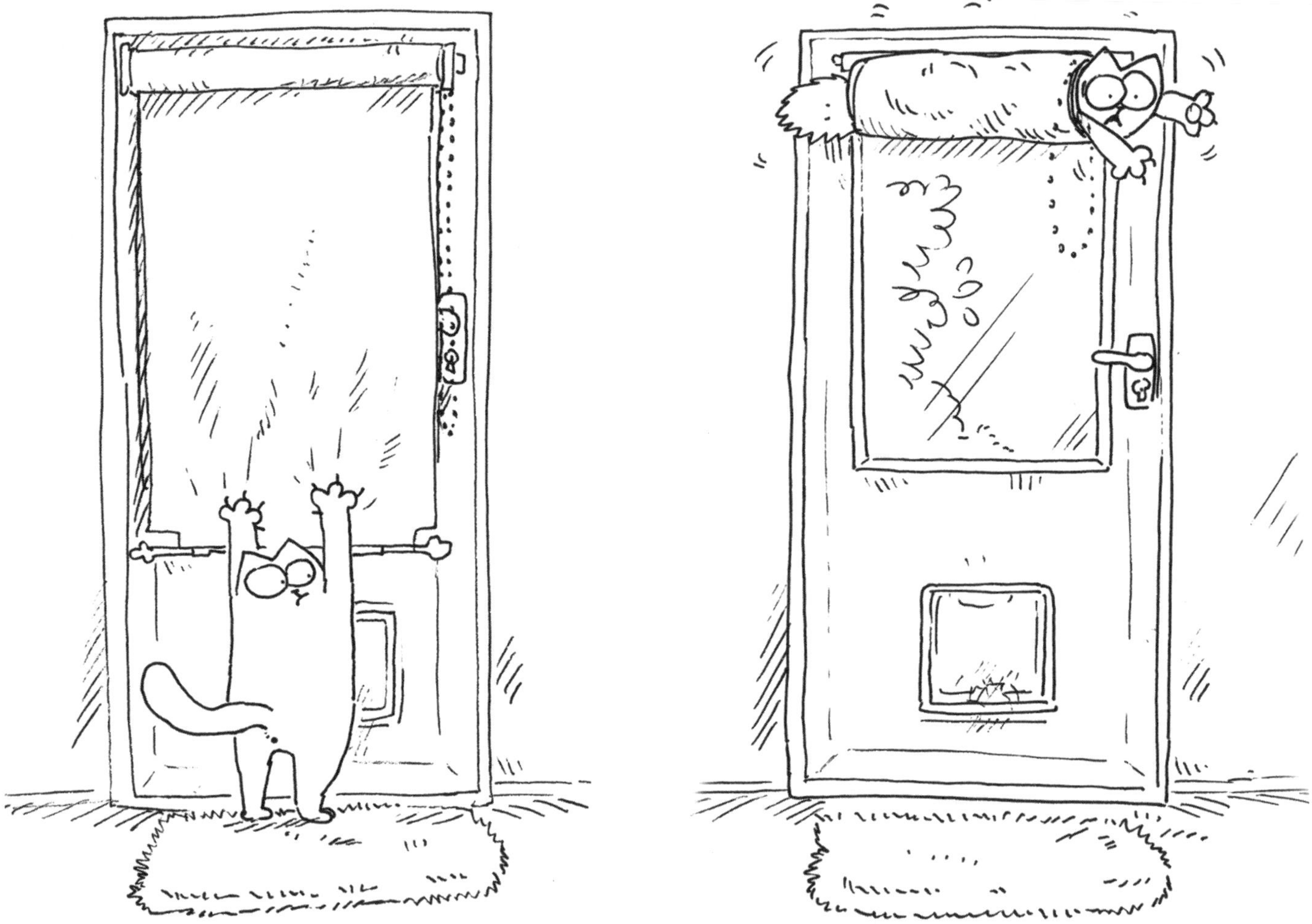

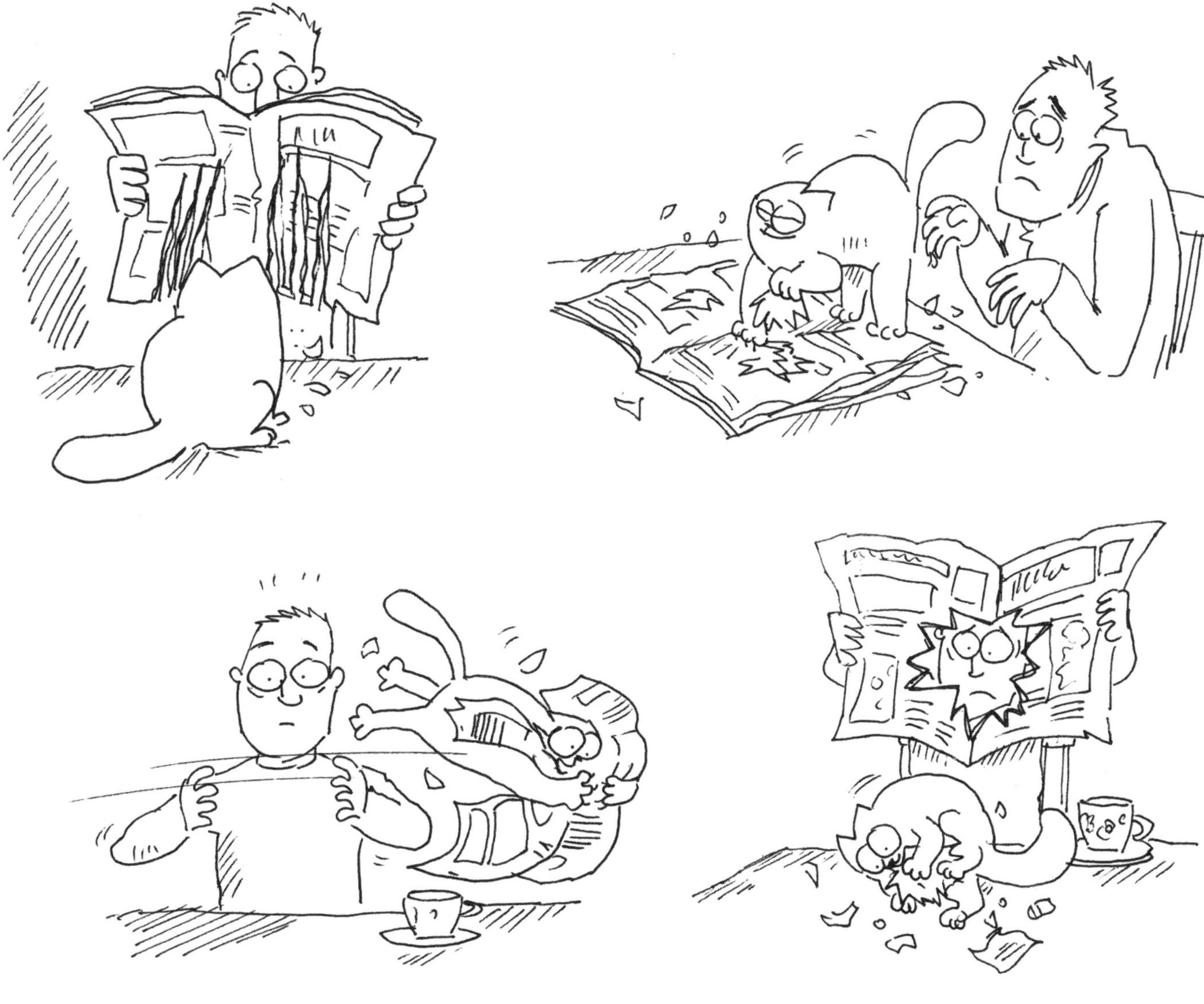

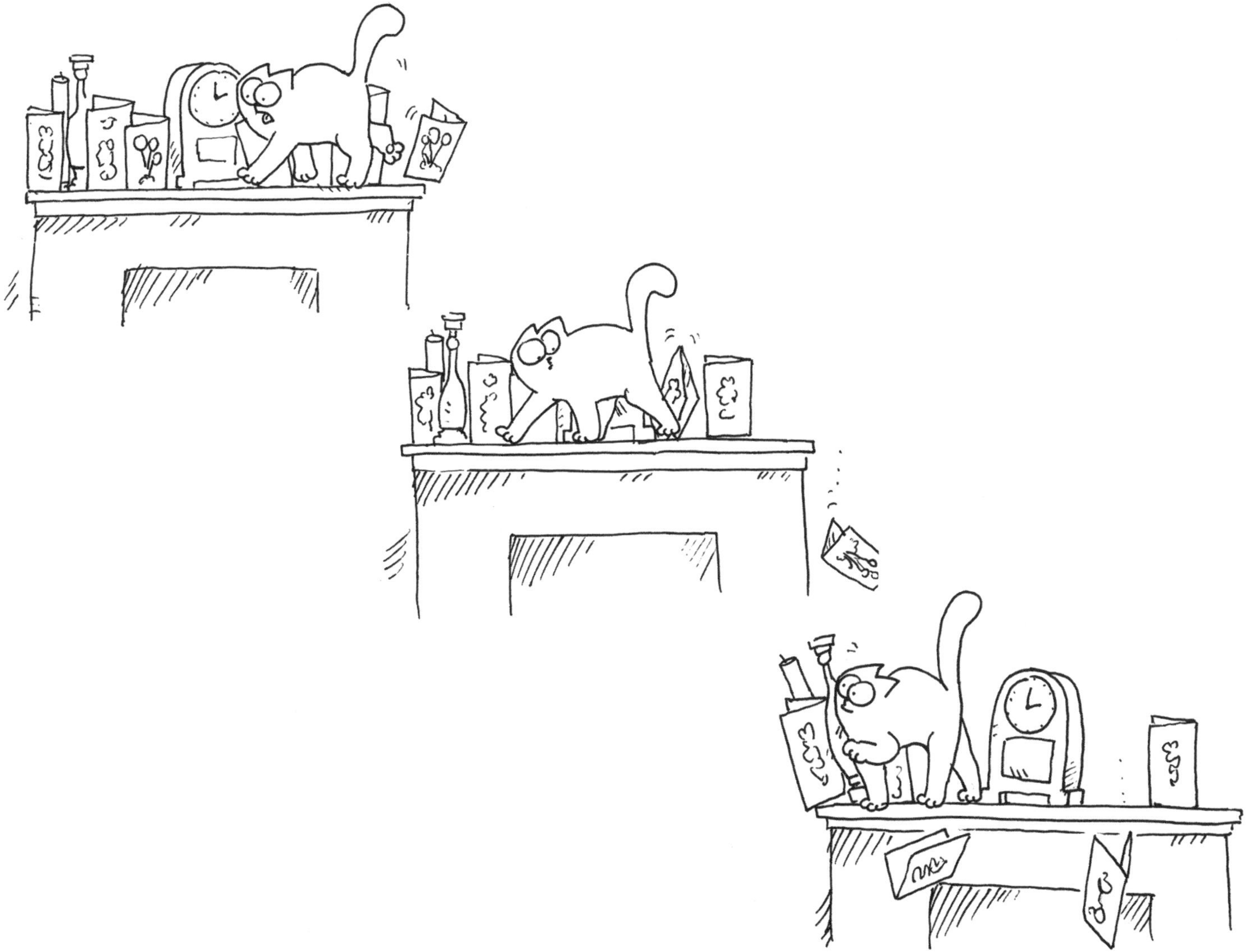

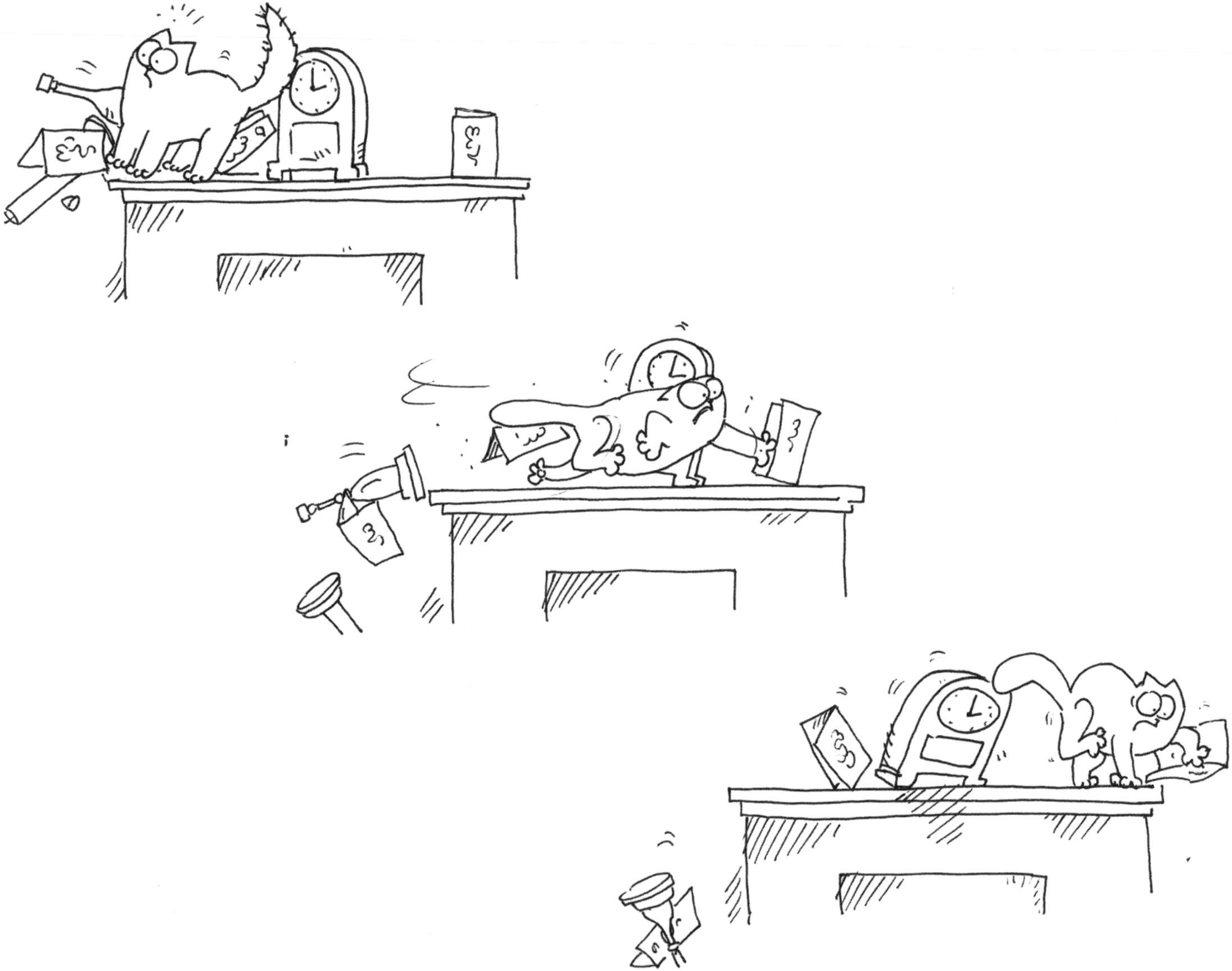

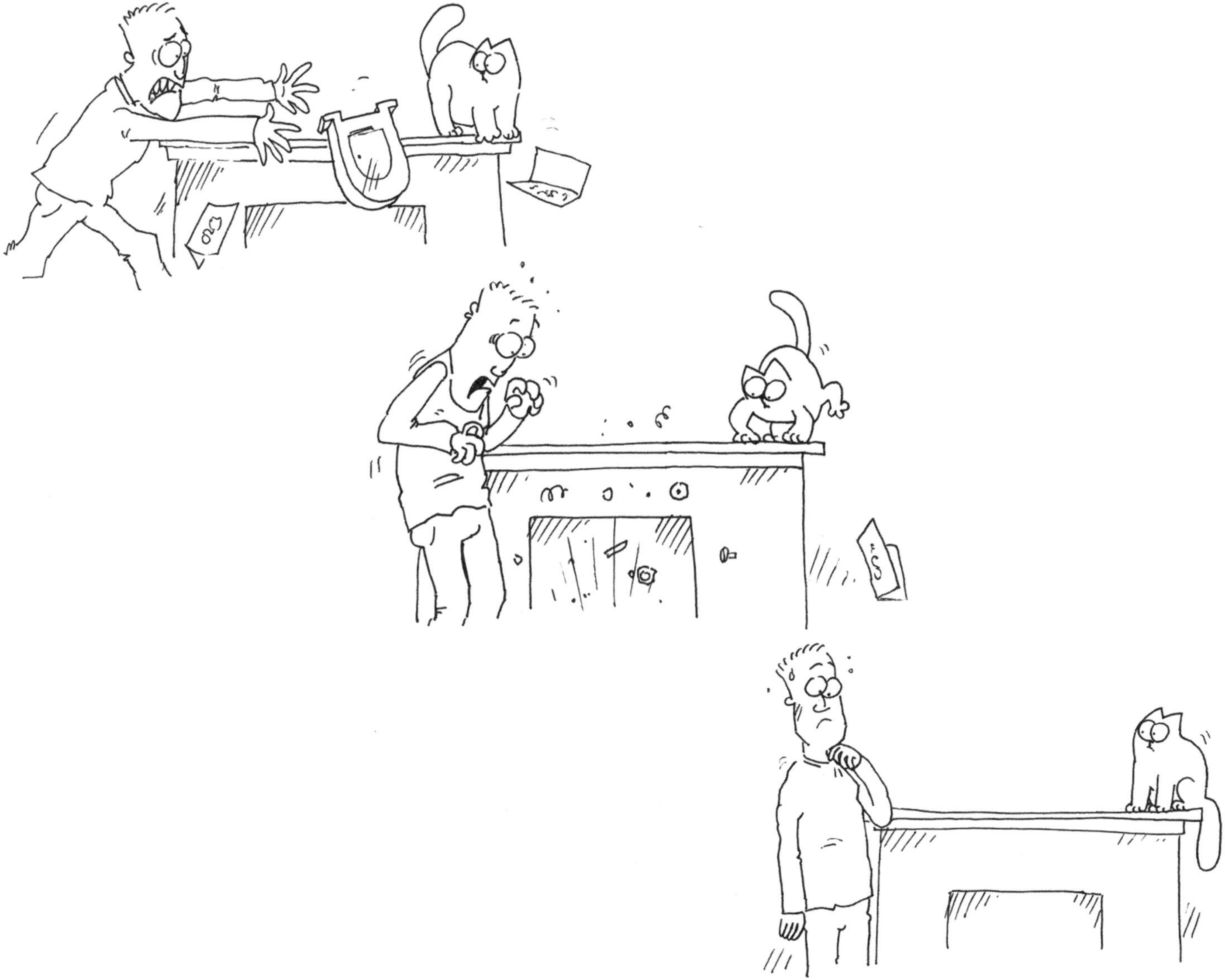

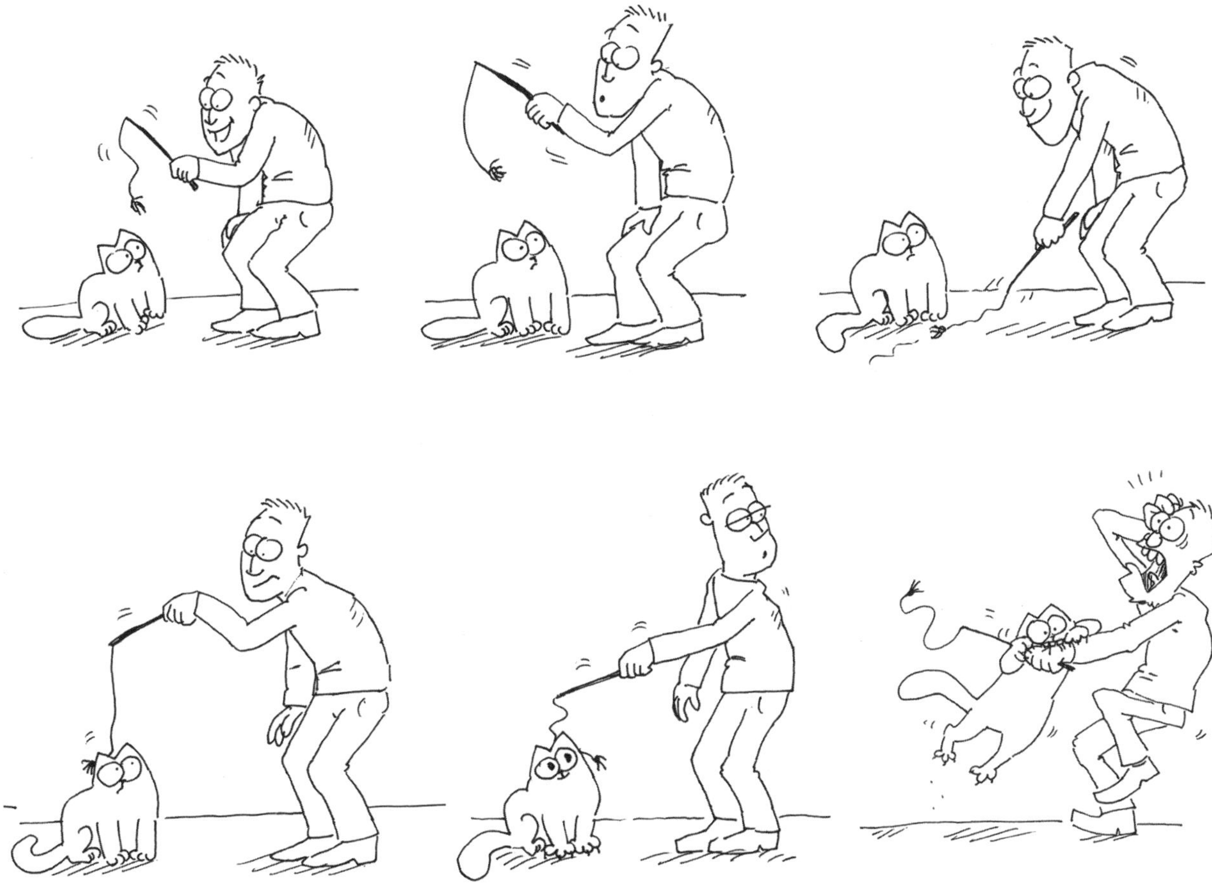

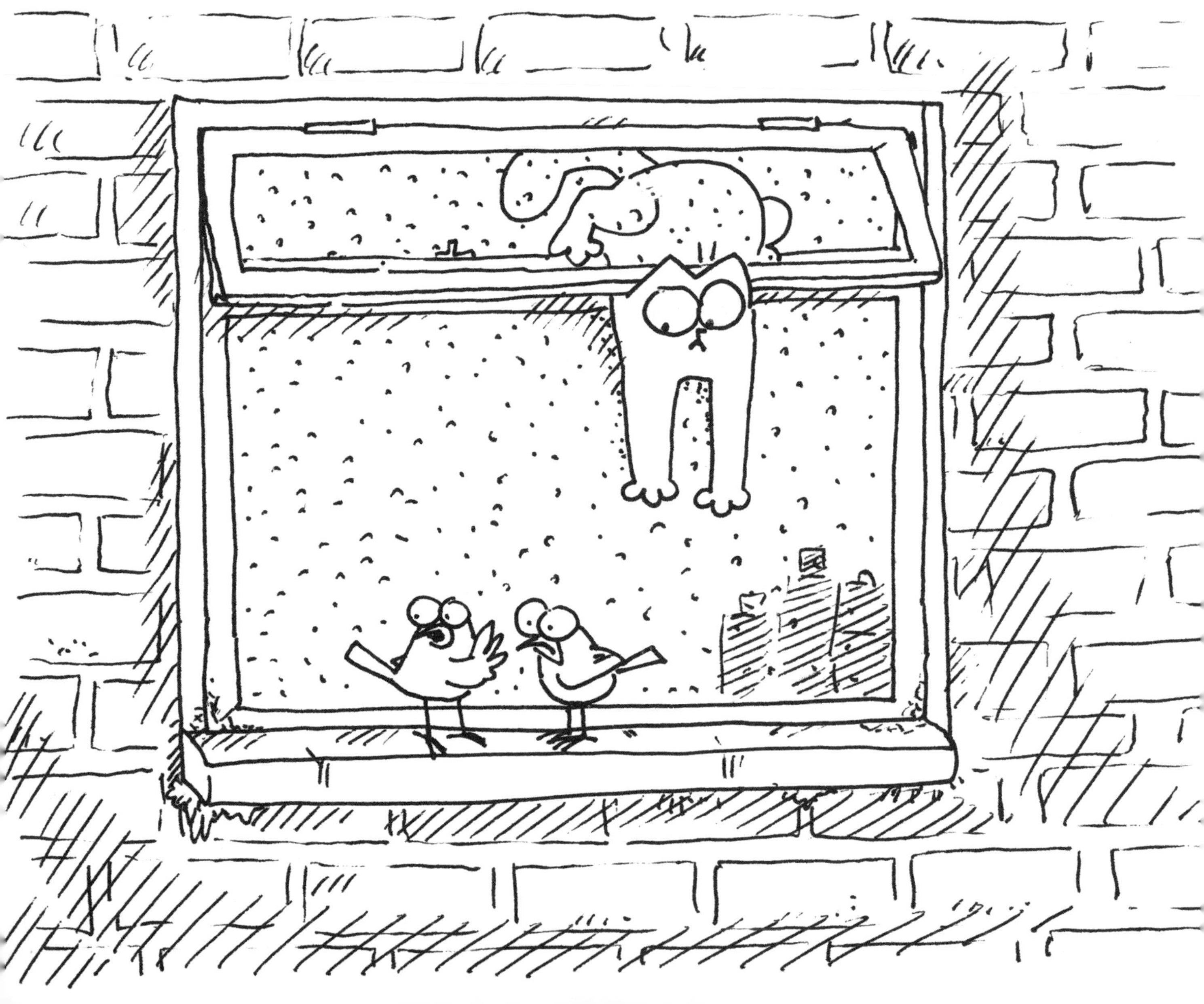

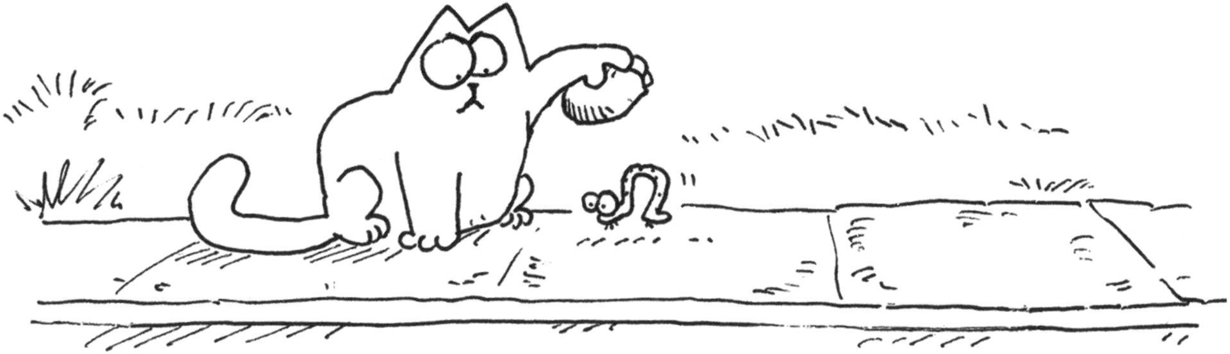

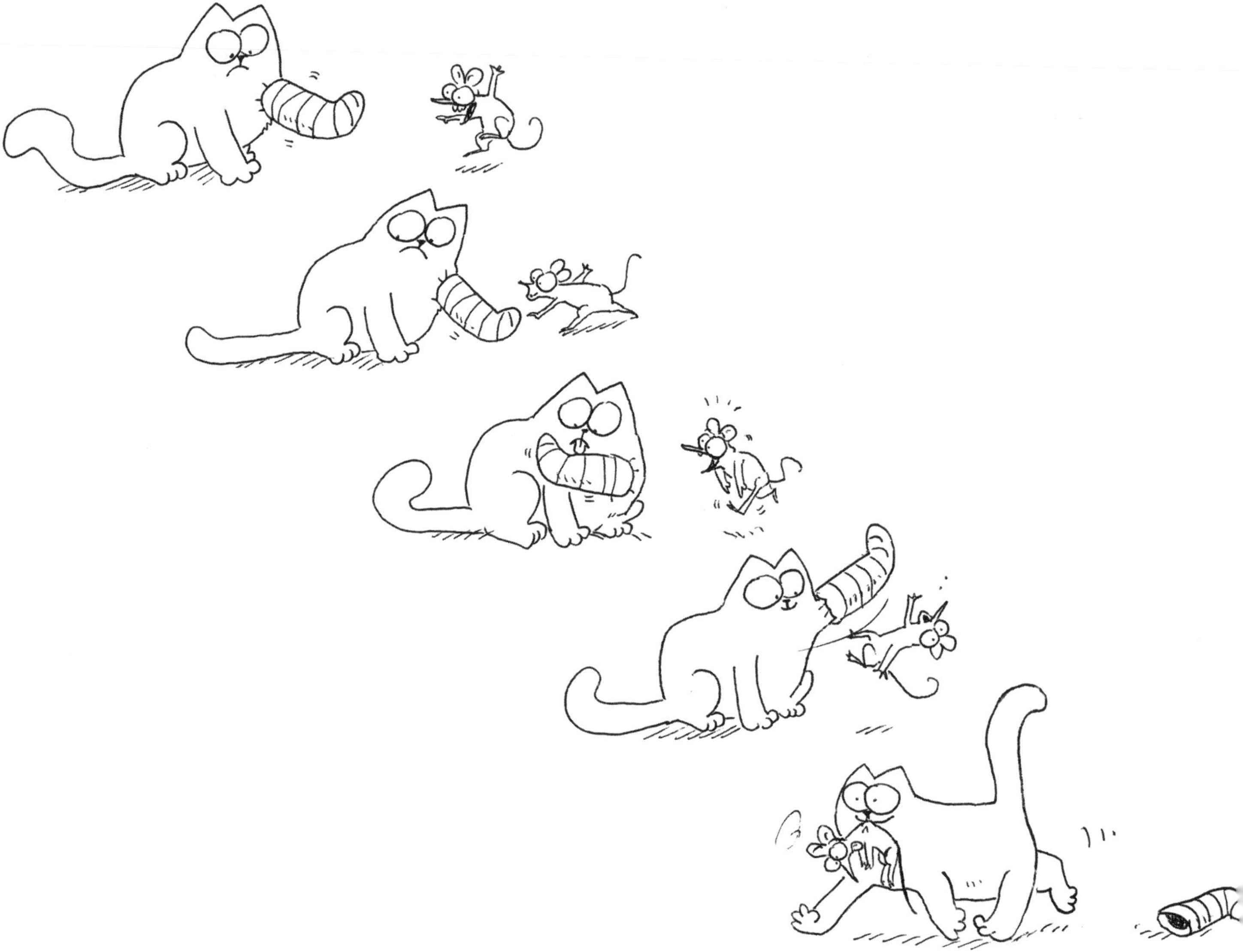

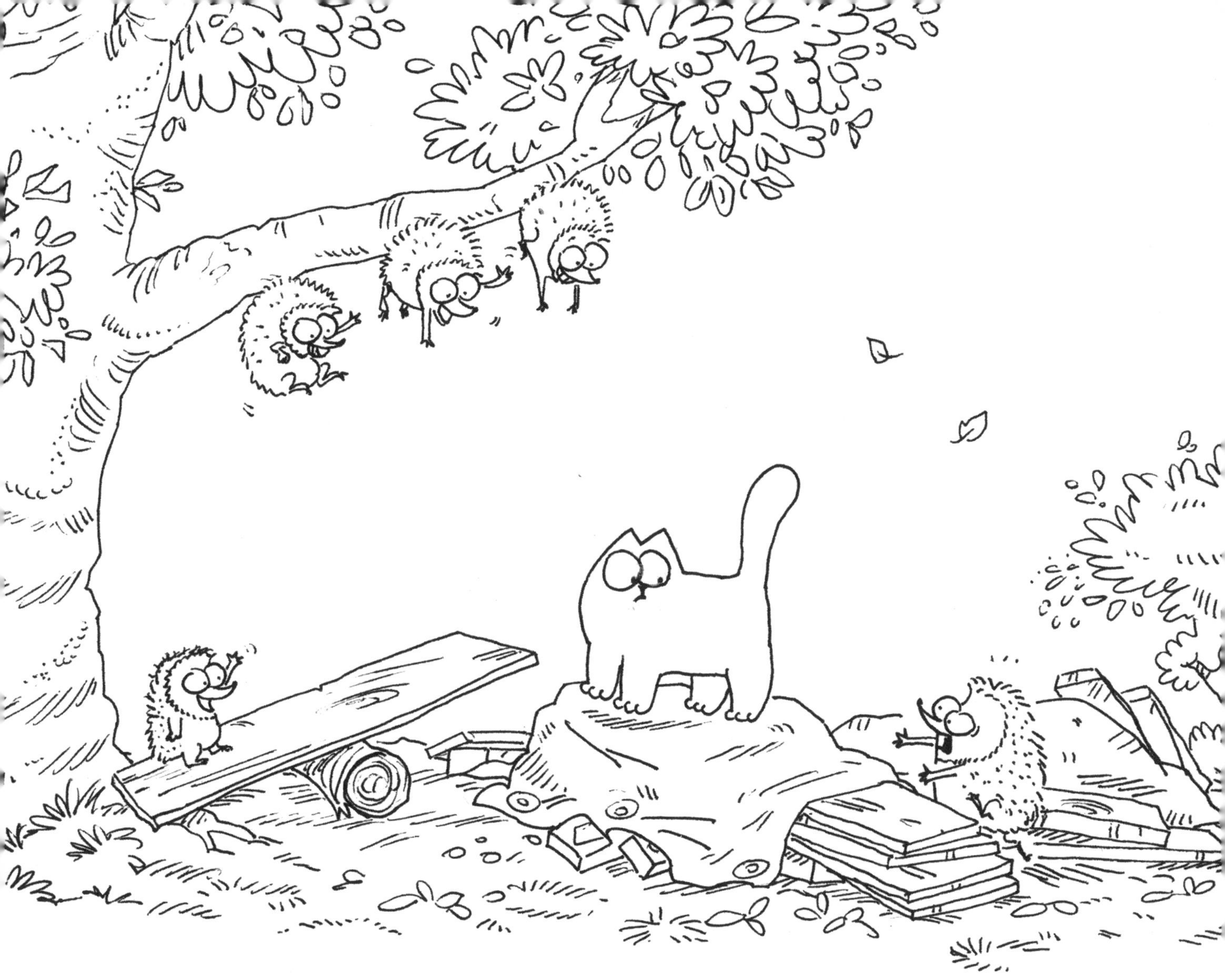

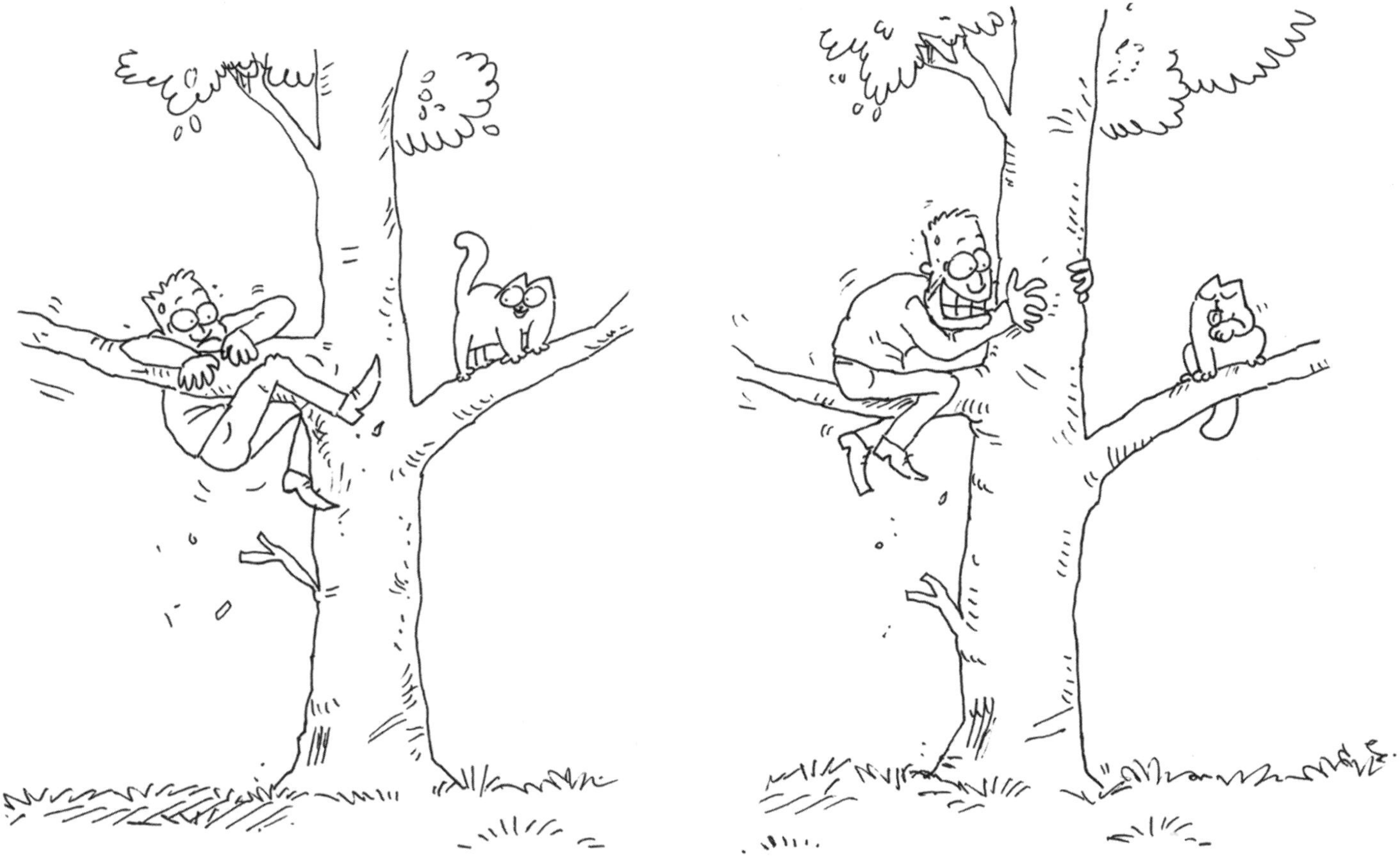

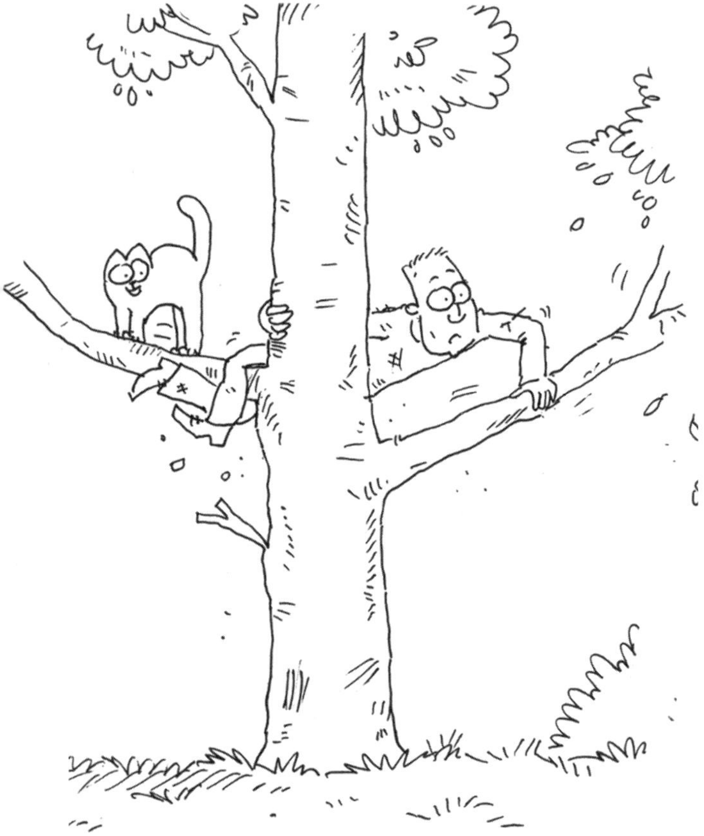

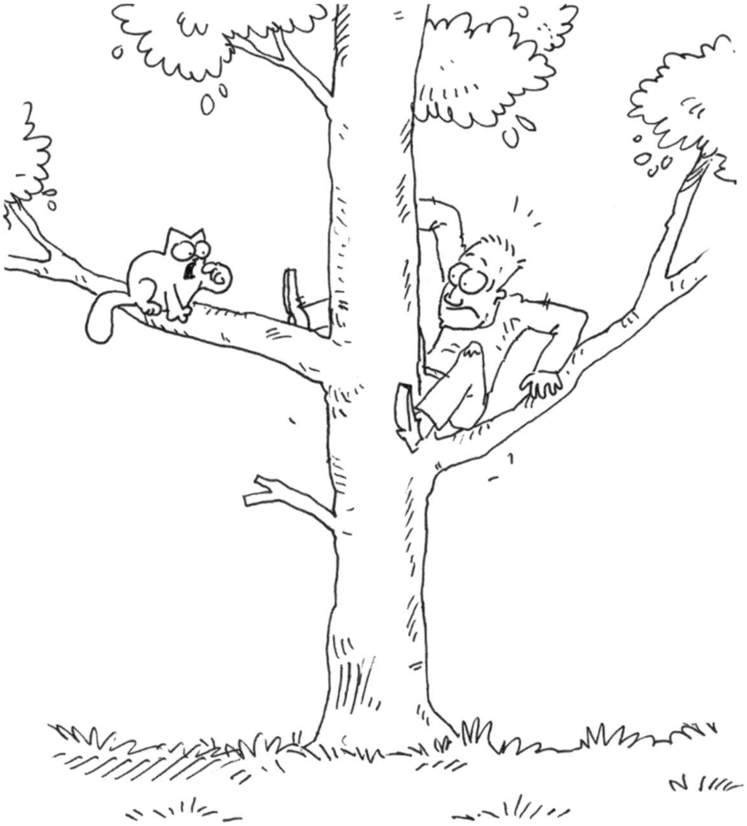

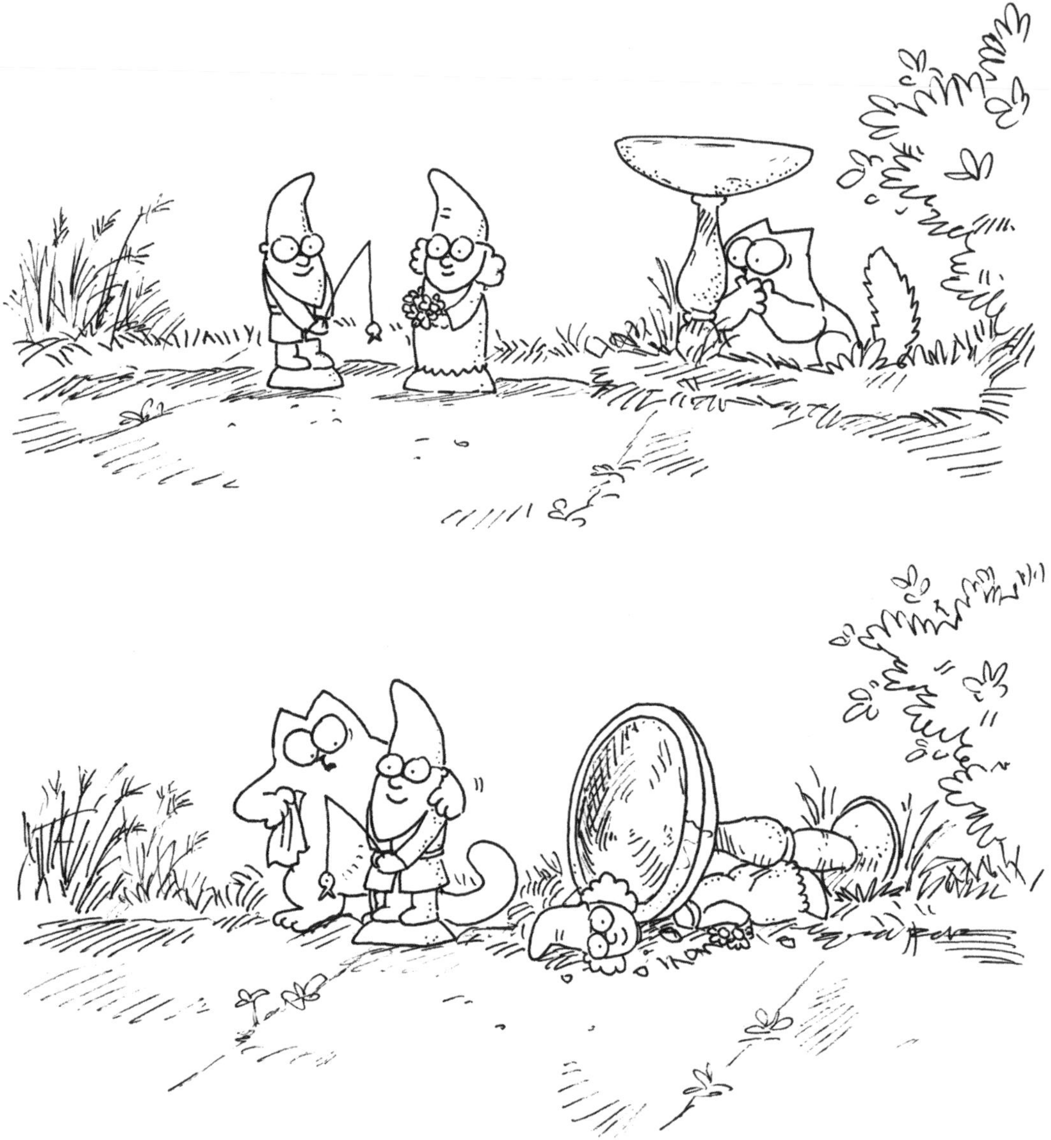

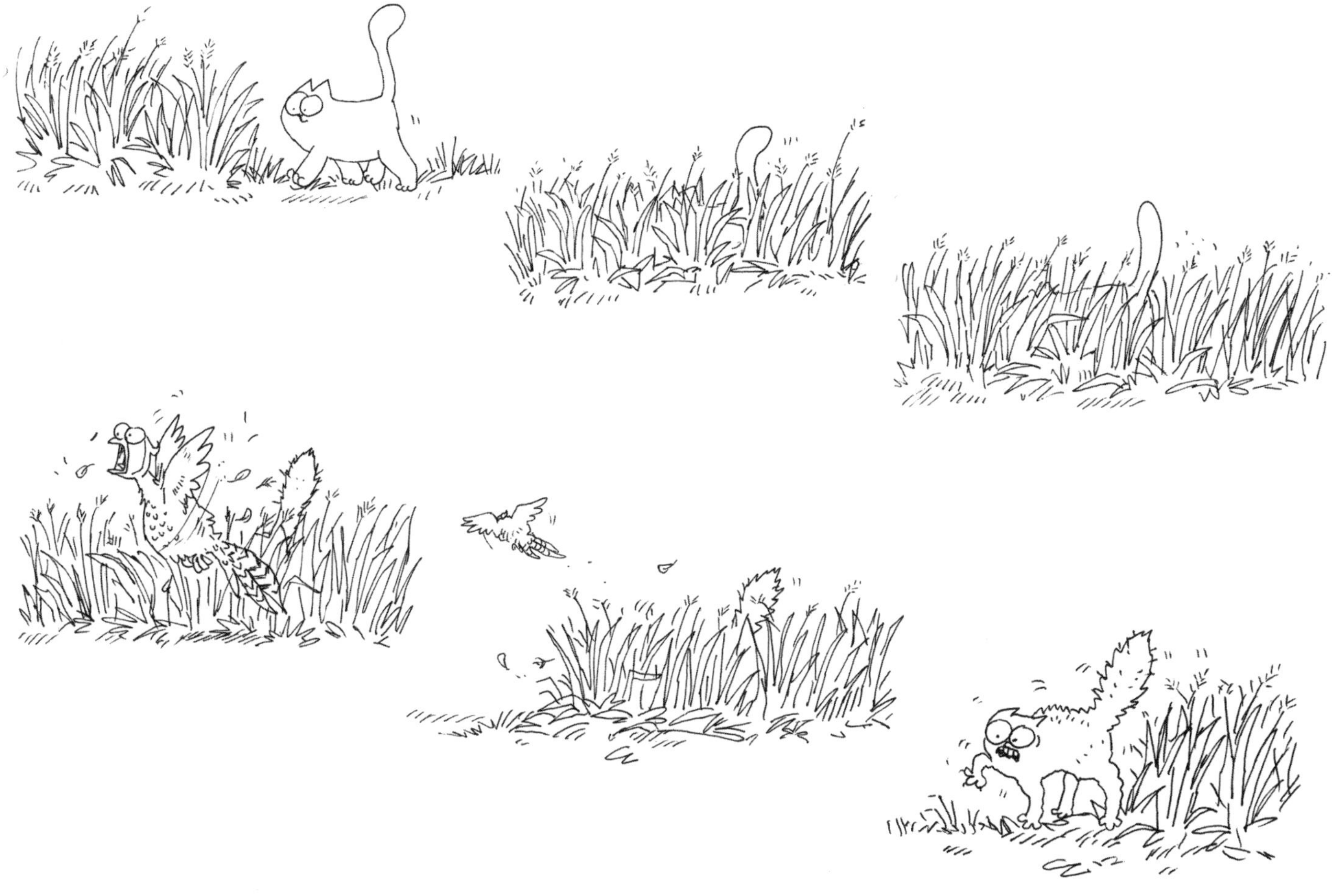

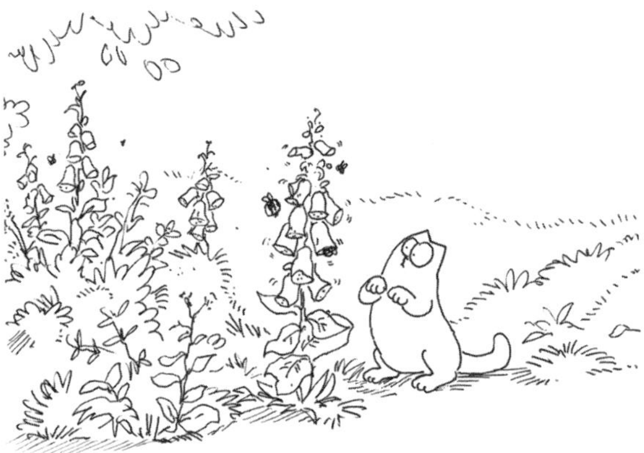
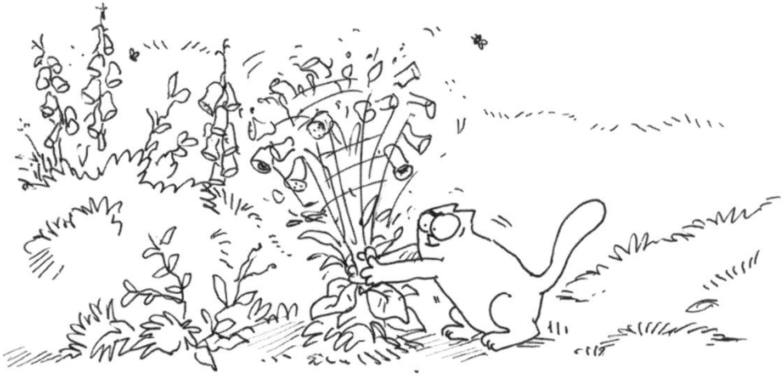
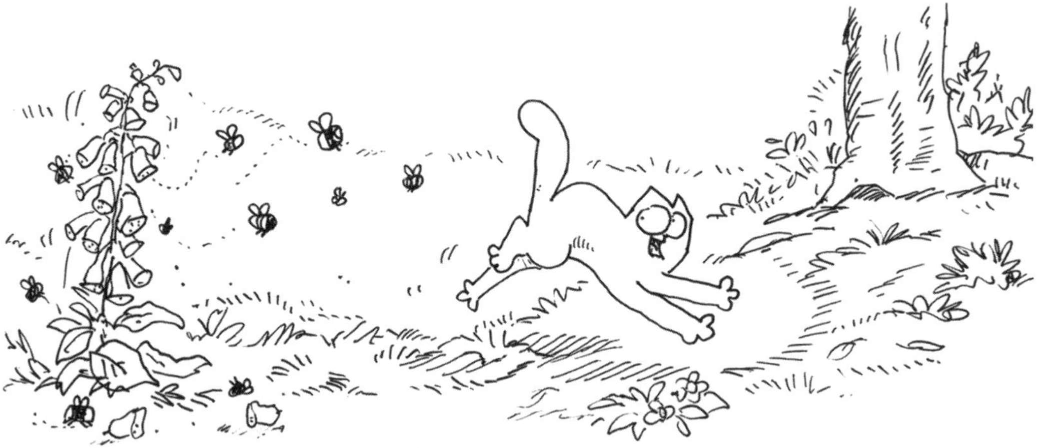

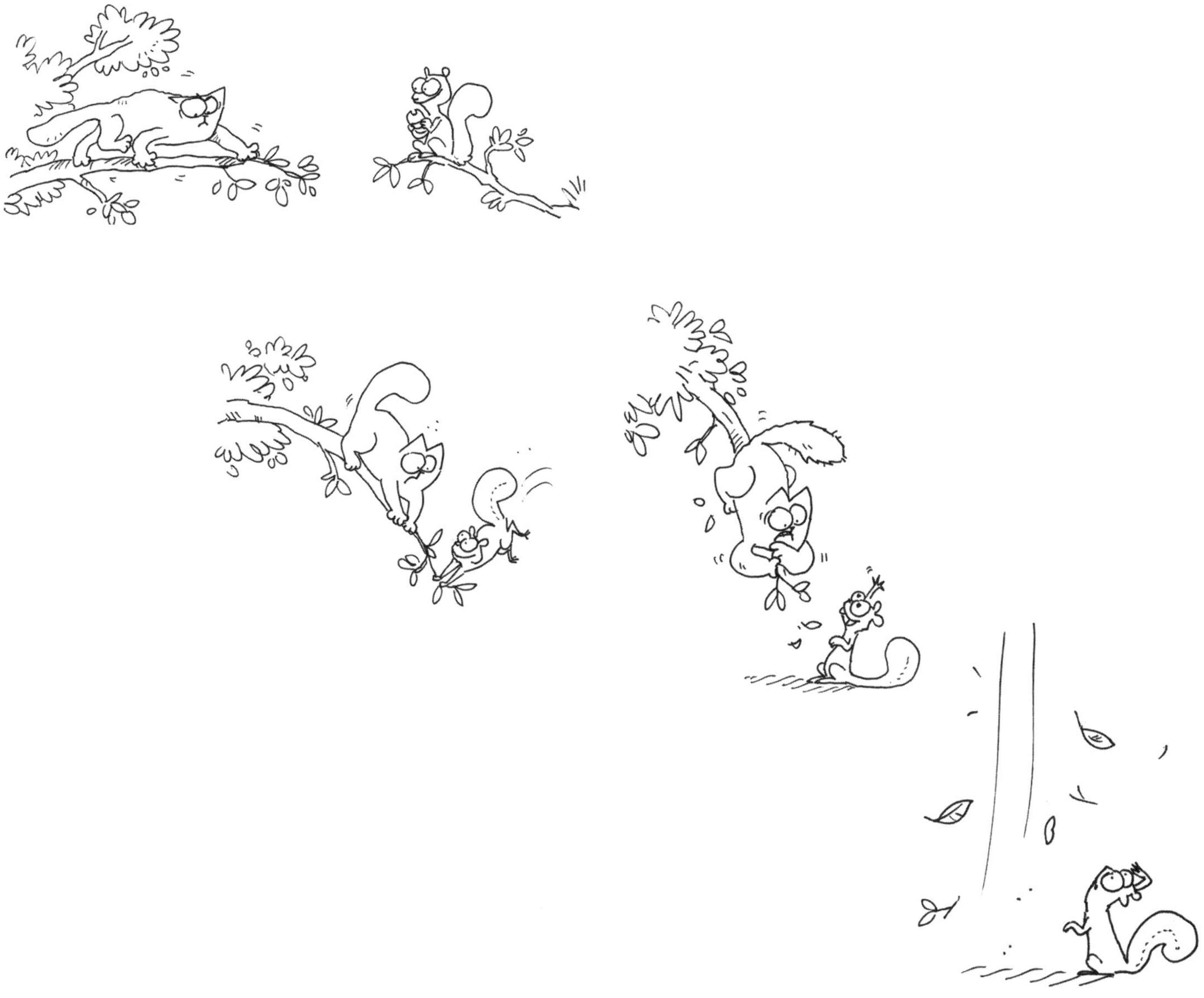

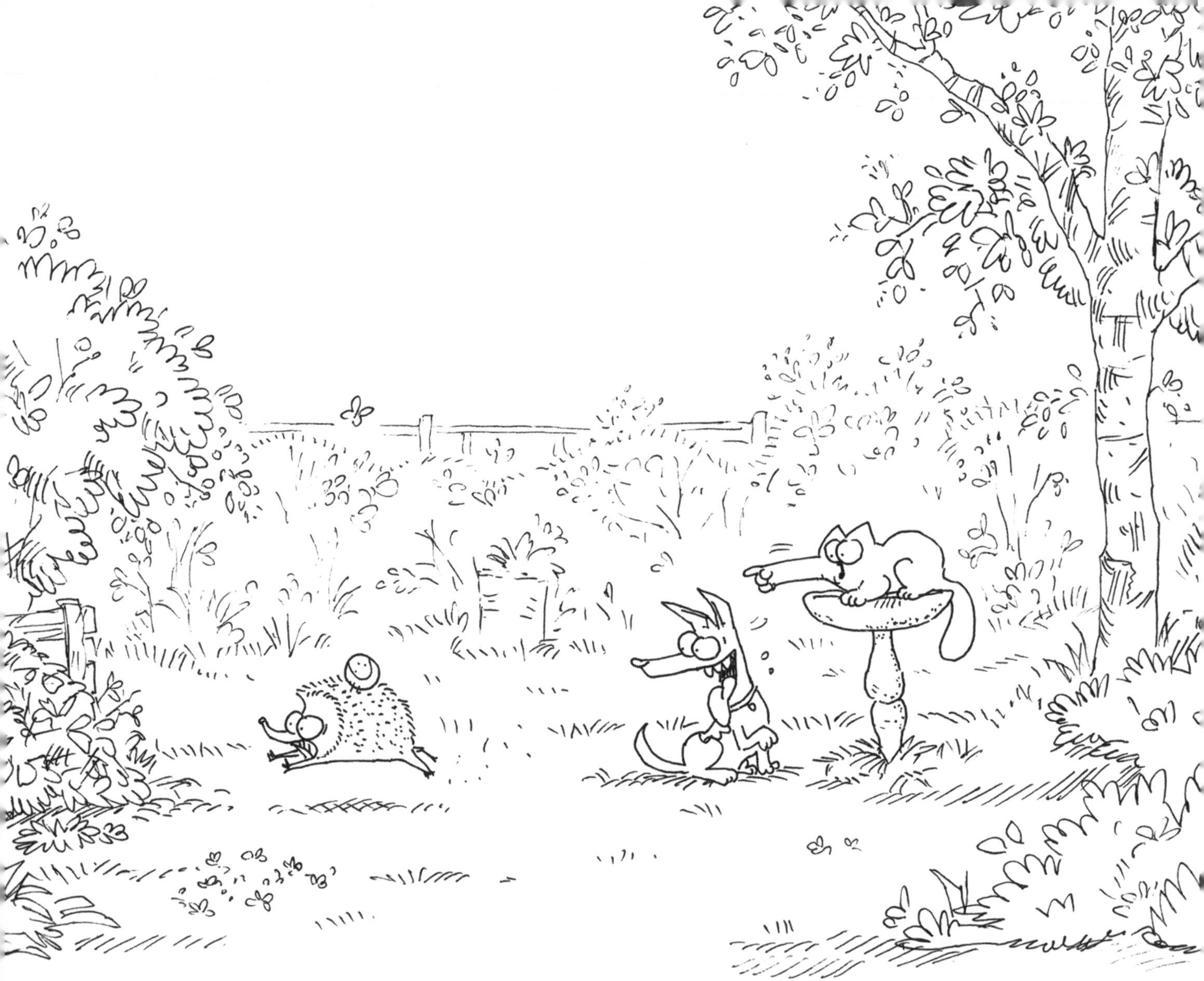

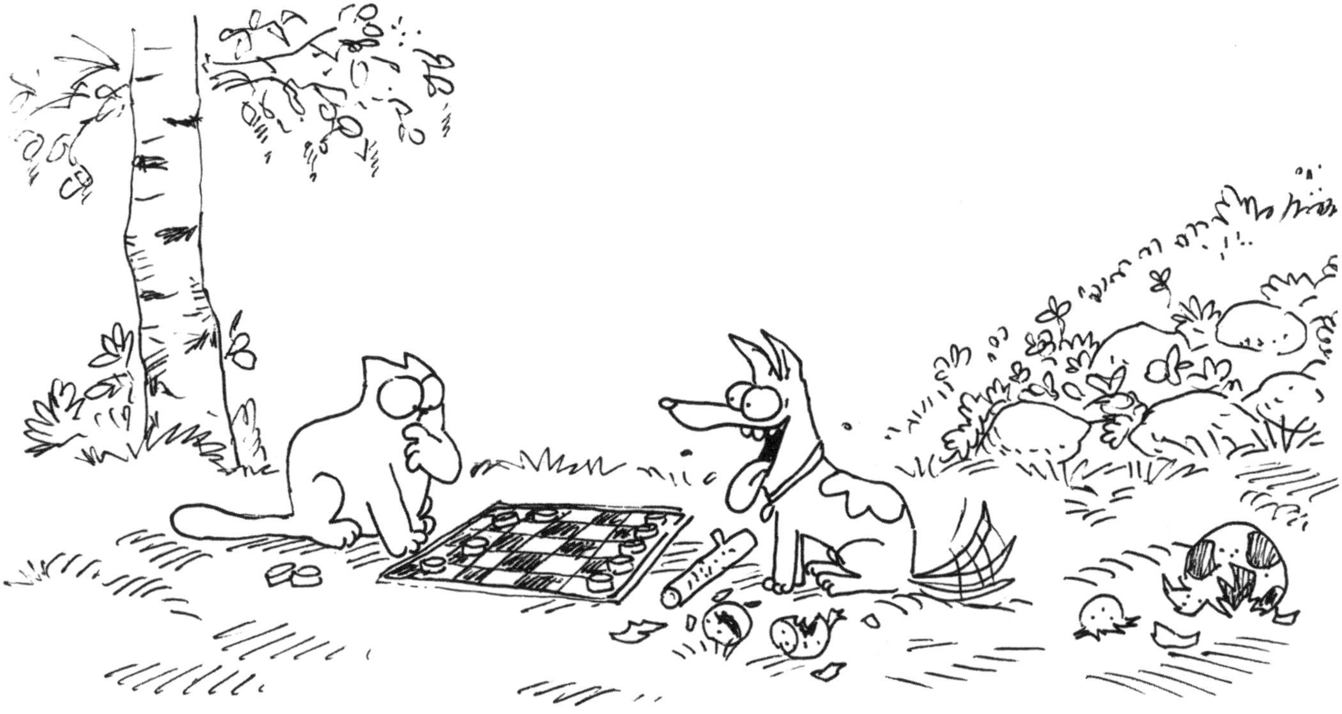

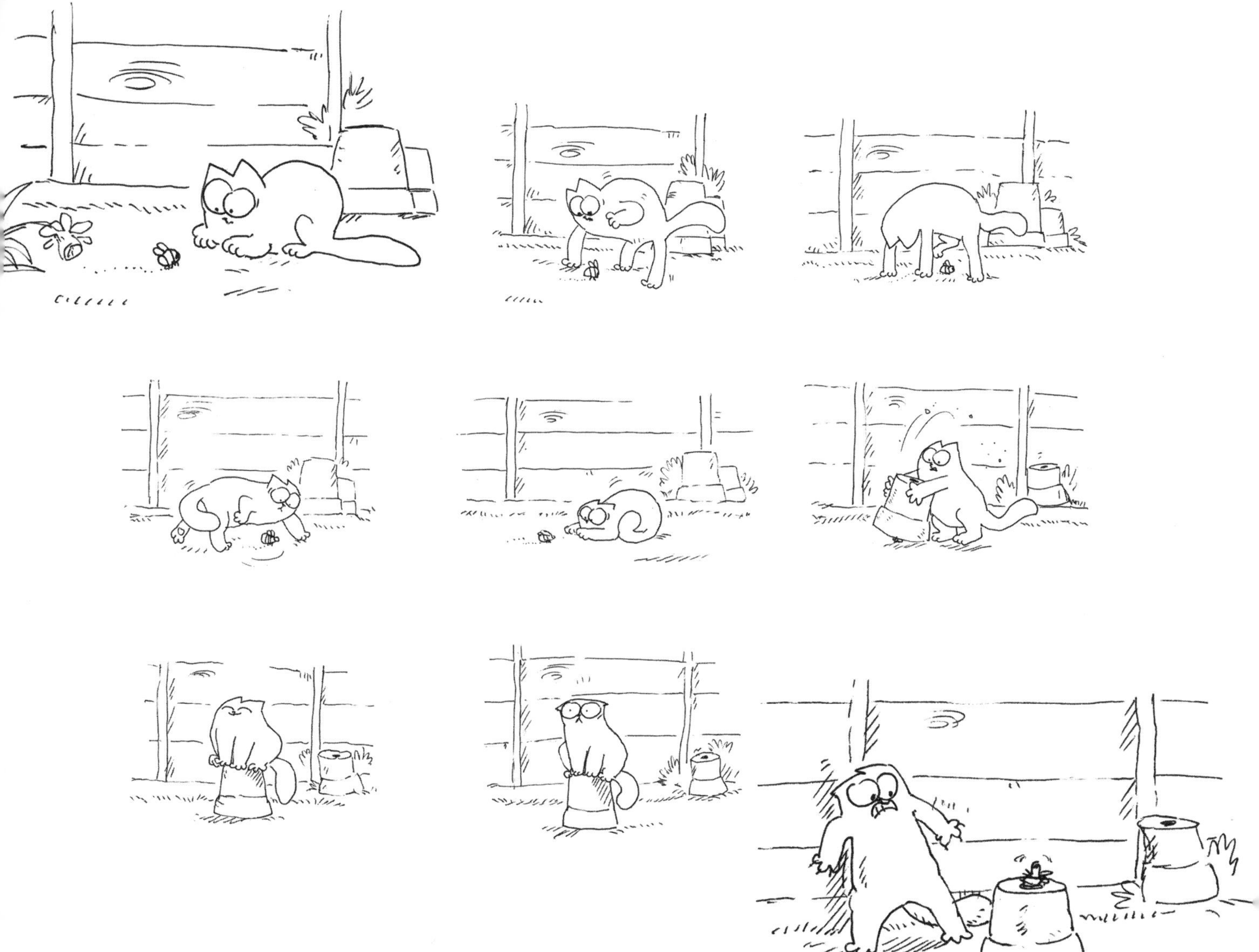

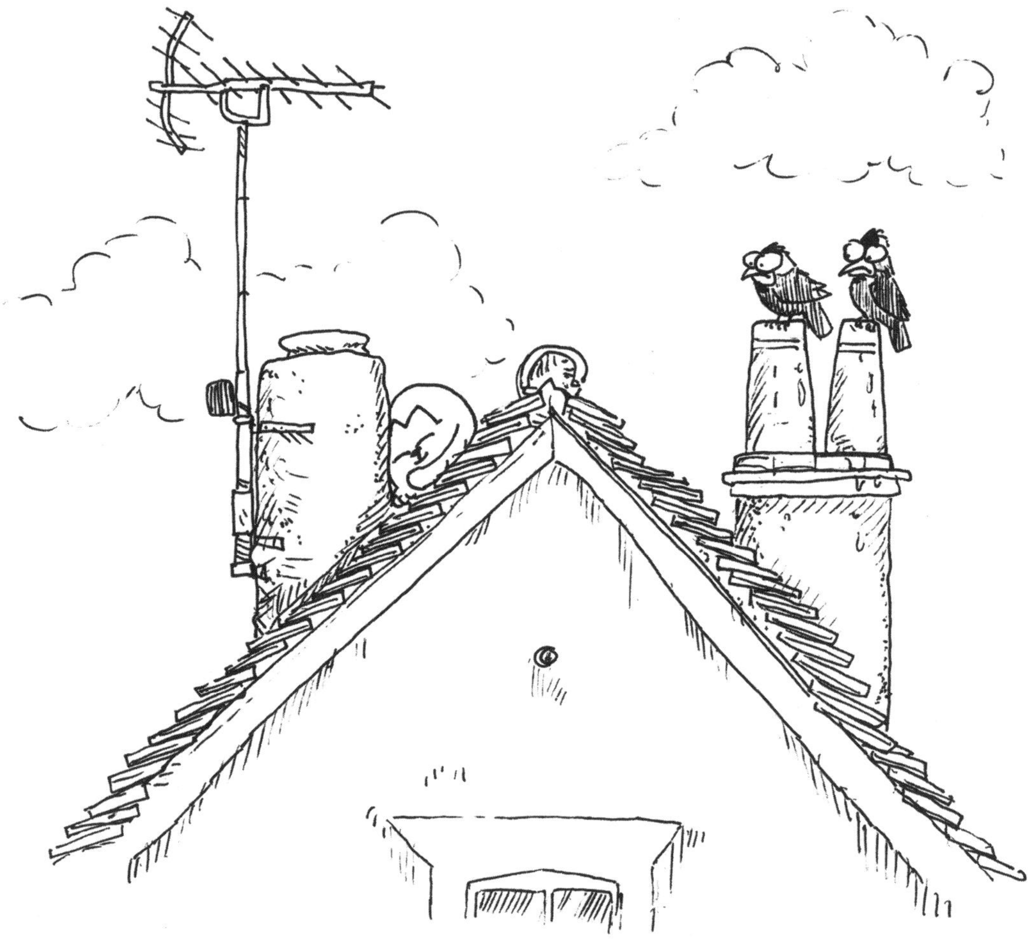

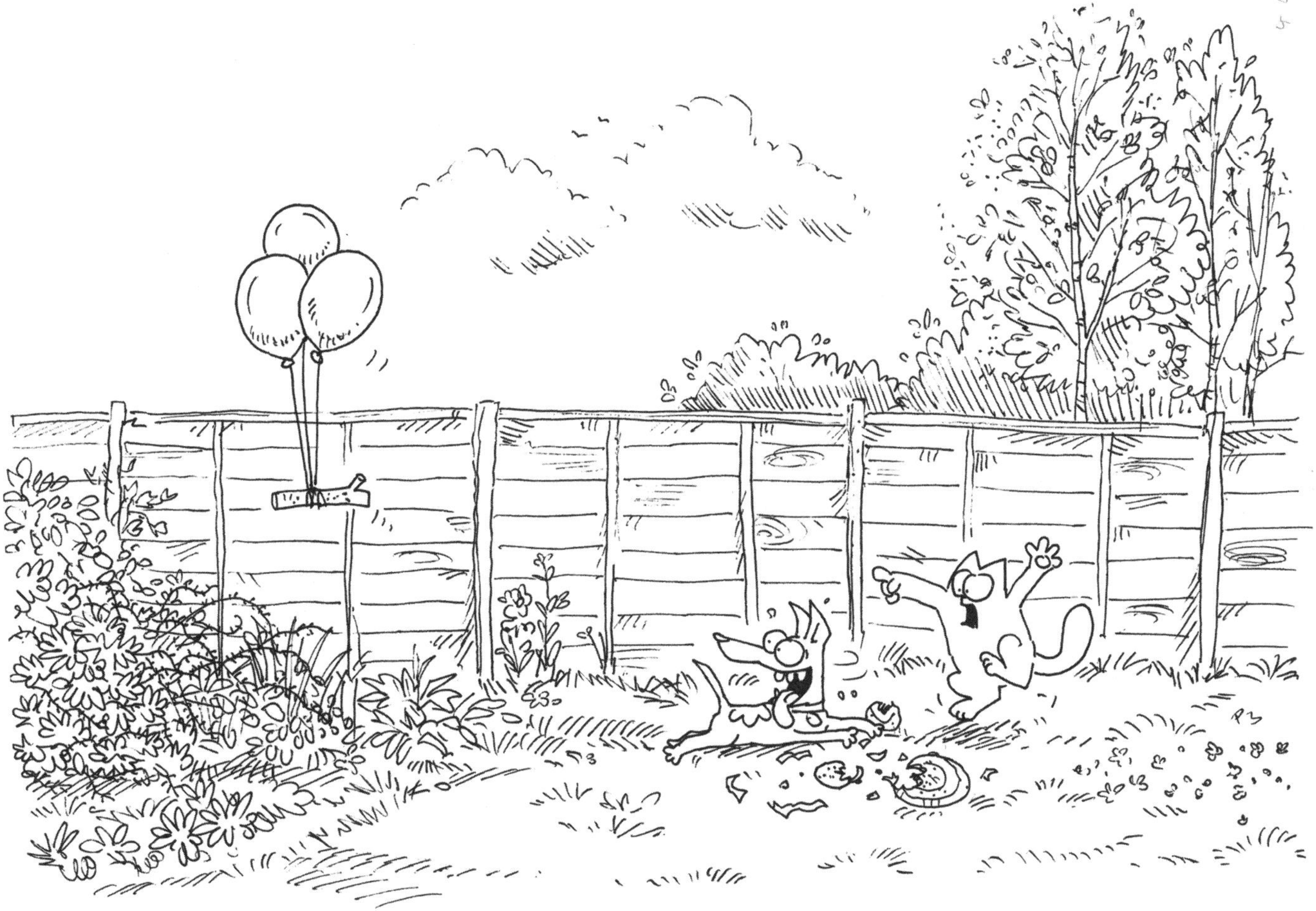

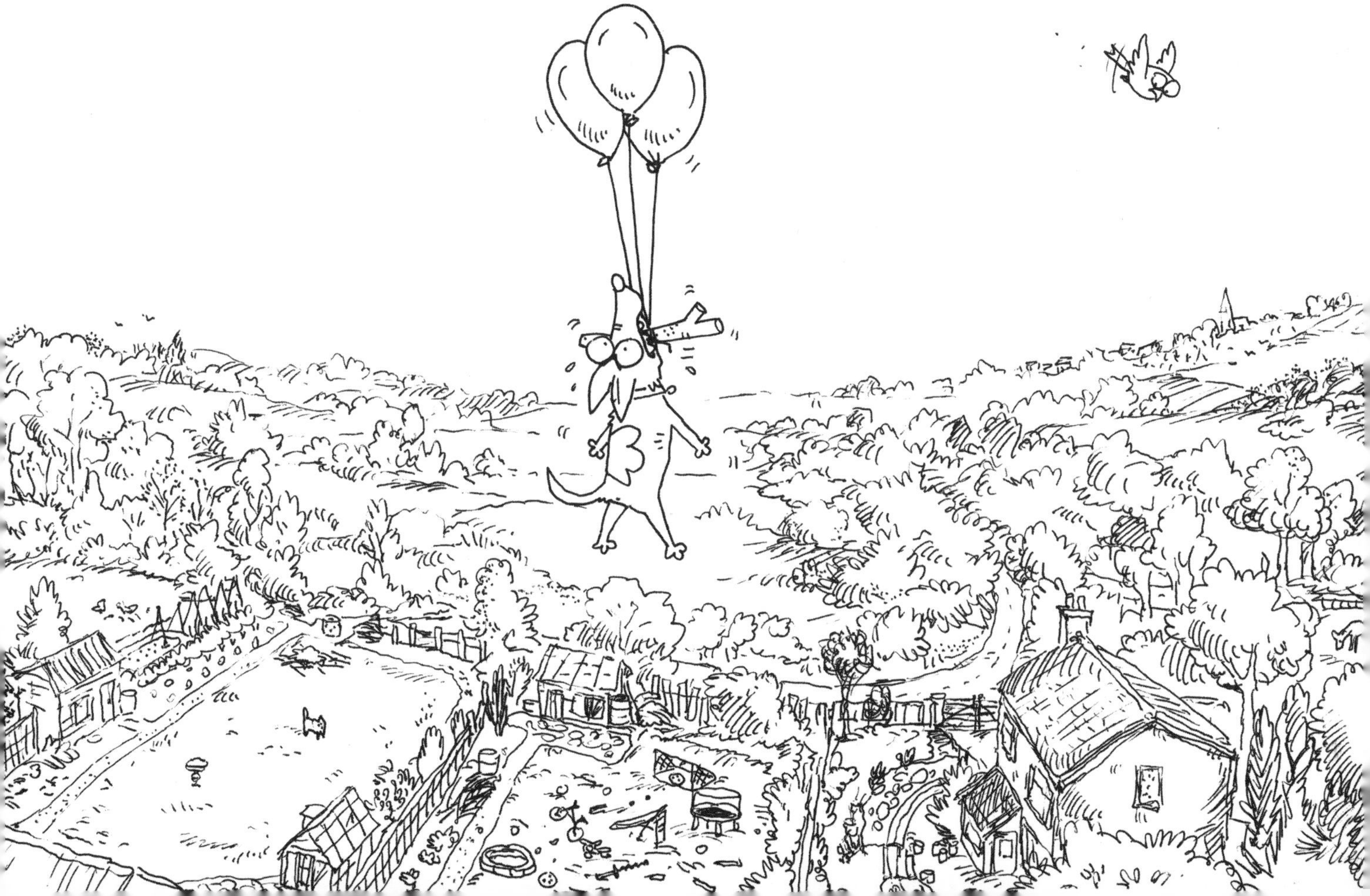

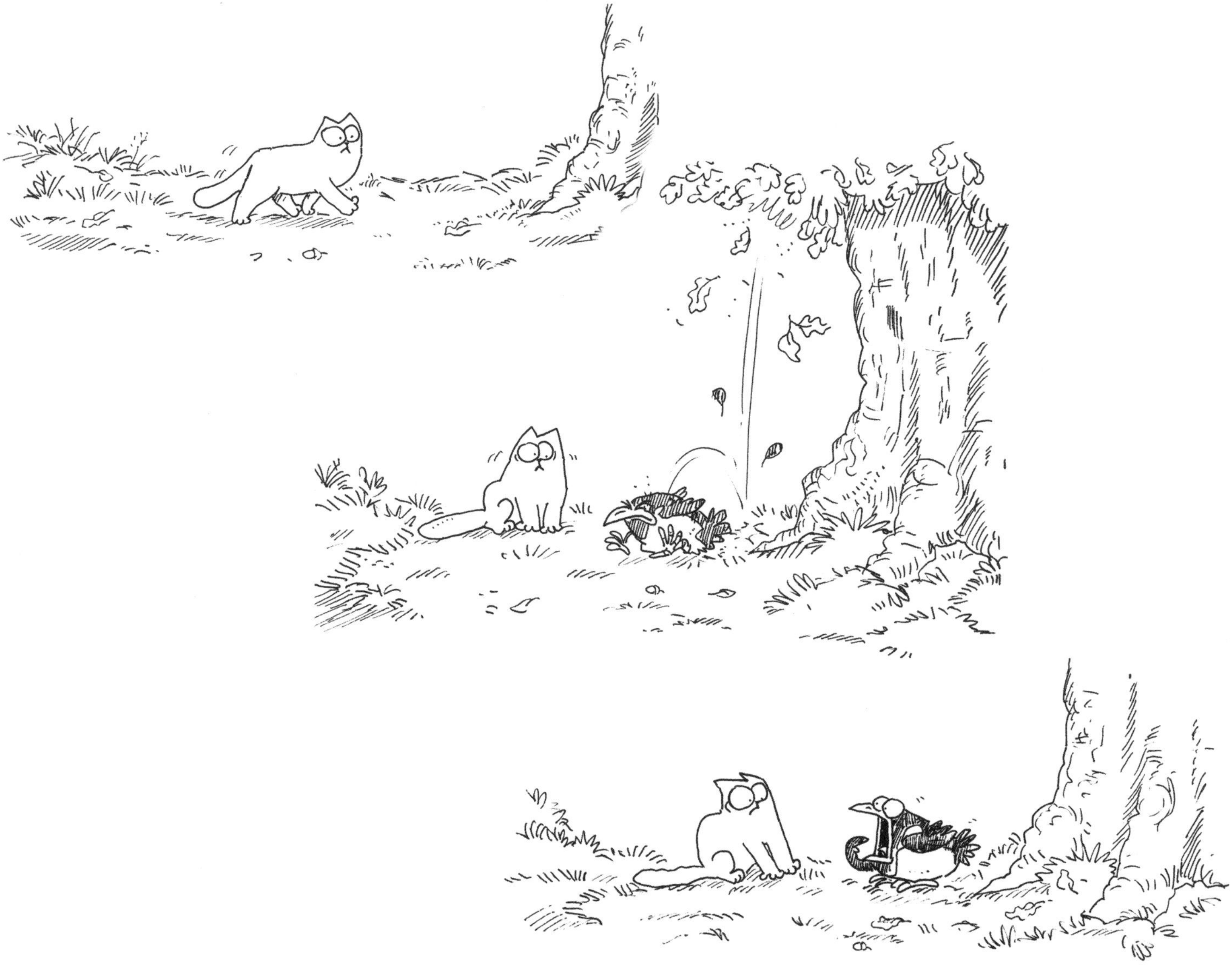

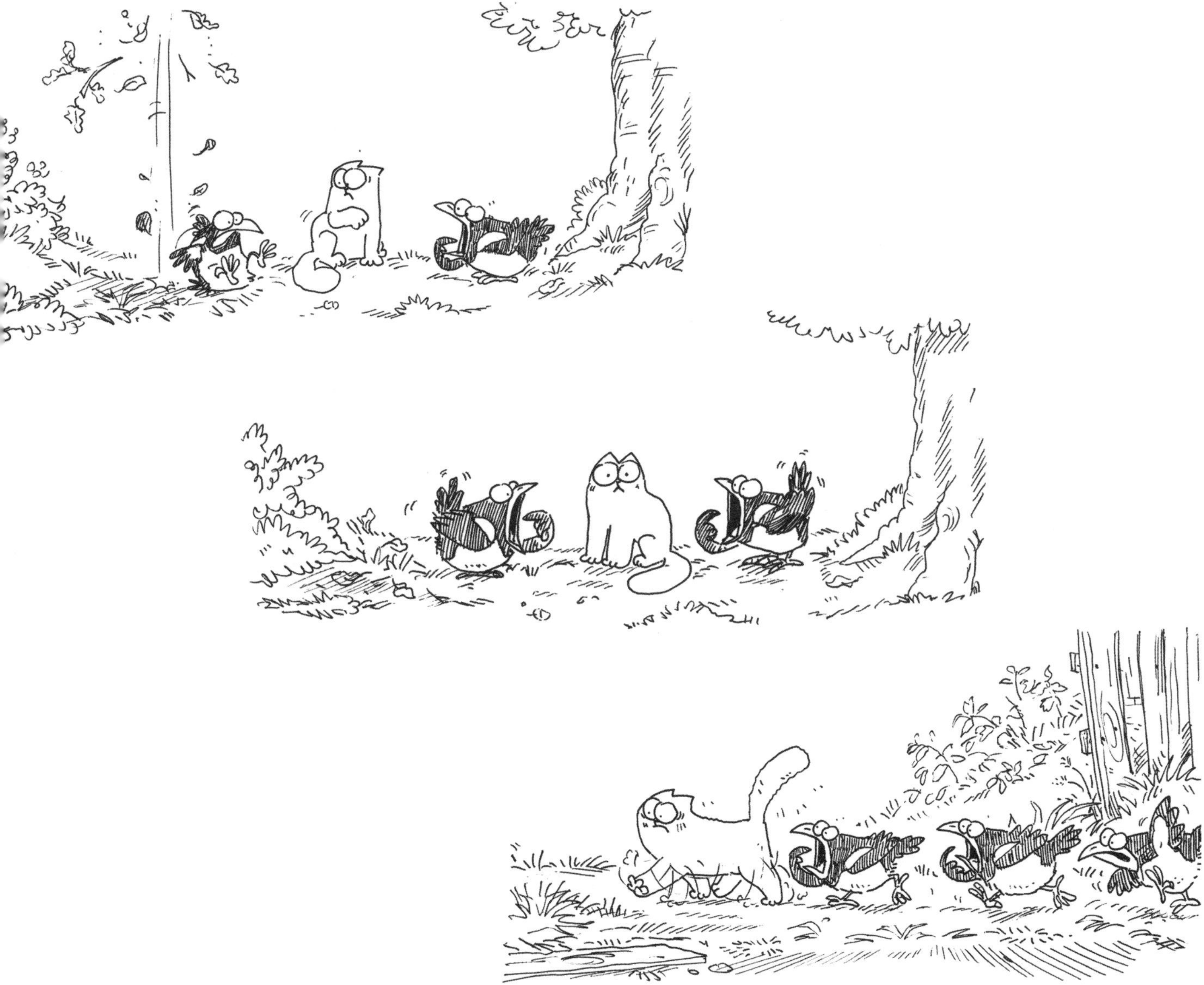

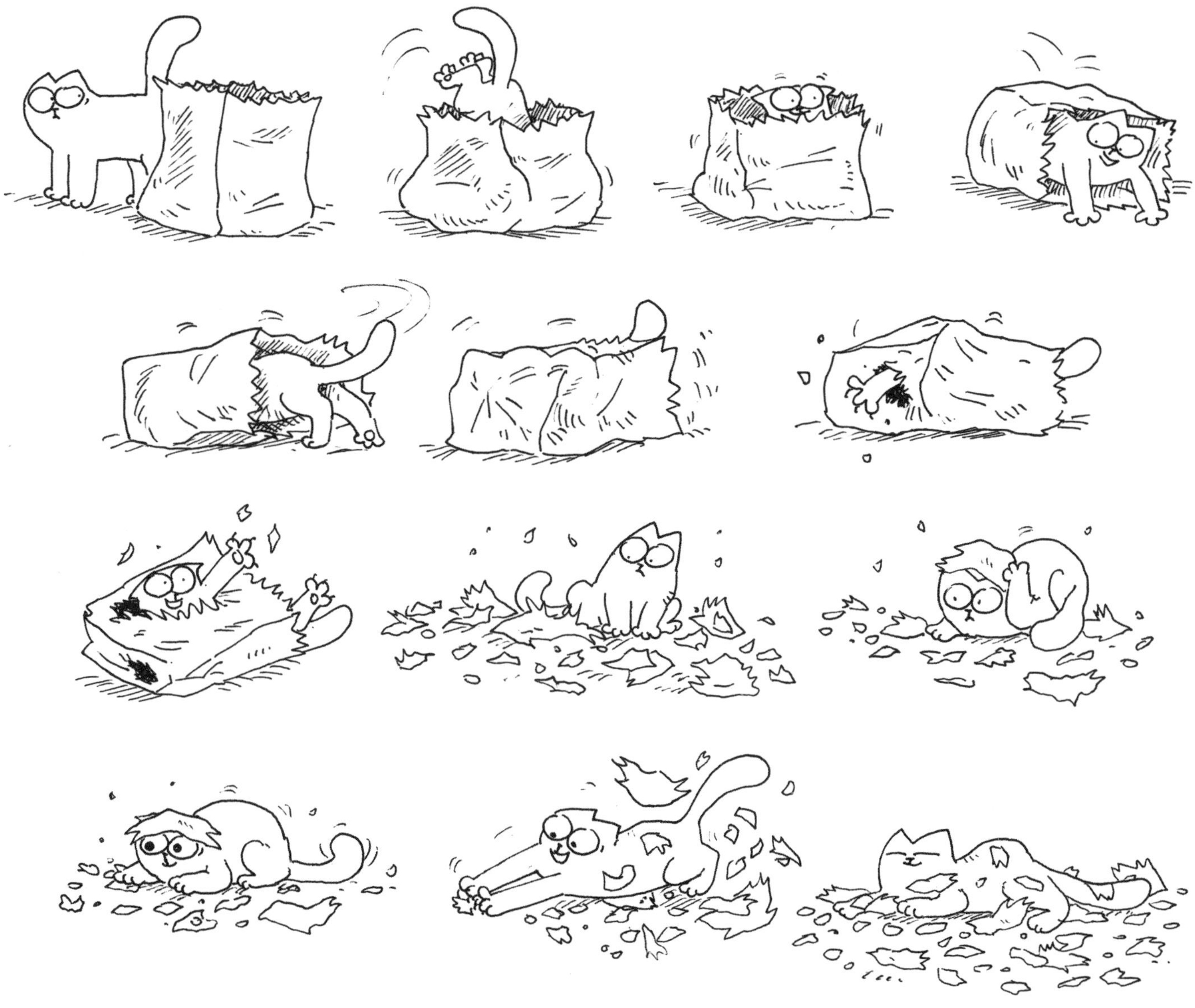

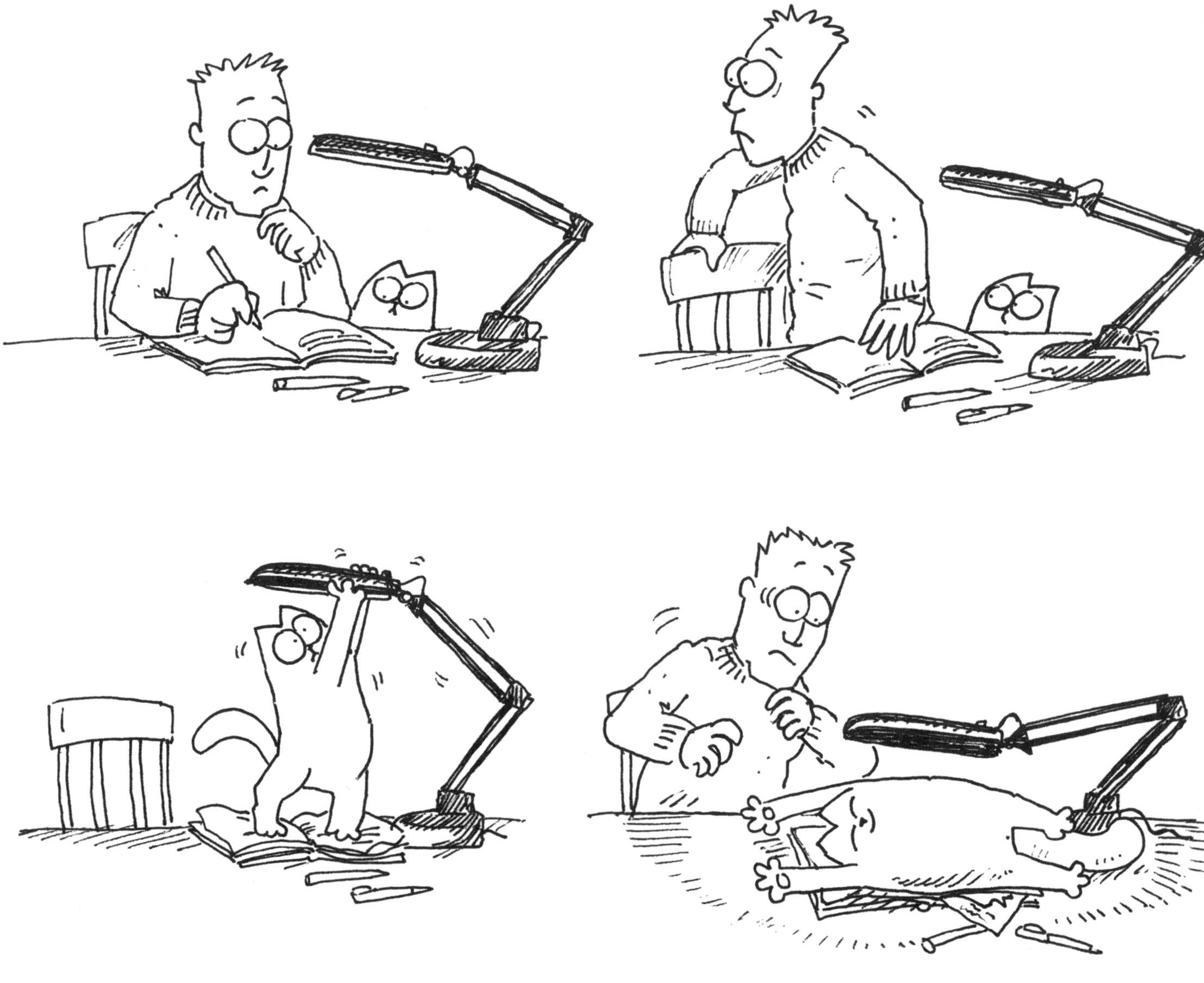

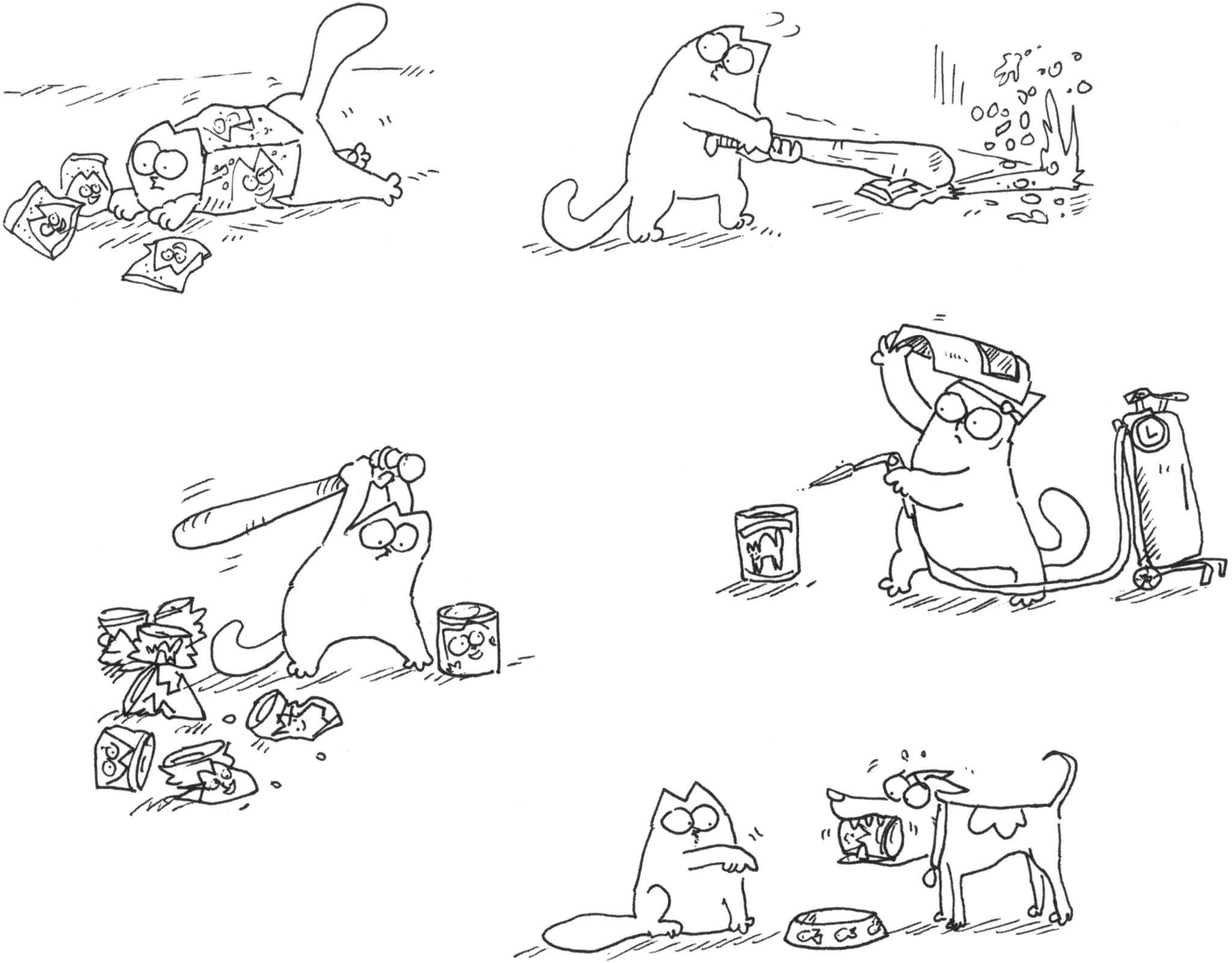

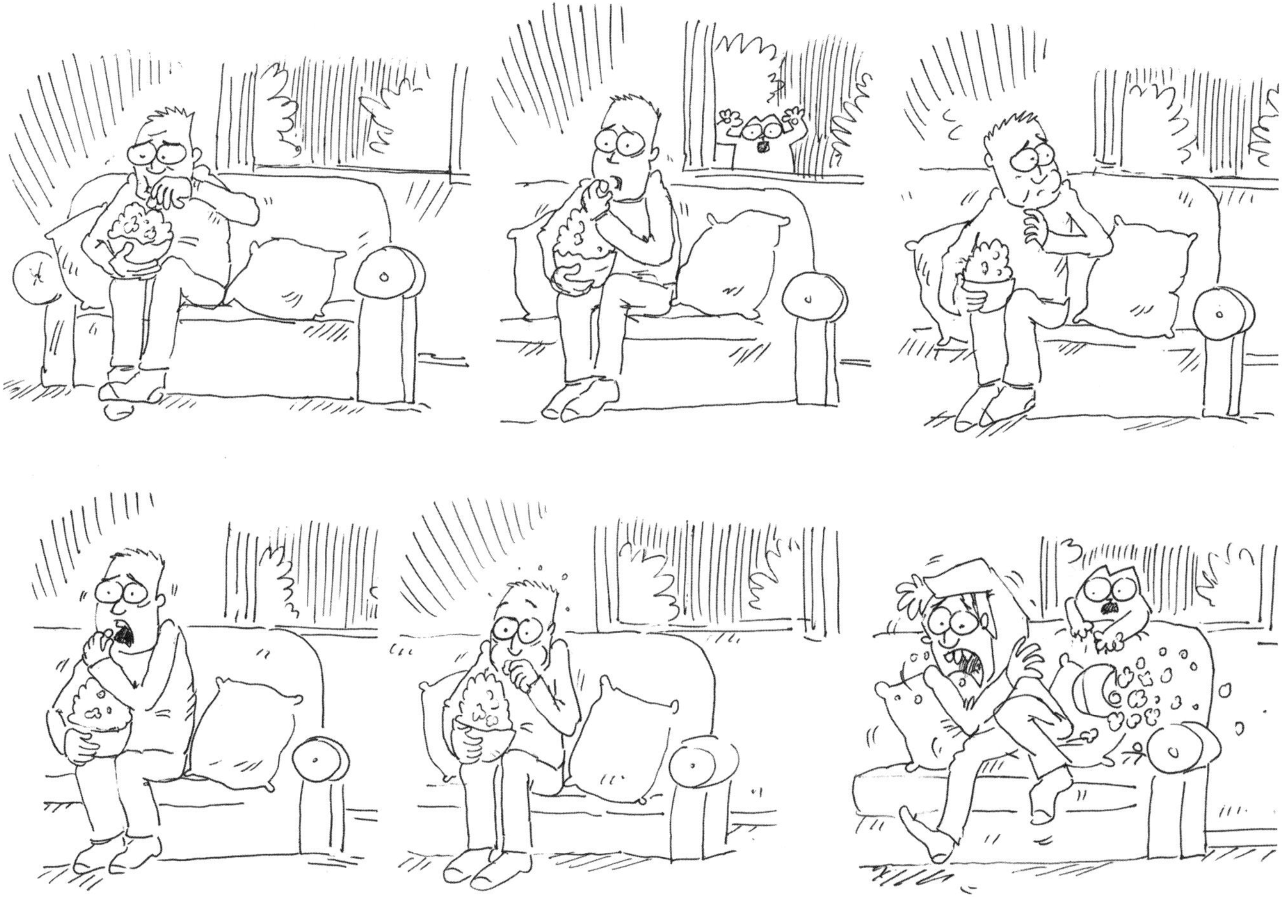

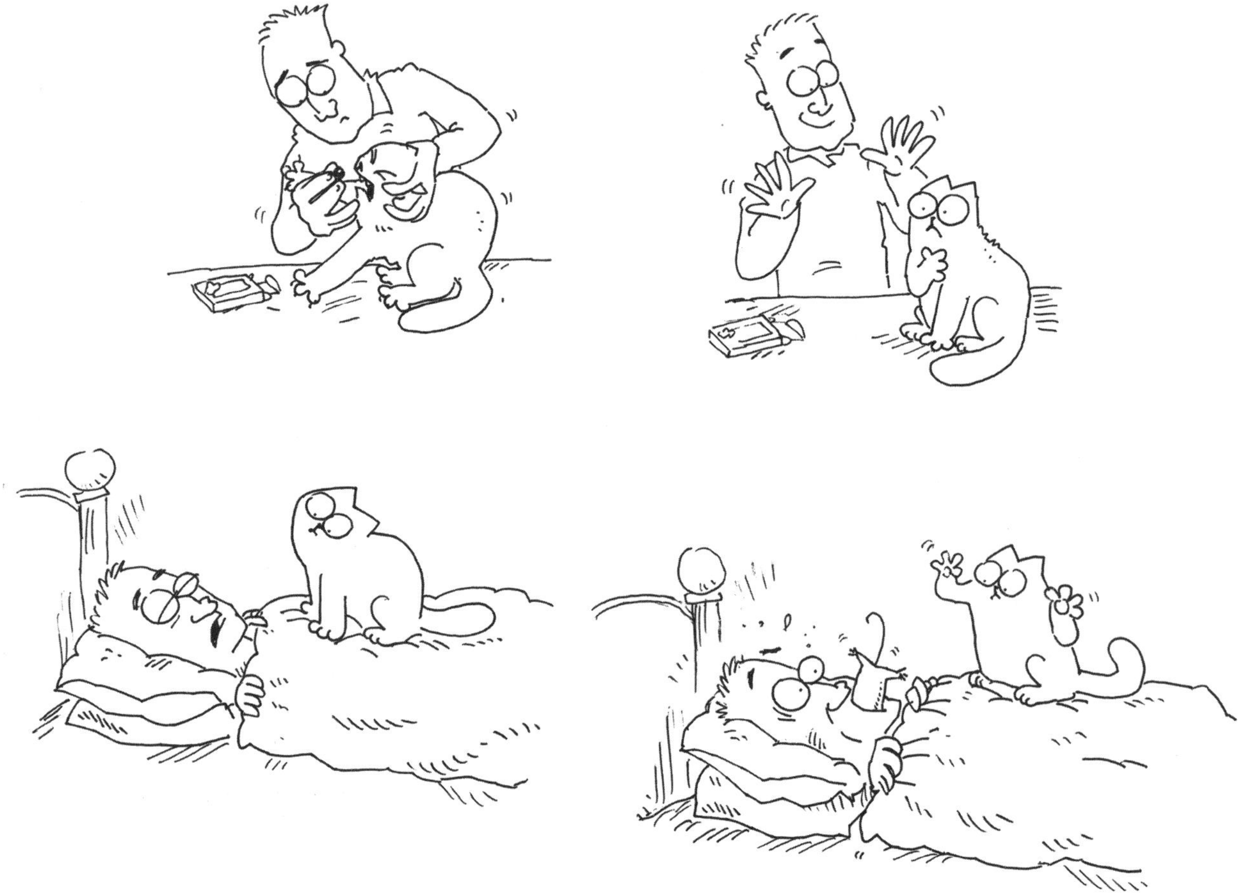

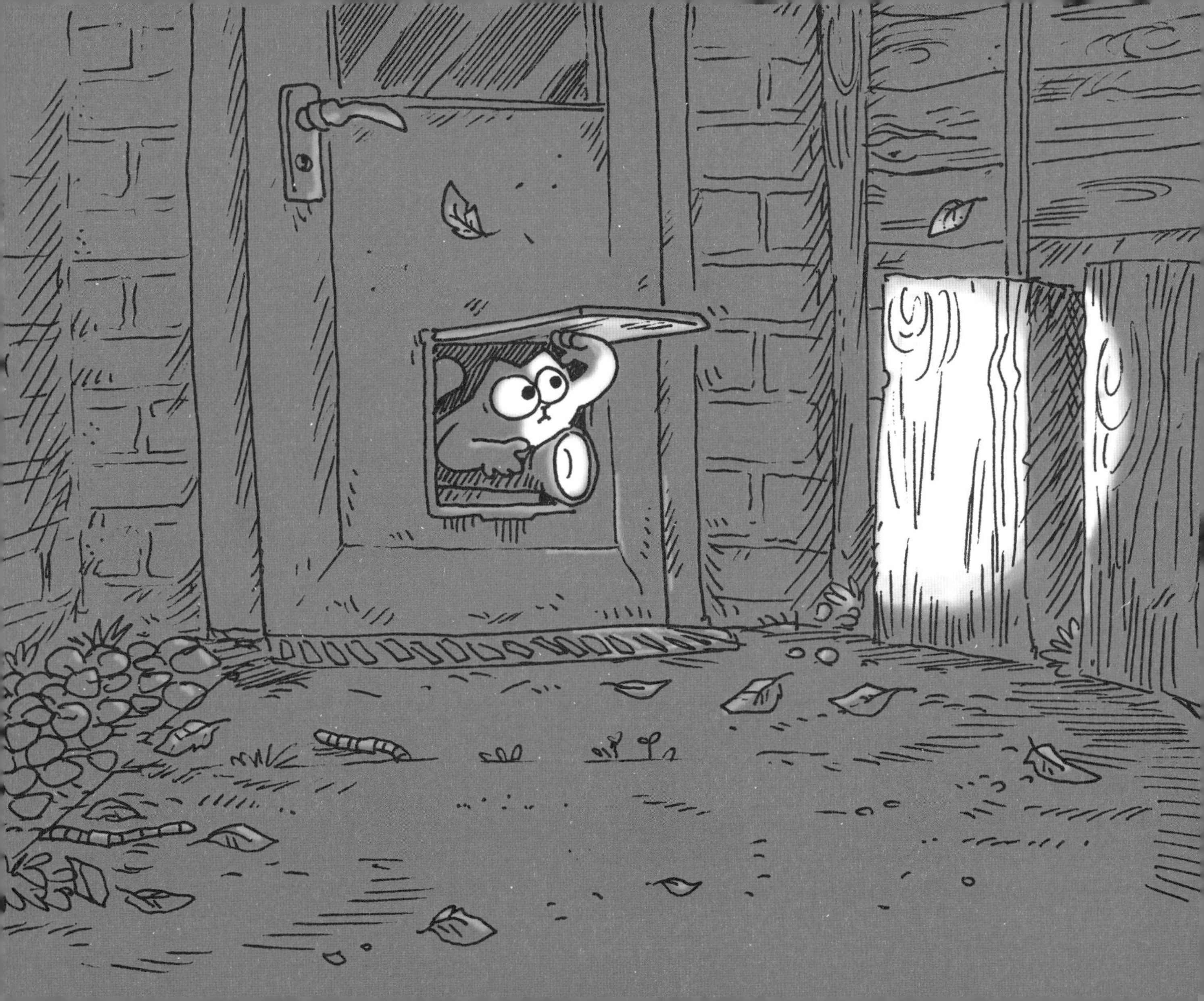

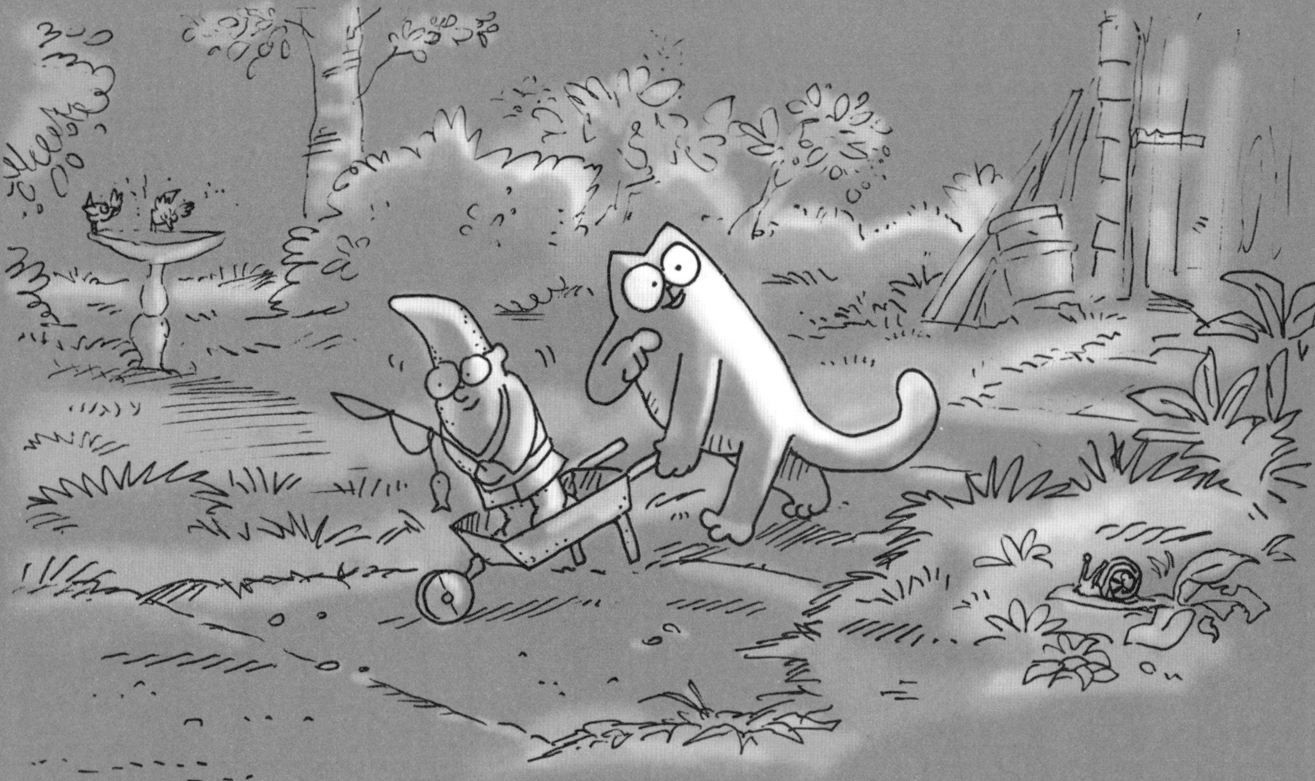

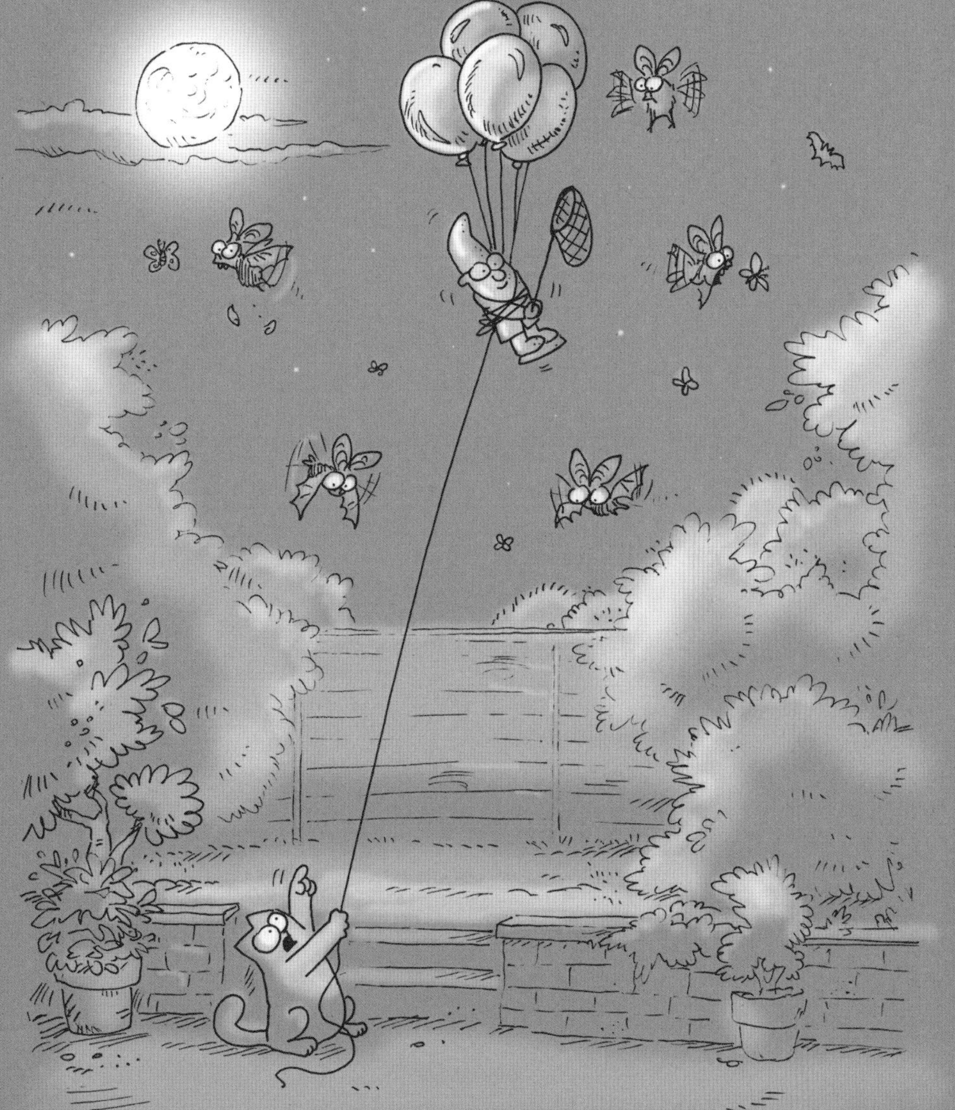

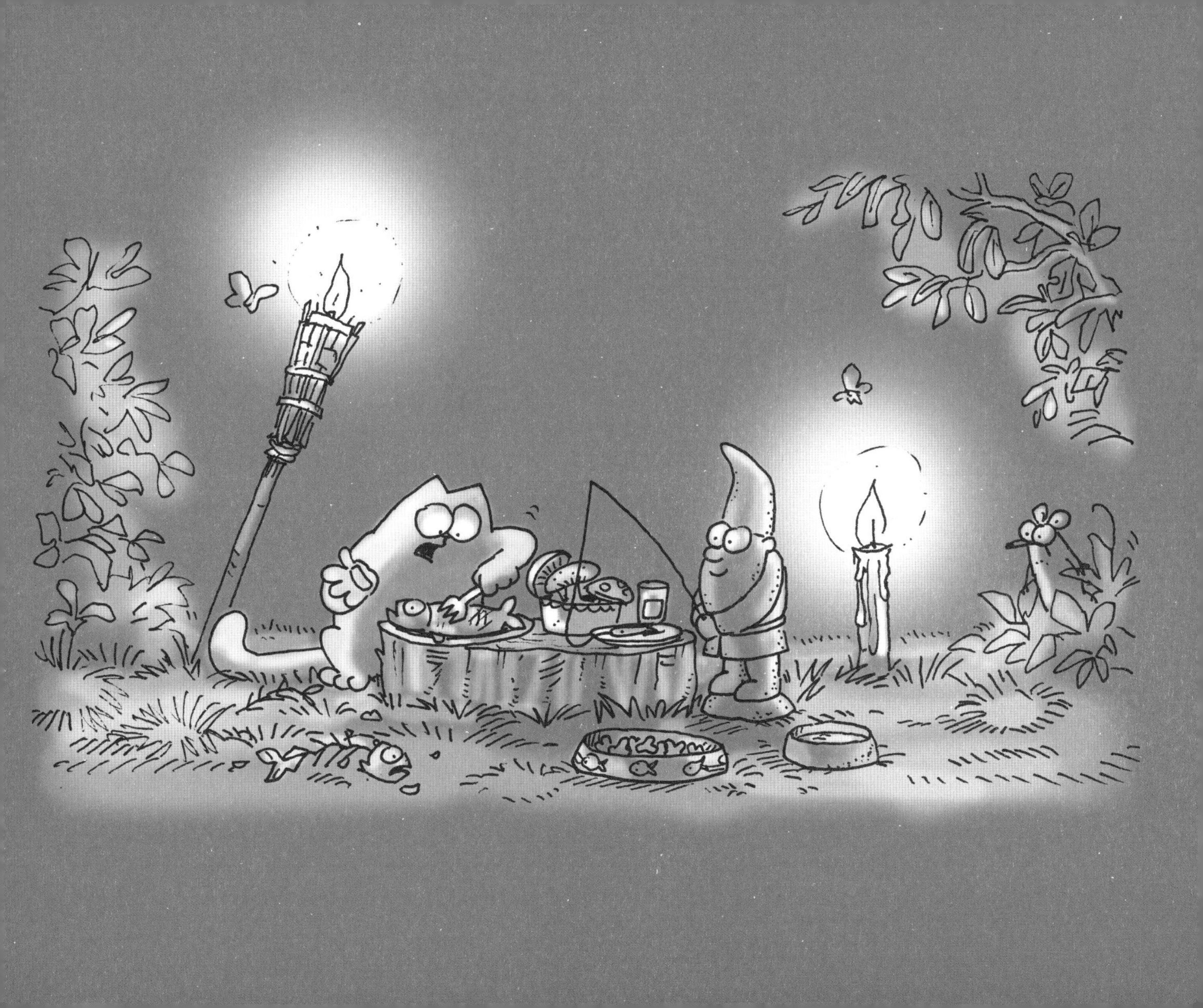

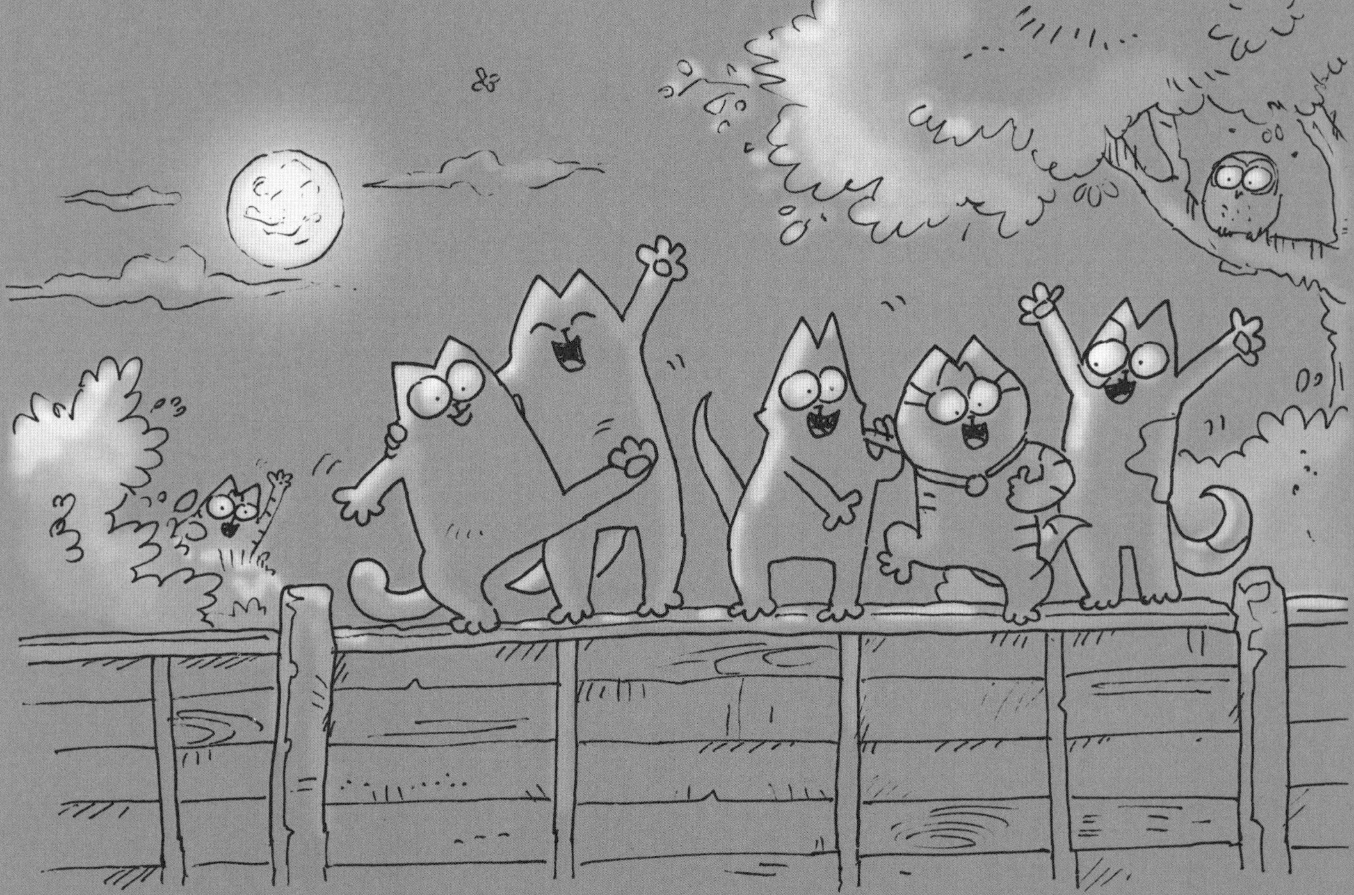

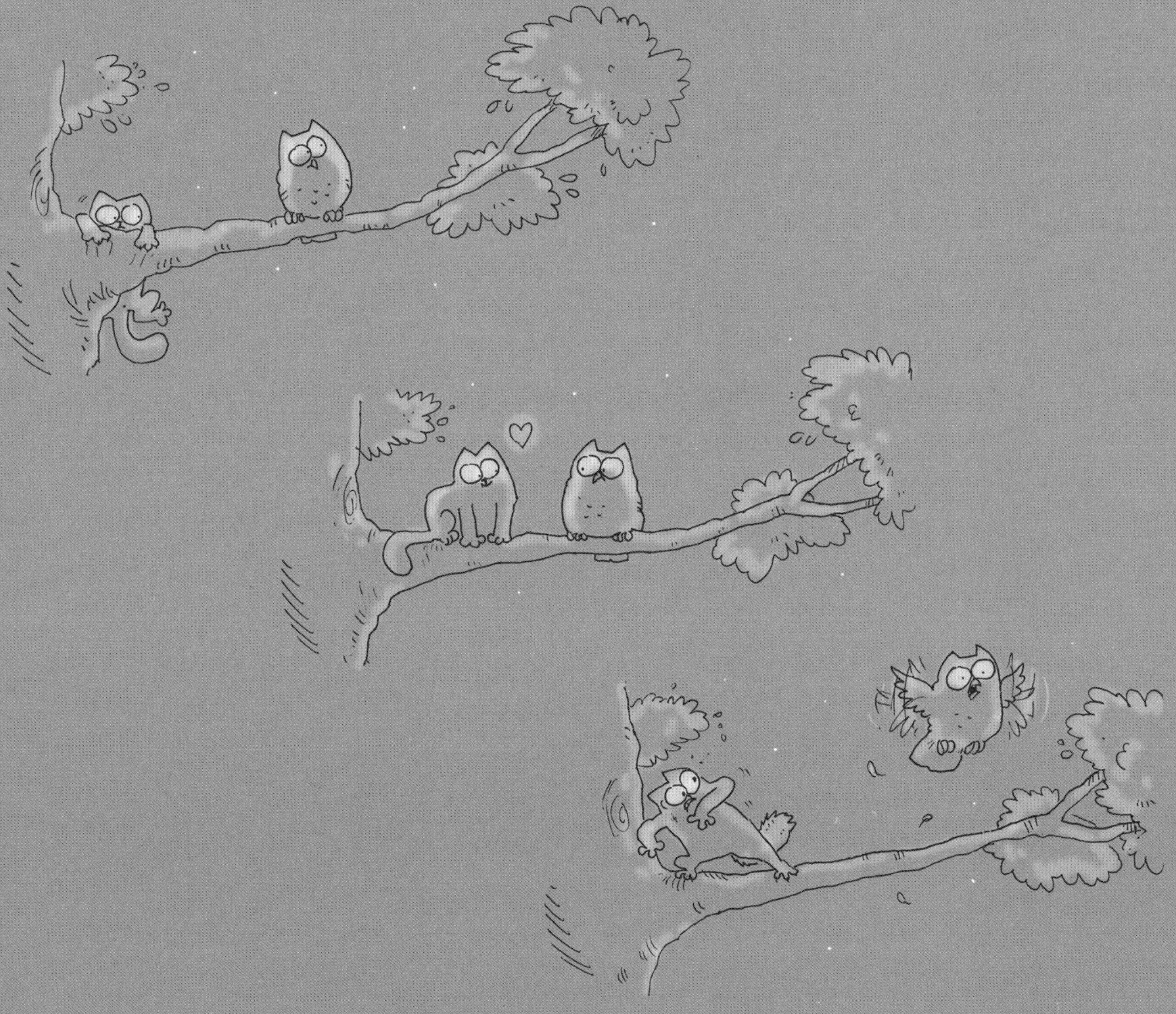

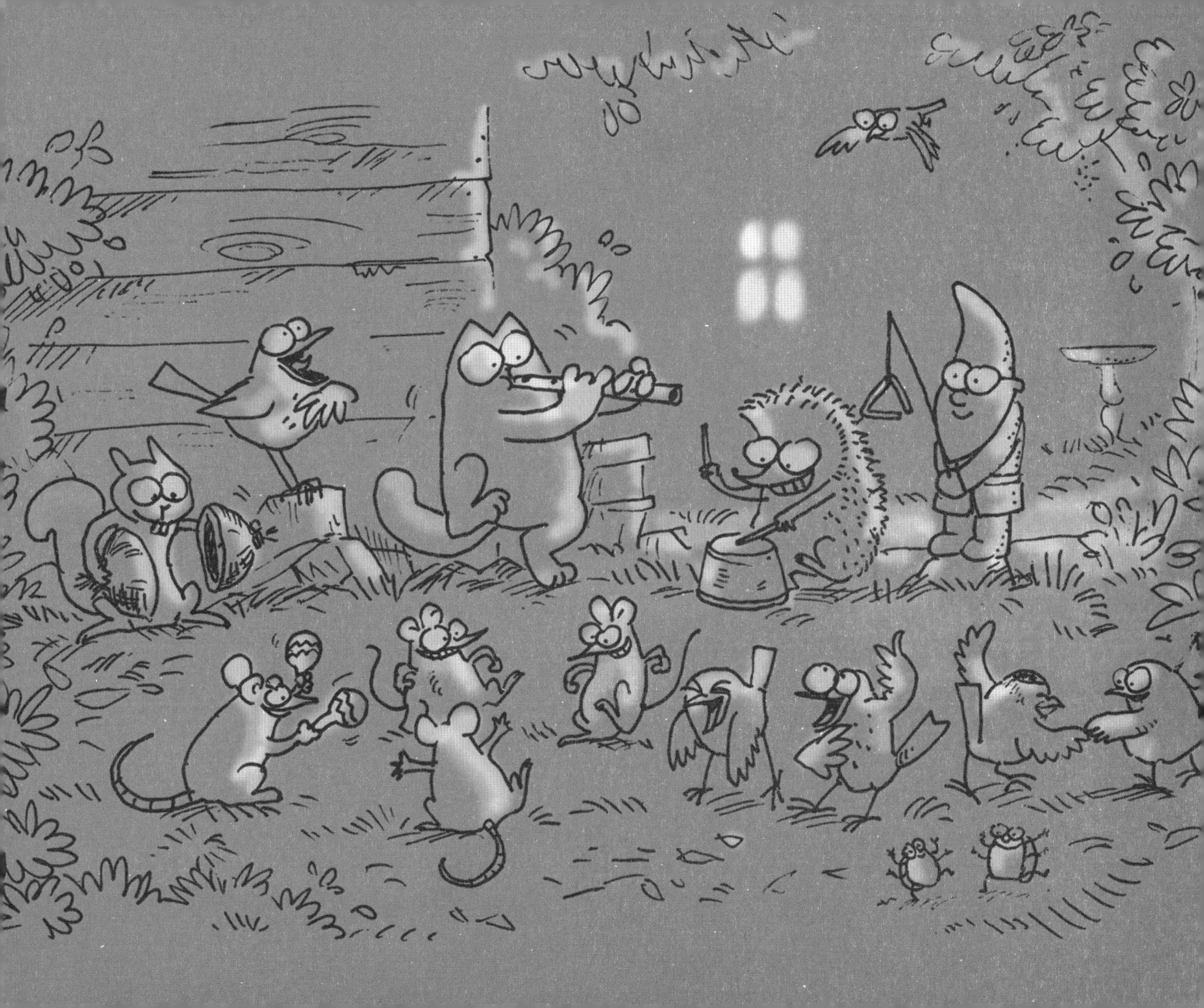

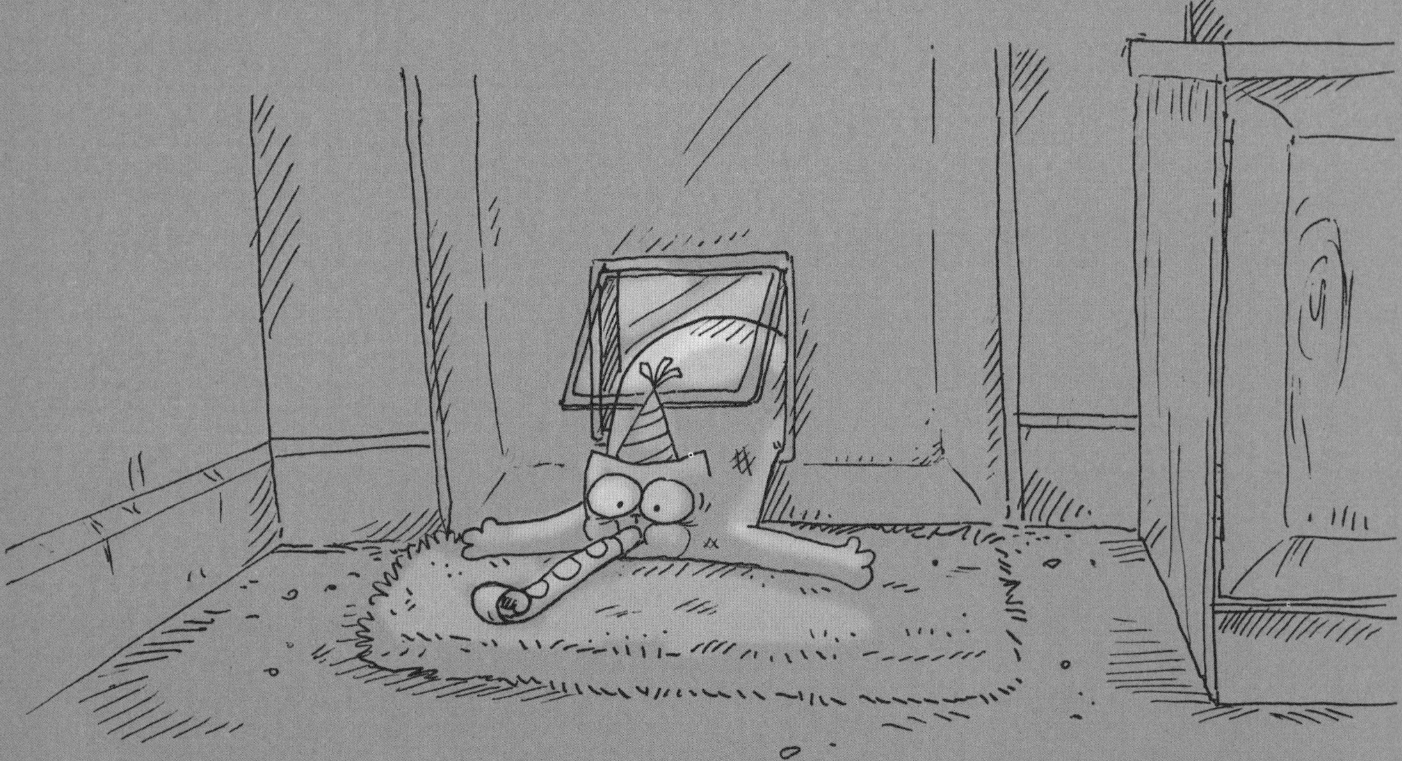

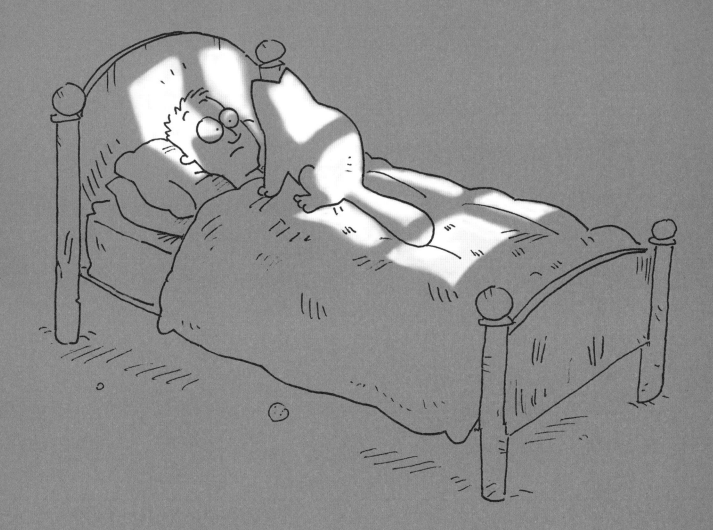

Acknowledgements

Thanks to Mark and Julie Shaw, Victoria Tobin, Nigel Pay, Daniel Greaves, Mike Bell, Richard Tofield, and everybody at Tandem Films for their support. Nick Davies and the Canongate team, Robert Kirby and Duncan Hayes at UA, and my three cats, Hugh, Maisy and Jess for their endless inspiration.

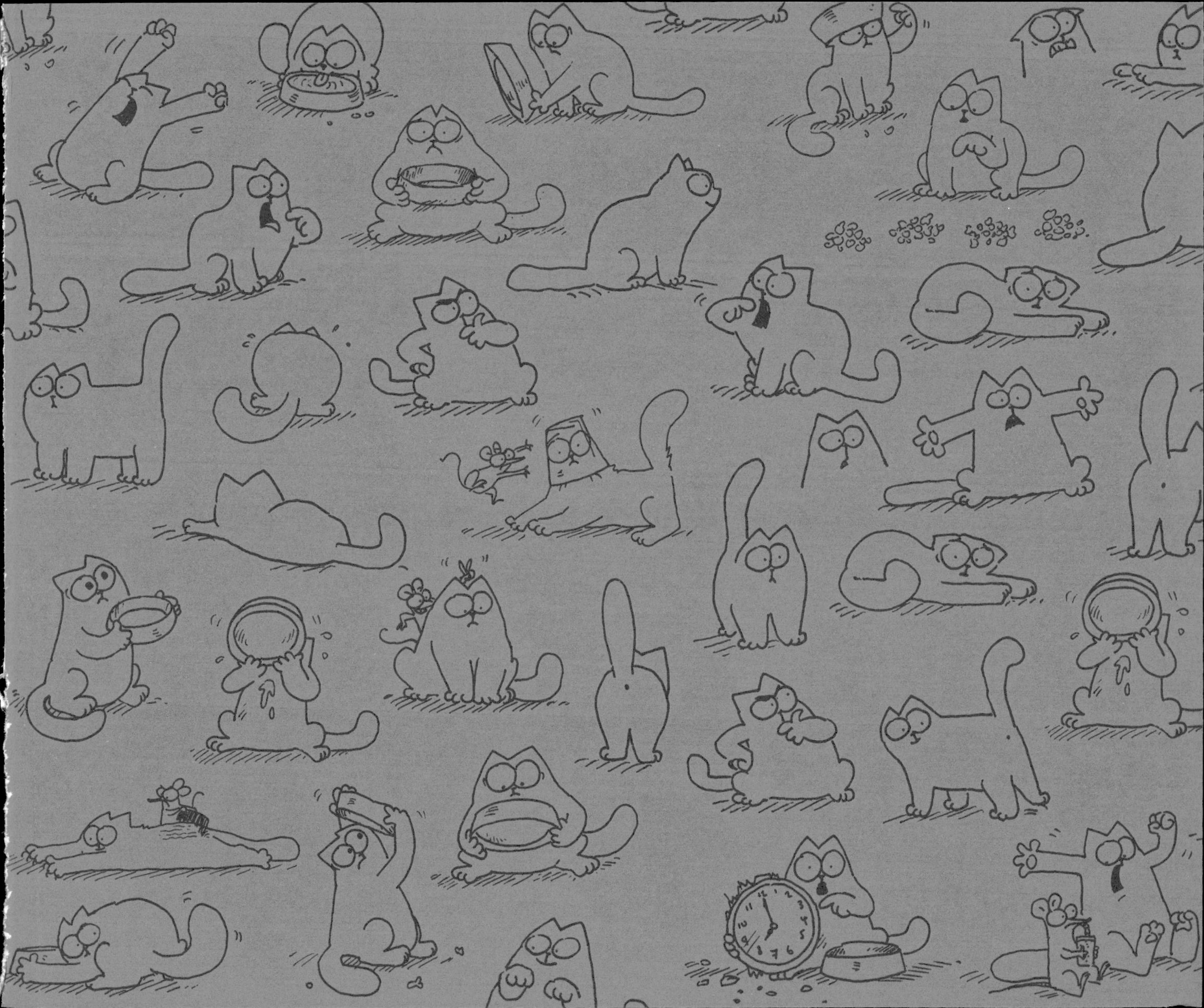

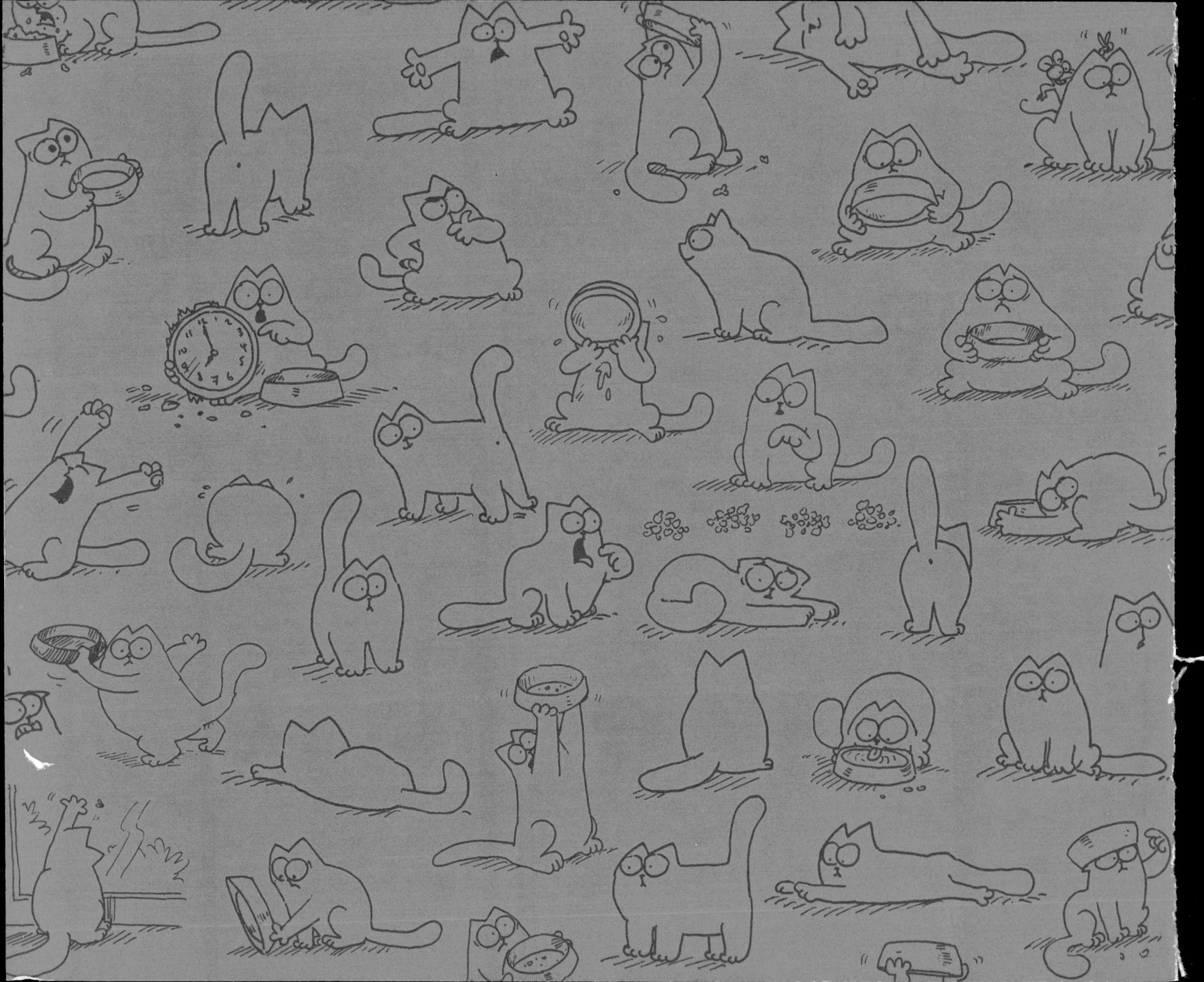